SoulFullJoy: A Better Path

SOULFULLJOY

A Better Path

My Sacred Journey from the Shadows to the Light

Marcia Wakeman

SoulFullJoy.com

SoulFullJoy LLC
Sarasota, FL USA

Library of Congress Control Number: 2026912144
Hardback: 979-8-9948238-0-4
Paperback: 979-8-9948238-1-1
Ebook: 979-8-9948238-2-8

Book cover design by Christina Thiele
Interior design by Christina Thiele
Author photo by Dy'Shone Hayes
Editorial production by KN Literary Arts

For Steve,
my brother, my rock, my friend—
grateful beyond words, always.

Contents

Part III: Embracing Wholeness: A Tapestry of Healing and Connection

SoulFullJoy: A Better Path

This poem is my sanctuary, a touchstone for moments of doubt or disconnection. It weaves the insights of my healing journey, guiding me back to love, alignment, and radiant joy.

When I choose love over fear, embracing the tender wounds that stir within, I uncover truths that light my way:

I cradle my pain, sitting gently with sorrow's weight, and as I turn to love, my heart blooms, luminous with a joy that spills like sunlight.

I surrender to life's flow, leaning in with open trust, and my world weaves into a rich tapestry of harmony.

I glimpse the clarity I seek as hidden truths—my sacred purpose,
life's deeper meaning—emerge from shadow, bathing me in unshakable peace.

I awaken to my power, shattering illusions and igniting boundless freedom, as I realize no one can dim my light unless I leave it unprotected.

I release suffering's grip, choosing love's warm glow, my thoughts shifting like dawn piercing an endless night.

I let go of old stories, once clutched like faded relics, and their heavy burden lifts, leaving my spirit unencumbered.

I unearth the love within, no longer chasing external praise, and my inner flame burns brighter, steady and fierce.

I yield to Spirit's guidance, and divine peace sweeps in—soft as a whisper, mighty as a tide—enfolding me in its warmth.

I reframe my perception, and miracles flood forth, painting my path with awe and wonder.

I honor every experience as a sacred gift, unwrapping it with reverence, and healing washes over me, tender and profound.

I embrace the truth that we are loved beyond measure, a revelation striking like a lightning bolt, illuminating all.

I reach for understanding beyond myself, my heart expanding, no longer yearning to be seen but to see.

I choose forgiveness, releasing buried grievances—even those that feel justified—and serenity cascades through me, a joyous river.

I awaken to my boundless essence, far beyond this fleeting form, and divine bliss erupts, uncontainable and free.

I rise above powerlessness, its shadow cloaked in pain, and reclaim the fire within, fierce and unbroken.

I see the spirit beyond the human mask, and love flows effortlessly, repainting the world in hues of grace.

I claim my worth, basking in soulful joy that warms me like sunlight on skin, coaxing my spirit to soar.

Introduction: A Beacon of Healing: My Journey Through Questions to Light

I share my healing journey here with a quiet wish: that even one soul might catch a fleeting glimpse of light, a spark of hope from my story that helps them survive in a world that often feels shadowed and bewildering. Like so many, I've been a seeker since childhood, wrestling with questions that stirred my soul: *Who am I? Why am I here? What is life's meaning? What is my purpose?* Growing up in a fundamentalist religious cult, these questions were not just curiosities—they were hauntings. The rigid teachings of right and wrong clashed with a deeper knowing that stirred within me, even as a young child. Life, as it was presented, didn't align with the whispers of my heart. I questioned everything, fearing I'd never find answers—or worse, that the answers wouldn't ring true.

However, don't mistake my journey for one of unrelenting struggle. My life has been woven with vibrant threads of joy—moments of profound peace, a thriving career, cherished friends and family, adventures across the globe, and the gift of abundance. Yet, beneath it all, a quiet ache persisted, a sense that something was missing. I made choices that led to suffering, but with time, I've come to see every experience—bright or shadowed—as a purposeful brushstroke on the canvas of my life. Even the painful moments held lessons, shaping me into who I am both in my career and in my personal life.

My journey is far from complete; as humans, the ego rattles the bars of our inner peace, giving us opportunities to grow, to learn. But today, I stand in a place of healing, joy, and clarity, eager to share the answers that have illuminated my path. In this book, I weave together the pivotal stories and experiences that carved my way forward, paired with reflections on the truths that anchor my heart. Regret, I've learned, is a heavy weight that serves no purpose. Instead, I offer hindsight's gentle wisdom—what might have been a better approach to certain situations—not to dwell on the past, but to light the way for others.

I'll start by recounting my childhood growing up in a cult, then I'll take you through my career journey, sharing the highs and lows and the beginning of my healing. Lastly, I'll offer you the wisdom I've learned over the last twenty-plus years. In several sections I start with my own poetry as a lead-in to the topic.

To those weighed down by the frustrations and burdens of the corporate world, I offer tools and perspectives to spark joy in your journey. To those who grew up in oppressive religious environments, haunted by fear, doubt, and guilt, I extend the promise of healing. And to those who simply crave a little more love in your life, I seek to offer inspiration. My hope is that these words shine like a beacon, guiding you toward your own radiant truth in the vast, beautiful mystery of life.

Part I

A Childhood Shaped by
Shadows Amongst a Backdrop
of Beauty and Kindness

FROM SHADOWS TO HAVEN

A fracture split my childhood,
A stranger lost in my own skin,
No belonging, no truth to hold,
Trapped in a smiling, patriarchal cage,
Why this life, this veiled control?

Fear wove rules, soft as whispers
Mind shaped by silent control.
No voice for the chaos within,
Us saved, them lost in sin,
God's wrath a shadow on my heart.

Play the part, a fearful child,
Subtle chains dressed as love,
Obey, repent, bow to doctrine—
Questions banned, naivete fed,
Sheltered in a world of rigid right.

Work bound us, hands worn proud,
Staff's kind smiles warmed the halls,
Sisters' laughter, brothers' games,
Yet rules choked joy, a silent blade,
Discipline carved a sheltered soul.

Sermons roared, love laced with dread,
Hellfire haunted lilac's bloom,
Communal meals, hands clasped tight,
But isolation walled us in,
Who am I beneath this rigid charm?

A haven flickered, cruelly bright—
A pulse of love beneath the lie,
Whispering: You are not this cage.

One question has echoed through the years, whispered in curious tones by friends and strangers alike: *How did you find the courage to leave home at eighteen, just weeks after high school graduation, and strike out on your own?* The answer burns as vividly now as it did then: Staying felt like a slow suffocation, like a life sentence in a world where I didn't belong. The weight of that place pressed against my chest, my thoughts, my very being. I was a stranger in my own skin, misunderstood, alone, adrift in a sea of unyielding certainties that made no sense to me. Leaving wasn't just courage—it was survival. I had to run, to break free, to find the edges of who I was beyond the confines of that world.

From my earliest memories, a quiet unease gnawed at me, a feeling I couldn't name. It was as if I'd been born into a puzzle with a piece missing, and no one else seemed to notice. Deep within, I knew something was wrong, but I lacked the words to pin it down. I was out of place, a square peg in a round hole, caught in a performance that felt like a costume I was forced to wear.

The world I inhabited was starkly divided: us against them, the righteous Kingdom opposed to the sinful World, God versus the Devil. Sermons thundered with threats of hellfire and brimstone, fear clashing with love in a relentless tug-of-war. I'd lie awake at night, staring at the ceiling, wondering, *Why am I here? Why this family? Why this life?* The only response I could muster was rebellion—a desperate, wild urge to escape, to run until I found a place where I could breathe.

Who am I? The question pulsed like a heartbeat, unanswered but insistent.

Growing Up at Fairwood, a Beautiful Cage

grew up at Fairwood, a compound in rural New Hampshire otherwise known as the headquarters of The Kingdom. This fundamentalist religious cult was led by my grandfather, Abram, until his death in 1977, and then by my father.

Fairwood, nestled down a dusty dirt road at the foot of Mount Monadnock's graceful silhouette, was a stunning place to grow up. A mile away, surrounded by whispering pines and buzzing with the hum of summer crickets, lay a pristine spring-fed lake, its glassy surface mirroring the sky. This breathtaking haven with its idyllic surface sang with nature's rhythm, yet its beauty could not hide the cage of strict doctrine and oppressive rules that shaped my childhood.

Early on, our family crowded into one cramped apartment inside the grand, creaking Main House, which was the heart of the compound, with little privacy. I shared a tiny bedroom with my sister Wendy (who is older than me by four years). Our metal twin bunk bed was pressed against one wall, and a shared dresser held our modest belongings. Down the narrow hallway, my older brother by two and a half years, Roger (Rog), and my younger brother by two and a half years, Steve, bunked in a mirrored setup, and the sounds of their laughter and their squabbles seeped through the thin walls. (It would be several more years before my youngest sister Rosie, whom I call Rose, would be born; she is almost ten years younger than me.) The apartment also included one bathroom, a small living area with a green vinyl couch, and my parents' bedroom, but it lacked a kitchen, so we joined communal meals in the Main House's bustling dining room, thrown in amongst the other residents and the Bible school students from the dormitories across the property.

Beyond our space, the Main House was a labyrinth of lives. It hummed with purpose. There were apartments for other families as well as single rooms for couples and elderly residents. There was a beautiful parlor with a window seat and heavy drapes that still allowed sunlight to stream in through tall windows; a meeting room where daily church services resounded with fervent hymns and prayerful pleading; and a large kitchen with a walk-in cooler big enough for tall milk cans from local farms, plus a separate pantry for supplies. A closed porch stored large egg cartons, boxes of bananas, bushels of apples, and seasonal produce. The communal laundry room thrummed with the churn of a commercial-sized washing machine, and outside, a sweeping veranda lined with rocking chairs overlooked an emerald lawn.

Fairwood's gardens and fields were a colorful patchwork, tended by devoted caretakers. Spring brought crocuses piercing snow-dusted earth, followed by daffodils and tulips in fiery reds, soft pinks, and blazing oranges. More flower beds burst with delicate petunias, stately irises, and cheerful zinnias. I'll never forget the way the lilac bushes along the curved driveway released a sweet, heady perfume, singing of summer's approach. Ancient grapevines framed another lawn, their heavy clusters ripening with dark, tart juice in fall. Vegetable gardens yielded all the splendor of fresh summer produce, and there was also a patch teeming with sun-kissed strawberries, so juicy and red. Autumn flared after Labor Day, the air crisp, the skies a brilliant blue, with trees ablaze in crimson, orange, and gold. We raked leaves into towering piles, diving in with gleeful abandon, as their earthy scent filled the air. Winter's first snow, which sometimes arrived as early as October, transformed the landscape into a sparkling wonderland, each flake a prism in the sharp, pine-scented air.

Beneath the Main House lay a shadowy cellar, our rainy-day playground, its cool, damp air thick with stone and soil. We played hide-and-seek, darting through its maze of narrow hallways, squeezing behind crates or dusty corners. Shelves groaned with mason jars of applesauce, peach slices in syrup, plump pears, tangy pickles, green beans, and stewed tomatoes, all of them canned during sweaty late-summer days. A dark root cellar held wooden bins of knobby potatoes, sweet carrots, and pungent onions, while a sacred corner stored the grape juice for monthly Communion.

Fairwood's grounds spread like a small village, each structure fit for purpose. The sanctuary was a hallowed space reserved for life's most sacred moments—weddings, funerals, and the grand Feasts that drew members from far-flung corners in March, May, and September. Fairwood's founder, Frank Sandford, had rooted these gatherings in the ancient Jewish traditions of Passover, Pentecost, and the Feast of Ingathering as times for prayer, worship, fiery preaching, and shared communion. The sanctuary's lofty ceilings framed the *Living Waters* painting, which hung above the baptismal tank, where ministers preached from a platform.

The men's and women's dormitories were filled with Bible school students and convention attendees, and the dining hall doubled as a wedding venue. Its industrial kitchen was filled with stainless-steel counters, sinks, ovens, a sterilizer, and a mixer. Frosty clouds billowed from the walk-in freezer that stored berries, vegetables, fish, and meat. There were more dormitory rooms above the dining hall with garages below for parking. A mechanical garage a few yards away smelled of oil and metal and roared with the sound of wrenches and engines. A workshop breathed out the smell of sawdust and varnish. A small red cottage, which would later become our home, stood near the dining hall. Clotheslines sagged with flapping sheets, swings creaked in the play area, the sandbox cradled our castles, and a basketball court and ball field echoed with shouts under summer skies. Later, new staff housing, a care facility, and a gymnasium all sprouted up, the latter hosting countless volleyball games.

At the top of the compound sat the Embassy. Perched regally on a hill, this was home to Grandpa and Grandma Abram and my beloved aunts. The Embassy stood in stark contrast to the rest of Fairwood's humble and sparse buildings. My grandfather insisted on only the best: A meticulously tended rose garden was viewable from the living room, with petals unfurling in shades of crimson, blush, and ivory, their fragrance drifting on the breeze. A bird bath in the center of the garden summoned bluebirds and chickadees alike. The garage housed a spotless blue Lincoln, and the basement held a green felt pool table upon which the striped and numbered balls clacked softly.

CHILDHOOD MEMORIES

Any moments of carefree fun in my childhood were inevitably laced with rules. I didn't understand until much later how inflexible and controlling they really were. Given how little privacy we had in our communal living environment, I frequently felt like I was in the spot-light. For example, I was often the last one sitting at the dining table, lingering glumly, pushing cold, overcooked broccoli or mushy peas around my plate, praying for rescue as the staff and student attend-ants cleaned up the dishes.

Like many others in those days, my parents were firm discipli-narians with us kids. There were spankings when we were "out of line" or "disobedient." But many times, I was left confused, wondering what I had done that warranted that kind of punishment. Upon reflection, I realize I was more sensitive than most people, even my siblings. (More on that later.) I also craved attention, and I recall often begging my mother for just one more hug and kiss before going to sleep.

At any rate, our behavior was monitored fiercely, especially in later years when my father became the leader. We were required to set the highest example of discipline, even during our growing years. This also meant we were not allowed to express our emotions fully or, really, to question anything. Life was just "follow the rules" and "do as we say."

Though my childhood seemed idyllic on the surface, beneath it ran an undercurrent of shame, fear, abuse, and control that I only recognized later. Though I don't recall experiencing any abuse myself, I've learned of countless stories of sexual abuse and coercive control in the years since I left. Over time, I've come to understand how the harsh doctrine of purity, common in many religious settings, contributed to these issues.

OUR NEW APARTMENT

After a few years in the Main House, our move to our new apartment felt like stepping into a world of our own, a thrilling leap from our previously cramped quarters, even though it was just a handful of yards away. Our new building stood proudly, with the word "Hosanna" etched upon its stone wall. Our humble apartment on the second floor was attached to the women's dormitory, with two smaller units below. For us four kids, it was a dream come true. We burst through the door, and our voices echoed through the rooms with excitement as we discovered *our own kitchen*, with a stove that readily hummed to life and a refrigerator just for us. Best of all, each of us claimed our own partitioned space, tiny retreats where we could pin up posters, stash treasures, and actually shut the door on the world. The hallway stretched like a small runway, perfect for impromptu races and games that sent thuds reverberating through the floor, no doubt completely annoying the elderly neighbors below with our shrieks and stomping feet.

Downstairs, the rec room became our winter sanctuary. Its walls rang with the sharp *thwack* of ping-pong balls, the commotion of other made-up games, and the laughter of countless snowball-dodging days spent indoors.

THE COTTAGE—OUR HOME FOR MY TEENAGE YEARS

We savored the years in our new apartment until my younger sister Rose was born. As our family expanded, we needed a bit more space. Then came the move to the Cottage, the red-shingled jewel that felt like a castle of our own. Tucked among the trees, its compact size didn't dampen our joy—it was *ours*, a private refuge at last.

Yet privacy was fleeting; the Cottage hummed with constant visitors needing support or advice from my parents. It housed my father's office, where he prepped for sermons and counseled members when he was not outside tending to the maintenance of the compound—fixing cars in the garage, digging ditches, repaving roadways, shoveling and plowing snow, felling trees for firewood, or driving the tractor to prepare the garden beds. I would come to dread that office, though, with its metal desk and book-lined shelves, for it was where "talks" happened. This was where rebellion met with consequences and where the very air felt thick with the weight of expectations.

The Cottage was warmed by a wood-burning furnace in the cellar, and it was notoriously hard to keep at a steady temperature. The extremes were palpable—swelteringly unbearable when the fire roared yet bone-chillingly cold in the mornings before it was stoked again. The rhythmic *thunk* of axes and hatchets echoes in my memory as Dad and my brothers chopped logs, the sharp scent of pine and sap filling the air while they stacked cords of wood near the furnace. Upstairs, the space was ingeniously divided into five semiprivate nooks for us kids—each a little haven with a bed, shelf, dresser, nightstand, and just enough room to dream. A small bathroom with a shower stall completed the floor.

Downstairs, the entryway held a closet stuffed with coats and boots, plus a washer and dryer that chugged through endless loads. The open main room flowed from a compact kitchen to a space for a dining table where we gathered for our daily suppers at 5 p.m. In one corner sat a desk piled with papers alongside my mother's sewing machine, its pedal humming whenever she sat down to create clothing and crafts. The living area had a couch and a pair of armchairs arranged near a piano that trilled under my mother's fingers during our lessons, its keys worn smooth from years of scales. My parents' bedroom, another bathroom, and the office completed the first floor.

⋮

2

Oases of Warmth

Amid Fairwood's unwavering rules, certain souls shone like lanterns in the dark, their warmth a lifeline. Over the years, the Fairwood residents shifted like seasons, a gentle rotation of familiar and fresh faces. I hold dear the memory of these relatives and friends, from the elderly with their weathered wisdom to the young newcomers with their bright, untainted spirits. For example, I cherished my time with Miss Craig, a kind old lady who lived to over one hundred years old. Her tiny room in the Main House was a place of comfort. Her silver hair glowed under the soft light of a single lamp, and her eyes sparkled as she taught me how to play Scrabble at a small, wobbly table. I loved words, their shapes and sounds, and Miss Craig nurtured that passion, game after game, her gentle voice praising my clever plays. Those moments shimmer in my memory—alive today whenever I pull out my own Scrabble board for another game.

In later years, treks up the hill to Grandma Abram and Aunt Toria's became a cherished ritual. Grandma would sit by the big picture window with sunlight streaming through, while she wove soft hats and scarves, darned socks, or hemmed dresses with meticulous care. A cluster of bright African violets bloomed in a nearby planter, their velvety purple petals a cheerful contrast to her focused calm. Aunt Toria, ever patient, wrangled us rowdy kids when my parents were away on church mission trips. Her gentle smile and knack for storytelling kept us enchanted, even as we tumbled through the living room like a pack of wild pups. Later on, after a television was purchased, we would gather together to watch the Olympics or movies like *The Sound of Music*.

Aunt Rea's visits from her Canadian home were bursts of joy. Her family would spill into Grandma's house, my little cousins' shy smiles so precious. Then Aunt June and her crew, who lived at Fairwood in its early days, would sweep in for family gatherings or church events. The dining room would come alive with deliciously cooked meals, the clatter of dishes punctuated by bursts of laughs. My aunts, each so distinct yet bound by love, wove a thread of warmth through my childhood.

The winding roads of New Hampshire would deliver us to Grandpa and Grandma Wakeman's house, located just a few miles from Fairwood. I recall a few Saturday mornings when we piled into the car, tires crunching onto their gravel driveway, the air alive with the scent of freshly mown grass. Grandpa would fling open the door, his smile as warm as the sunlight spilling across the porch. Grandma put the final touches on breakfast, standing in the kitchen proudly wearing her apron, a colorful canvas embroidered with the names of all her grandchildren in playful, looping script. The kitchen was a symphony of comfort: The waffle iron hissed and sizzled, sending up clouds of buttery steam, while the sweet aroma of these golden treats wrapped us in an olfactory hug. We'd cram around their sturdy table, our fingers sticky with maple syrup, savoring each fluffy, golden bite.

When they later moved to Maine, our visits became more rare, but now they glow ever-brighter in memory. Their new mobile home was a place of comfort, its tiny kitchen alive with the hearty perfume of a boiled dinner simmering on the stove. Corned beef, tender and salty, mingled with wedges of cabbage, potatoes, and carrots in a steaming pot, each spoonful of warmth lingering on the tongue and in the heart. Each St. Patrick's Day I'm reminded of those precious meals as I make the same corned beef dinner. Those trips also meant time with Uncle John and his family. Their hospitality—always welcoming us with open arms and easy smiles—was cozy and familiar.

When Grandpa and Grandma Wakeman came to visit us, their arrival was a celebration, like a holiday bursting into bloom. They'd step out of their car, arms cradling a "goody box" overflowing with delights that Fairwood's plain pantry never held, such as cheese pops that crunched with salty joy. My eyes would especially widen at the sight of fizzing orange soda bottles; I anticipated how their bubbles would tickle my nose with each sip. Every treat was a thrilling rebellion against Fairwood's simplicity, a taste of the wider world. Tucked among my keepsakes is a card from my grandparents, sent not long before my grandfather passed, congratulating me on a work promotion. Grandpa's humor sparkled through, as he cheekily inserted *not* into the preprinted message, "You're *not* always on my mind," signing it with a flourish from "Aunt Ruth and Uncle C." That card still brings a wry smile, a snapshot of his playful spirit.

Other joys of my childhood included visits to see Aunt Betty in Massachusetts. She'd spoil us with feasts that outshone Fairwood's fare—plates of homemade lasagna, layers of rich marinara and creamy ricotta bubbling under a golden crust, paired with warm garlic bread. Best of all were the trips to the nearby beaches, where the Atlantic roared and sparkled, waves crashing against sun-warmed sand. We'd run barefoot, chasing the tide, the salty air tangling our hair as Aunt Betty watched with a grin, her love as abundant as her garden's bounty. Those days—filled with laughter, feasts, and the sea's wild song—created a joy that still shimmers in my heart.

⋮

3

A Legacy of Hustle

Fairwood was a world unto itself, a hive of industry that thrived on our collective sweat, and from dawn to dusk, my parents instilled in us a fierce work ethic. Their own hands were never idle, except during the Sabbath, their movements swift and purposeful. We kids mirrored their hustle, diving into the rhythm of Fairwood's self-sufficient heartbeat. For us girls, that meant caring for the bounty of the gardens along with the other women of Fairwood, our fingers becoming stained with the juices of the ripe fruits and vegetables. After harvesting pails of green beans, and wheelbarrows full of corncobs, we'd gather on the veranda or crowd into one of the kitchens to begin the canning process. Meanwhile the boys—Roger and Steve—tackled their own tasks: pulling stubborn weeds from the garden beds, their knees dusted with earth, and riding with my father to neighboring farms, hauling brimming cans of milk and dozens of eggs.

I swelled with pride watching my parents and strove to emulate their tireless energy. They moved like well-oiled machines—fast, efficient, never faltering. I'd perch at the table, mimicking my mother's deft movements, snapping green beans with a crisp *pop* or husking corn as fast as I could manage. It baffled me when some women arrived late or, worse, skipped the work entirely, their absence a stark contrast to my mother's unwavering presence. I don't recall either of my parents ever taking a sick day; their stamina was legendary among the staff. Praise for their reputation of excellence was a melody I loved to hear: others often marveled at their speed, their skill, their constant dedication.

That dedication shone brightest during Feasts and Conventions, when Fairwood transformed itself through a whirlwind of preparation. My parents and the other staff worked relentlessly, readying the compound for the flood of additional members who would soon descend on the land from afar. Dormitories were scrubbed until they glistened, and beds were made with linens that smelled of the crisp outdoors from drying on the clotheslines. Menus were planned with precision, each meal constructed to feed a crowd—hearty stews, casseroles, and plenty of homemade rolls. Groceries were bought in towering stacks, and the kitchens came alive with the clatter of pots and pans. Every corner of Fairwood readied itself to welcome the gatherings that beat with the Movement's fervor.

I looked forward to those events, not for the doctrine but for the faces they brought—my Grandpa and Grandma Wakeman with their warm smiles, not to mention aunts and uncles who doled out boisterous hugs, as well as cousins and friends I otherwise rarely saw. The long services, though, tested my patience. While the singing could spark joy—especially when the music occasionally strayed from the somber old hymns to newer lyrics that felt more alive, their words carried by the strum of guitars—otherwise the Sanctuary's chairs grew hard beneath me as speakers thundered about fear and repentance, their voices booming through the high-ceilinged room. Baptisms initiated the newly converted, those who were eager to join the Kingdom; their earlier baptisms from other churches were dismissed as invalid.

I know that this culture of hustle shaped me, fueling in me a drive to carve my own path. But a quiet question lingered: Was this relentless pace a choice, or another chain of the Kingdom's making?

⋮

4

A Growing Unease

As I grew into school age, the world began to shift—or perhaps my eyes began to see it all more clearly. Public school was a lifeline, yet it wasn't exactly a safe haven. I was different, marked by Fairwood's peculiar ways, and my classmates didn't hesitate to point that out. Their teasing branded me a Goody Two Shoes, a label that clung like a shadow. Teachers adored me—my conscientiousness, my quiet diligence—but that only deepened the divide, further tainting me as teacher's pet. I was terrified of stepping out of line, my naivete a shield and a shackle, rendering me blissfully unaware of how the world operated beyond Fairwood's borders.

When John Lennon died, the grief that swept my school baffled me. Rock music, with its forbidden drumbeats, was anathema to Fairwood, as was most pop culture. Though we owned a radio, its dial was tuned only to catch a bit of news from the most conservative stations. The records we played spun tales of faith or filled our home with the solemn chords of pious hymns. Television came late, a rare treat we enjoyed sparingly, mostly for Olympic races or, when my brothers pleaded, Patriots, Red Sox, and Celtics games.

The screen would of course be snapped off with a click during beer commercials. But my social awkwardness, my sheltered heart, would only dawn on me years later, a quiet ache showing me how naive I really had been, how little I was actually taught about the world. We weren't allowed to debate or question things, to have a voice, especially on *worldly* subjects like politics, religion, music, science, or, really, most anything. Curiosity wasn't encouraged. So life just didn't make sense to me.

In the fourth grade our class was scheduled for a field trip to Boston University's Sargent Camp, a break from the classroom's monotony that I usually loved. But this time, dread took shape. The day would include a ropes course, which we had to wear a harness for. For most kids, it was no big deal, but for me, it was a nightmare. My strict upbringing meant I could only wear dresses—no exceptions. We were following an old-school symbol of modesty based on a reference in the Old Testament that women were not to wear that which pertained to a man. A dress and a harness? A recipe for disaster. I pleaded with my mother for pants, even though I didn't even own any at the time. Her compromise was to make me a pair of hand-sewn jean gauchos. Mortified, I pictured how all the other kids and camp counselors would snicker at me. I had no choice but to go.

That certainly wasn't the last time I felt like I stuck out, a sore thumb in a world that seemed to fit everyone else. Time and again, I was singled out, isolated by rules I didn't understand. Why was wearing pants so wrong? It haunted me daily.

Friends and strangers would chant, "Marcia, Marcia, Marcia," their voices gently teasing as they repeated my name thrice. I'd mimic them back, puzzled, my smile masking ignorance. It wasn't until my twenties that I learned they were quoting *The Brady Bunch*, a cultural touchstone I'd never watched. But Bible verses? Those I could recite with ease, their cadences etched into my soul from daily readings. Church was my second skin—more services in a week than some attend in a lifetime.

⋮

5

The Kingdom's Shadow

In truth, I didn't realize that Fairwood was the headquarters for the Kingdom until I got a bit older. Its mission was grandiose: "The Restoration of All Things"—that is, a return to Old Testament ways while preaching New Testament grace. This paradox certainly sowed seeds of confusion in my young mind.

Life at Fairwood revolved around the Old Testament's ironclad rules, weaving a rhythm of sacred precision into our days. Each morning began with mandatory Bible readings, our parents' voices intoning the daily passage, followed by each of us offering prayers to bless the day ahead. The Sabbath was honored twice—on Saturday, as scripture commanded, and then again on Sunday, in a nod to other churches, to avoid their judging us as heathens. The air in our home hummed with reverence, heavy with the weight of ritual. Pork and shellfish were forbidden, their absence a silent echo of ancient Jewish customs. Shopping was also off-limits, another boundary etched into our lives that set us apart from others.

On Thursdays the staff and Bible school students fasted from 9 a.m. to 3 p.m. as a solemn reflection marking the day of Jesus's crucifixion (though in later years I puzzled over why we observed it a day early). The light supper to break the fast consisted of pea soup, stewed tomatoes from the jars in the cellar, and Jell-O for dessert since it could be prepared mostly in advance.

Daily prayer services echoed the ancient Jewish hour of sacrifice at 9 a.m., while Sabbath services at sundown on Fridays and Saturdays framed our weeks. Aside from participating in the Friday Sabbath service, us kids were granted a reprieve from the weekday services during the school year. But on the days when we attended service, I learned at a young age to sit still, my body quiet while my mind wandered, questions simmering: Why did we believe and worship so differently from those I knew at public school and in the wider town's community? The answers, like so much else, lay just beyond my reach.

My parents, like all Kingdom staff, worked without a salary, their lives a testament to their faith. They were taught to trust that God would provide, so their prayers rose like incense for every practical need—food, clothing, shelter. To keep Fairwood's lights on, the Church leaned heavily on its members' tithes, a mandatory 10 percent that flowed from those who held outside jobs. My dear Aunt Betty, a nurse with a modest income, gave selflessly. Each month, her envelope arrived with a check tucked inside to cover the costs of what the Church wouldn't—school supplies, winter boots, and sundry small necessities that helped make our lives a little better. Come September, she'd send bolts of fabric that my mother tirelessly transformed into dresses and jumpers for Wendy, Rose, and me, our back-to-school outfits a badge of her love. We also cherished the generosity of hand-me-downs from other family and church members, thrilled as we were with more variety.

The Kingdom's origins were a murky tale I never fully grasped as a child. Some rules had softened over time, left to members' discretion, but its roots ran deep. A member once penned a book called

The Sublimity of Faith, which exalted founder Frank Sandford, but its pages held no allure for me. Later, I would learn some more of Sandford's story: He was a charismatic young baseball player in the late 1800s, gripped by a divine calling to build a grand headquarters near Portland, Maine, that he would call Shiloh. Its immense but eerie structure, crowned by a golden turret that gleamed like a watchtower, still lingers in my memory. Sandford's mission was relentless—recruiting "heathens" worldwide, even poaching from other Christian denominations, including both of my parents' families.

His fervor swelled Shiloh's ranks until a bitter split in the 1920s caused a scattering of the once faithful members. His radical trust in God led to tragedy—sickness, starvation, and even death. Two of his own children fled, tales of their footsteps echoing in the hushed conversations I overheard, some voices dripping with disdain, others with fervent praise. Sandford's claims—that he was Elijah reborn, destined to fulfill prophecies already fulfilled by Christ—branded him a false prophet. Convicted for wrongful deaths, he served time in prison before fleeing to the Catskills in New York, where he lived out his days in seclusion, my Grandfather Abram by his side as his aide.

In the Catskills, they'd settled on a sheep farm, sharing a rambling house with other family members. The bleating of lambs and the rustle of wind through the trees filled the air on this land where my mother, her sisters, and five of their cousins were born. After Sandford's death in the late 1940s, my Grandfather Abram took the Kingdom's reins. Upon the purchase of the land at Fairwood, they moved again, this time to New Hampshire (though the Catskills property, known as "the Hills," remained part of the Kingdom, a quiet outpost of the Movement).

Articulating precisely what was wrong with the Kingdom—what made it a cult—is like trying to catch smoke. On the surface, it shimmered with biblical virtue, grace, and forgiveness, and many members cherished its transformative power. But beneath that veneer lurked darker truths: psychological manipulation, fear woven into most every sermon, oppression that silenced questions, and an elitism that elevated us above "the world." The hymnbook, titled *Warrior Songs for the White Cavalry*, betrayed an obviously racist undercurrent, while sexism also ran deep—men ruled as heads of households, their decisions final, often requiring Sandford's or, later, Grandpa Abram's approval for major choices, from marriages to moves. Women were to be subservient, their voices muted. A rigid list of rules demanded unwavering obedience, each dictate a link in the chain of control. Even the younger women at the Bible school were required to follow strict rules such as "Don't wear your hair wet to breakfast" (since it might make men imagine you in the shower) and admonishments against visible bra straps or form-fitting clothes. I learned that the list of don'ts had previously been even more endless: no bare legs, no sleeves above the elbow, no haircuts, no skirts above the knee, no bare feet, no open-toed shoes, no makeup, no nail polish. The message was clear: Cover yourself with no adornment in order to keep men from stumbling.

The Kingdom's doctrine twisted goodness into a rigid formula. Salvation wasn't about helping others but about avoiding sin—and nearly everything I longed to do was considered a sin. Dancing, rock music, movies, and pierced ears were all forbidden, each a potential step toward damnation. This conformity dulled our spirits, numbed our personalities, stifled expression, and crushed any hope of choosing our own paths. We were taught we were the elite, part of the 144,000 destined for the Kingdom of Heaven, the chosen few elevated above the world's "heathens." The weight of that belief suffocated me, leaving me to question how I could believe in a God who demanded such extreme perfection.

When Grandpa Abram died in the mid-1970s, my father stepped into the role of lead caretaker and preacher at Fairwood. However, upon assuming this role, his conditions were clear: A board of directors must replace the previous generations' sole-leader model. It was a bold move, a crack in the Kingdom's foundation. But he didn't want the responsibility or the limelight like my grandfather had.

Long after I had left Fairwood's grasp, he and others eventually began nudging the Movement toward change, challenging Sandford's false claims and outdated beliefs. The progress eventually caused a fracture, which led to a schism. Each individual church property held a vote on whether to honor Sandford's doctrines and remain part of the Kingdom or move away from his controversial beliefs. This was a divisive time, causing rifts between many family members. By the mid-1990s, my parents and many others chose to leave the Kingdom. This more progressive faction sought a new path, unburdened by the Founder's shadow, but the Kingdom's legacy—psychological manipulation and fear-soaked sermons—remained etched in my soul. I just couldn't grasp how or why a God that had created us demand that we suffer and sacrifice for our own humanness. Ultimately, the answers lay, for me, far beyond Fairwood's borders. These were truths I was desperate to find.

⋮

6

A Soul in Chains

As the preacher's kids, my siblings and I lived under a magnifying glass, our every move scrutinized as if we were the embodiment of the Kingdom's ideals. Expectations hung heavy, like a fog that never lifted. As I got older, I despised the fact that my sisters and I couldn't wear pants. My mother tried to soften the blow, much like when she created the gauchos for me to wear under the harness on the ropes course, and sewed a skirt for me that was meant to mimic the look of the marching band's royal blue pants with a yellow stripe. Even with this attempt at assimilation, I still felt like I was parading my difference through town. This also meant that participating in sports was nearly impossible for us girls; gym classes didn't make concessions for shorts or sweatpants until junior high, and then only when they were deemed "modest" enough. Skiing? Forget it— who wants to wear a long dress over ski pants? Even among church friends and cousins, many of whom could wear pants, I was the odd one out.

Music, like so much else at Fairwood, was bound by endless restrictions, its melodies locked behind additional rules. On long bus rides to school, before I had a car, I'd relish the joy of the radio crackling to life, pulsing with rock music's uplifting beat. The songs I heard on those rides were a fleeting escape, a window to a world beyond the compound's grip. But even that experience was short-lived—zealous Fairwood staff, ever watchful, phoned the school, demanding the radio be silenced.

The ridicule didn't stop at school. Each summer when Kingdom members from across the country descended on Fairwood for camp, I faced ostracism again. These kids, tied to the Movement but raised with looser reins, saw me as a curiosity. I can still hear a group of girls, their voices sharp and mocking, chanting the Adam and the Ants lyrics, "Goody goody two shoes / don't drink, don't smoke, what do you do?" Their words cut deep, leaving me stranded in a sea of isolation, my cheeks burning as I stood there, lost and aching for belonging.

Finding someone who understood was like searching for a star in daylight. But salvation came through my journal, its blank pages a refuge where I poured out my confusion, my doubts, my dreams.

As soon as I could in my preteens, I took on jobs—babysitting neighbors outside of Fairwood at first, then inheriting my sister Wendy's house-cleaning gig for a kind elderly couple down the street. Their home, a short walk from Fairwood, was a world apart. I'd step into their beautiful house, the air scented with perfume and fresh flowers, and lose myself in cleaning, ironing their crisp linens or polishing silverware until it gleamed. On special evenings, I helped serve the meals at their elegant dinner parties, the clink of crystal glasses and the glow of candlelight a stark contrast to Fairwood's austerity. They were Catholic, different from us, and though no one spoke ill of them, the divide was clear. I secretly admired their life, though, with its ease and warmth. Witnessing it helped ignite a quiet rebellion in my heart.

Those moments sparked a resolve: I could break free. Yet, the severity of expectations—salvation through obedience, not kindness—suffocated me. I questioned everything: Why was I here? Why was I tethered to this faith? The Kingdom's elitism, its control, felt like chains on my soul; their weight urged me to run.

⋮

7

Rebellion and Longing

My teenage years blur like a faded Polaroid, edges frayed, colors muted. Memories slip through my fingers, half-suppressed, half-forgotten. Even though my family and the other members of the Kingdom were kind, Fairwood didn't feel like home—it was a suffocating tangle of family and church, where lines between the two dissolved. The air always felt heavy, thick with expectations I didn't understand and couldn't meet. I rebelled in secret, sneaking to parties under the guise of babysitting, my heart pounding as I sipped forbidden drinks or smoked.

Around this time, a bombshell from an older teenager shook me to my core: my grandfather Abram had been involved with at least a couple of women in the congregation. At first I reeled from shock and disbelief. Later, I learned these weren't mutual relationships at all but acts of manipulation, his controlling nature casting a long shadow. This discovery deepened the chaos in my already troubled soul, layering new questions onto my search for my own identity. In later years, I reflected on why I'd never felt close to him. His dismissive nickname for me—Marcia Pest Wakeman, or "MPW"—always stung like a slap, and it was repeated often enough to lodge in my heart. Perhaps as a child, I'd sensed something unsettling in his presence or unwittingly stood in the way of his secrets. It would take years for the truth to come out later.

I also carried a quiet ache—that I was never pretty enough, thin enough, smart enough, *enough*. My buck teeth, a jagged badge of insecurity, finally softened under braces, a kind gift from my Grandpa and Grandma Wakeman. At school, I drifted like a ghost, never anchoring to any group. Not a jock, not a scholar with Ivy-League dreams, not a pothead lost in haze. I was just . . . there, trying to fit into a puzzle that didn't have my shape. By my last couple of years, I found slivers of belonging, fragile as spun glass.

I continued to work my babysitting and house-cleaning jobs, saving every penny I could. With every paycheck, I inched closer to freedom. Eventually I finally had enough to buy my brother Rog's blue Pinto. It became my chariot of liberation: chipped paint, rumbling engine, and all.

The day I turned sixteen, I clutched my driver's license, the plastic warm in my hand, and felt the world crack open. No more long, bumpy bus rides to school—I could drive, the wind whipping through the open windows, while listening to the forbidden thrill of the radio turned low. An unexpected connection started to form with my younger brother Steve. Though he'd once just been a typical sibling with whom I bickered, he soon became my closest ally. The Pinto brought us together, our shared adventures forging a bond that deepened with every mile. He was my rock—nonjudgmental, always ready to listen and to laugh together. Steve was my accomplice, and those moments—wild, free, and filled with joy—remain treasures we will always share.

I continued to struggle with all the rules. Working a job on Saturday, the sacred Sabbath, was unthinkable, though my father eventually relented when I got hired as a teller at Peterborough

Saving Bank when I was a senior. He insisted that I at least keep it discreet. But pierced ears, movies, dancing, and even bowling? All of them forbidden, each a sin in the Kingdom's eyes. At school, these restrictions made me a target, my classmates' taunts stinging like nettles. I still recall my mother finding my Huey Lewis and the News cassette hidden in my nightstand drawer. She didn't need to listen to "I Want a New Drug"—the title alone was enough to deem it scandalous, and her disapproval was abundantly clear.

My bathing suit's sewn-on skirt for "coverage" advertised my shame every time I went to the beach as a teenager. I envied my cousin, who stayed with us some weekends while attending a nearby school; she wore jeans like it was nothing, and I burned with jealousy.

My mother, aunts, and the older women didn't get it. In their Catskills childhoods, dresses were the norm, regardless of faith, so they easily blended in, at least at school. My sister Wendy, too, seemed relatively unbothered by the restrictions. I, on the other hand felt like I was drowning in them.

RENEWED HOPE

Fairwood's sister property, Chestnut Hill, was about an hour away. It always felt a little less rigid there. Beyond its church, the grounds buzzed with life—staff houses dotted the landscape, and a massive barn loomed, its weathered boards alive with the lowing of cows and the clucking of chickens. The teenagers who lived there, including some of my cousins, were a fun crew I began to click with starting in my early teens. Many attended the Bible school at Fairwood after high school, their dormitory rooms a hub of laughter and secrets. After school, I'd hurry over and slip into their rooms, where we'd lay on bunk beds, sharing stories and dreams. Those girls became my anchors, their friendship a gift to my confused soul, each memory a warm glow—laughter and shared confidences and the simple joy of being understood.

Then one summer during high school, while visiting an older friend in Maine who was part of the church but looser with the rules, everything changed. She took me to a thrift store, where I bought my first pair of jeans. I was electrified. Back home, I started wearing them in secret, rolling them up under a long denim skirt until I was out of sight from the house. Shedding that skirt felt like shedding chains. At school, kids noticed. They warmed to me, saw the spark of someone new. I'd never fully fit in, but I felt a little less like an outcast.

There was also a boy, another secret spark in a world where dating was forbidden. "Date when you're ready to marry" was the rule. So, I wove lies—about babysitting or meeting a girlfriend—to steal moments with him. One Saturday evening, we pulled into Carr's, the only gas station in our sleepy town, its neon sign flickering like a tired heartbeat. He ran in for snacks, leaving me in the car, my breath fogging the window. Then, headlights sliced through the dusk. A Fairwood staff family. My stomach dropped as I ducked, heart hammering, but their eyes caught mine. They *knew*. The next day, the office's stale air pressed against me as I faced "the talk." My parents, resigned, eventually asked to meet him, but then the spark between us fizzled. He moved on to someone brighter, bolder, more *worldly*. My heart cracked, a quiet fracture. Crushes bloomed and withered—boys from church, boys from school—but their eyes never lingered on me. I craved to be seen, to be wanted, to be loved.

I dreamed of escape, of my sneakers pounding the pavement in fleeting rebellion, but the world beyond didn't open its arms. No one wants the weight of a runaway who isn't theirs.

In late spring, just before high school graduation, I was headed to a party with friends. We stopped for pizza, and I waited in my car—a brown Chevrolet sedan, a trade-in from the blue Pinto— unaware that cans from the case of beer they'd stashed inside my trunk were opened and being consumed. As they drank outside, police lights flashed, and chaos erupted. My friends were cuffed, and I, underage with alcohol in my vehicle, was hauled to the station. My heart pounded, frantically calling friends over twenty-one to no avail.

With no other choice, I dialed home. Dad's voice was a low rumble as he arrived, his face stern as he asked the officer if I was intoxicated. I hadn't touched a drop, and the officer, sensing my fear, softened, his pity a small mercy. But the jeans I wore—forbidden at home—were a glaring sin in Dad's eyes. He followed me to retrieve my car, then to my friend's house, where I'd planned to spend the night. I begged to stop there to reassure her I was okay, and he relented, tailing me closely. The drive home was endless.

As graduation loomed, I knew: Fairwood wasn't home. Escape was my only path, the open road a promise of a self I'd yet to find.

Some friendships flickered like candlelight, warm but brief. When my rebellion flared—sneaking out, questioning the rules— many eyes turned cold. I was too wild for the church yet too tame for the world, caught in a liminal space where neither side claimed me. I coped, piecing together moments of laughter, defiance, and longing, but now those memories slip, elusive as shadows.

⋮

8

The Leap to Freedom

When I left Fairwood, it was with naive courage and no real plan, just ninety dollars in my pocket and a burning need to escape. I headed north, crashing with friends at first and then moving in with several roommates until I could find a foothold. My mission was simple: independence.

Work was my anchor, a habit ingrained by my parents' own relentless ethic. I wasn't afraid of long hours or hard tasks; babysitting, cleaning houses, and my bank teller job had all taught me perseverance. So I found a job and enrolled in college courses, each accomplishment a brick in the foundation of a new life.

Fairwood wasn't home; it was a place I'd survived. The open road, with its uncertainty and freedom, was all I needed to start again, to find the Marcia who'd been waiting beneath the weight of the Kingdom's rules.

Part II

A Winding Path to Purpose:
My Thirty-Five-Year Career Odyssey

Boldly I venture, breaking free from chains,
Chasing independence where freedom reigns.
Ever learning, my spirit's ascent,
Through highs and lows, with forward intent.

Goals conquered, new friendships ignite,
Bosses varied—some dim, some bright.
Mentors encircle, their wisdom a guide,
Lifting my soul as I stride side by side.

A woman carving paths in a man's domain,
Finding my rhythm, savoring the gain.
Clients, a spectrum—brilliant, yet some a trial,
Setbacks spark new starts, each step worthwhile.

Paying it forward, I champion those behind,
Planting seeds of change, vast and entwined.
Wisdom blooms through lessons hard-won,
Successes shine; detours lead on.

One chapter closes, yet my heart beats strong,
Onward I soar, where my soul belongs.

Over the past thirty-five years, I've been blessed with an extraordinary career in financial services, the last stretch in consulting, a journey I never meticulously planned but one that unfolded with a rhythm of its own. I never chased specific titles or corner offices; my only ambition was to keep moving forward, to grow, to see where the path would lead. Hard work was my compass, but looking back, I see the synchronicities—uncanny moments of alignment, both joyful and challenging—that guided me like invisible hands. I sought that guidance intentionally, praying for direction, trusting I was being led. My mission became clear: to help others. Whether it was empowering clients to navigate complex financial landscapes or mentoring colleagues to shine, their successes filled me with a joy that fueled my own drive. In time, I discovered my "why"—a purpose rooted in service, in making a tangible difference. Regrets hold no value for me; every experience, smooth or jagged, sculpted who I am. In reflection, I offer some considerations for others walking similar paths now. There are lessons I've woven into these stories I share.

Let me paint the picture of my career's winding road.

9

Roots of Resilience: Forging a Path Through Work and Healing

In 1988, fresh out of Fairwood, survival meant finding a way to earn money fast. My first job was in Lincoln, New Hampshire, behind the deli counter of a grocery store, the air sharp with the tang of roast beef and cheddar as I sliced meat and cheese with precision. My diligence caught the manager's eye, and soon I traded the deli's hum for the chime of the cash register, scanning groceries with a rhythm that felt like progress. Yet, when asked about my work, shame crept in—I wasn't on a traditional path like my college-bound peers, and I wondered where this would lead. But I pressed on, somewhat naively believing all would work out.

I'd savored my high school teller job at Peterborough Savings Bank, the crisp rustle of bills and the satisfying click of the drawer a quiet thrill. Weeks after leaving home, I landed another teller position, this time at First NH Bank, gratitude washing over me like a warm tide. To make ends meet, I kept the grocery store gig, working seven days a week, stretching a twenty-dollar bill to cover meals with canned soup, pasta, and the occasional apple. That fall, I enrolled in night classes, diving into banking, economics, and accounting, my mind like parched earth drinking rain as it soaked up these new concepts. Promotions came swiftly: personal banker, then branch manager, each step up evoking a burst of pride. I wasn't chasing a grand plan, just fueled by a hunger to learn, to advance, to stay true to my mission of growth.

In 1992, at the age of twenty-two, the bank launched a project to automate the typewriter, that clunky beast that haunted branch work. I'd spent hours typing up certificates of deposits and loan notes, each mistake forcing a restart. When the IT group sought frontline help, I leapt at the chance, leaving my branch role to join a small team as a business analyst. The world of project work electrified me, and I dove into learning basic programming, crafting requirements, and writing technical specifications. It felt like unlocking a new language. My confidence surged as I thrived in the dynamic chaos of different projects, a stark contrast to the predictable cadence of daily bank operations.

At the bank, after the automation project was deemed a major success, I dove deeper into project work, tackling bank acquisitions and merger integrations with zeal. We revamped systems and processes to meet new regulations like Truth in Savings, a regulation that provided greater transparency to consumers on how much interest could be earned from the bank on interest-bearing accounts, each challenge a puzzle I loved solving. I'd travel to different branches, the road humming beneath my tires, to guide staff through new software features, their faces lighting up as they grasped the updates. The work was alive, ever-changing, and it fed my soul, each success a step toward a future I couldn't yet see but trusted was unfolding as it should.

STRUGGLING WITH MY PAST

In my late teens and early twenties, as I carved out a career, my personal life felt like a battlefield, each step forward a struggle against the weight of my upbringing. I occasionally would fight depression, panic attacks, and even suicidal thoughts. I didn't feel like I belonged anywhere. The confusion from my past, the fear, plagued me. Something deep down didn't feel right.

A lifeline came from a dear friend, her words a spark in the dark: "Marcia, you can be mad at God—He's big enough to take it and understand." The moment her words sank in, it was as if a locked door swung open. Relief flooded me, a rush of freedom I could taste like cool water after a long drought. For the first time, I felt permission to question, to challenge the teachings that felt wrong deep in my bones, without fear of divine retribution. It was the beginning of my emancipation, a path to thinking for myself.

In my early twenties, I sought out therapists to help untangle the knots of confusion and pain from my upbringing. They became my guides, helping me navigate the emotional fog. They encouraged me to write to my parents, to share the weight I was carrying and disclose my need for space, even from holiday visits. It took months to summon the courage, but I finally penned a letter, raw and honest, telling them I was struggling and needed room to breathe. My dad's response came swiftly—a letter of his own, filled with understanding and support. Over the next few years, we exchanged several letters. He shared his own awakening, realizing how the Kingdom's teachings had oppressed not just me but others too. He even met a therapist who compared the impact to PTSD, a clarity that validated my emotions. I wasn't crazy; my feelings were real, rooted in something deeper than I'd known.

In one of his letters, he wrote to let us kids know that finally they would be sending a formal acknowledgment to Kingdom members regarding my grandfather Abram's indiscretions. For years, many members had revered him, only to feel betrayed by the deceit surrounding his manipulative affairs with women in the congregation. The members' demand for truth had grown louder, and the letter was a step toward accountability.

Although I had left Fairwood years before, I'd stayed connected to the Kingdom, even visiting other churches on occasion. When I finally realized I needed to distance myself from even those churches, I nevertheless managed to keep in touch with friends and relatives from the Chestnut Hill area. They were a comfort, as they knew about my background but weren't tied so tightly to the rules. I have fond memories of outings with them like Sunday breakfasts at Bickford's, drinks at the Salty Dog, and ice cream at Friendly's, as well as countless dinners at their homes. And I met more new friends through them that weren't from the Kingdom. One friend introduced me to a guy that I started dating when I was twenty-three and would eventually marry.

As I broke free, I wrestled with why I was the first to leave. Why didn't my family see what I saw? Over time, they too moved away, and when my parents finally left the Kingdom, embracing the very "sins" they'd once condemned—my mother piercing her ears and wearing pants—I was caught in a storm of conflicting emotions. While I wanted to celebrate their freedom, all their past certainty, the rigid lines they'd drawn between heaven and hell, left me reeling. How could they seemingly pivot so easily? Those rules had shaped my childhood.

Slowly, I began to see the invisible chains that had bound them too, the mind control woven through generations. I judged them at first, frustrated they hadn't pushed harder for change, but I came to understand that each generation nudged the needle forward, even if just a fraction. My parents' small steps were victories, hard won against the tide of tradition.

MENTORS AND FRIENDSHIPS

During those early years at the bank, I was surrounded by an array of mentors who lit my path. My boss, Dawn, was a powerhouse of wisdom and encouragement whose belief in me was unwavering. Under her guidance, I soaked up lessons in leadership, problem-solving, and resilience, each one a building block for my future. I also forged bonds with colleagues at the technology provider behind our core banking systems, Systematics. Learning their systems—with their intricate dance of data and functionality—was like mastering a new language, a skill that became a cornerstone of my career, opening doors I couldn't have imagined.

Another person I'll never forget is Nancy, the office manager and executive assistant for one of the senior vice presidents. The memory of our first meeting still makes me smile: She asked for my birth date to update a form, then glanced at me with a playful smirk, exclaiming, "Oh, that is your birth date, haha!" I was so young, barely out of my teens, and her teasing broke the ice. We became fast friends, her kindness a balm for the belonging I craved. Nancy invited me into her world, welcoming me into her home for holidays and gatherings, each visit a treasure. I can still recall the smell of the freshly baked blueberry muffins that greeted me on Christmas morning, their sweet, warm aroma mingling with the glow of twinkling lights and sweet peals of laughter. Nancy and I shared countless adventures— lazy days at the beach, games in the pool, or lively Christmas Eve parties in her neighborhood, the air filled with carols and clinking glasses. Nancy was a gift, a touchstone of belonging I'd yearned for. Her Christmas and birthday cards still arrive like clockwork, each one a cherished reminder of our enduring bond.

BURLINGTON, VERMONT

In 1994, a new chapter opened for me when I heard about a year-long opportunity with the bank's technology provider, Systematics, in Burlington, Vermont. I interviewed with the account manager, Mark, my nerves jangling but my determination steady. When he offered me the role—a project manager leading a branch system and network upgrade—I was elated (though I also knew my lower salary expectations had tipped the scales for me over another candidate). I dove in headfirst, thriving on the challenge. Mark became another mentor, a fatherly figure whose coaching shaped me profoundly. His advice—on managing teams, navigating setbacks, and trusting my instincts—still echoes in my mind, guiding me even now. As the work ramped up, I traveled across Vermont with Unisys tech installers, our weekends a blur of action. We'd descend on branches after Friday's close, yanking out clunky IBM hardware, the air thick not just with dust but also with the hum of anticipation. By Monday morning, the newly installed Unisys equipment shined, loaded with updated software, ready for the day's transactions. Each successful install fueled my confidence, the rhythm of the work becoming a song I loved to sing.

ATLANTA

The triumph of the installation led me to a bold move: relocating to Atlanta in 1995. I would be working with the same company (now called ALLTEL) and trading New England's biting winters for the South's warm embrace. The city was in full swing getting ready for the Summer Olympics the following year. My then-fiancé also landed a job there, and the cherry on top was that my siblings Steve and Wendy were already living nearby. At that time, Steve and Wendy both still had some ties to the Kingdom but had moved away from the stringent rules and would also eventually leave altogether. In many ways, this move to Atlanta felt a bit like coming home.

I moved in with Steve for the first few months; he had a midtown apartment in the Georgian Terrace, a slice of grandeur across from the famous Fox Theatre. The building was a marvel—ornate architecture, a rooftop pool shimmering under Georgia's sun, and a vibe that was filled with possibility. Being close to Steve again, now as adults, was a gift. We dove into Atlanta's energy, sharing nights I'll never forget: my first U2 concert, the music thundering through us like a shared heartbeat, and meeting at the Ritz downtown, where Steve worked, to share conversation and fun, the city lights painting our evenings.

Wendy and her husband Joseph lived nearby, and their two small children were a delight. Being an auntie warmed my heart—their bright smiles and tiny hands tugging at my sleeve sparked pure joy. Rog and his wife Robin had made me an auntie years earlier, but their move away from New England meant I rarely saw them during those days.

Yet, as I settled into this new rhythm, change swept through again. Wendy and Joseph soon packed up for Texas, chasing new horizons, while Steve set off for San Francisco to pursue his own dreams. Around the same time, I married and moved in with my new husband, planting the seeds for a fresh chapter. Atlanta became my home, a place to paint a new life and enjoy a career that continued to unfold like a map to an unknown but thrilling destination.

In Atlanta, I plunged into the exhilarating chaos of a pioneering start-up, the first to venture into internet banking—a realm as thrilling as it was uncharted. The work was a whirlwind, often leaving me overwhelmed and bone-tired, but I drank in knowledge like a parched traveler at an oasis. The friendships I forged were electric, and the experience launched my career into a new orbit. I spent countless hours mastering the intricacies of online security, guiding banking clients through the brave new world of digital transactions. The software was raw, still toddling in its infancy, and the sales team's lofty promises often outstripped what we could deliver. Those of us in implementation scrambled to bridge the gap, racing against deadlines in a high-stakes dance.

For the first few months, I was blessed with an exceptional boss whose brilliance and calm demeanor were a necessity amid the start-up's frenzy. His steady hand guided us through the chaos, but when he left sooner than expected, we pressed on under less inspiring leadership. The void he left was palpable.

One of my proudest roles was as a problem solver, a mediator between groups practically speaking different tongues. I sifted through error reports and audit logs, my eyes scanning lines of code under the glow of my monitor, then connected with the right tech experts to untangle the issues. I became the bridge between the new Cisco internet developers—who were young, brash, and full of jargon—and the seasoned banking network engineers, whose skepticism was etched in their furrowed brows. When connections failed, blame ping-ponged between them, but as they found their way toward a newfound ability to communicate, each resolution felt like a small triumph. I savored each victory. The team was an assembly of remarkable people, many becoming dear friends. Those years also honed the skills that would, much further down the road, come to define my consulting career: translating, mediating, building bridges where none existed.

⋮

10

Beach Trip Escapades: A Sisterhood Forged in Laughter and Waves

In the fall of 1996, I found a sisterhood that wrapped me in warmth and acceptance. These women, unconnected to my past, saw me for who I was—no judgment, just open hearts. It all began with Nancy (not my Nancy from the bank), a firecracker who joined the project at ALLTEL just after me and who had a spark that drew me in. She was funny with a little sarcasm mixed in, and I kept nudging her to hang out, but she was laser focused on training for Atlanta's Peachtree Road Race over the Fourth of July. By August, though, we finally connected—likely over cocktails and dinner at a bustling neighborhood spot. Her humor was electric, coaxing cheek-burning, belly-aching laughs from me, the kind that left me gasping. But she could pivot to deep, soulful talks, as our conversations wove effortlessly from silly to serious. That night, a friendship was born that felt like home.

Nancy introduced me to her girls' night out (GNO) crew. This lively mix of women, many hailing from elsewhere in the South— Kentucky, Arkansas—had accents that dripped like molasses, leaving me, the New Englander, struggling to keep up. They'd say "ice tea," and I'd hear "Asti," picturing cheap champagne, as my confusion caused chuckles. Their drawls presented a puzzle at first, but I learned to love the cadences, each phrase emerging like a warm hug from a different world. Our nights out—clinking glasses in dimly lit bars, sharing stories over our Southern-inspired plates—were pure joy, a connection that felt freeing.

The next summer, I joined about ten of them for a road trip to Destin, Florida. That six-hour drive was an adventure! We all piled into a caravan of cars, excitement filling the air, stopping at a Wendy's for lunch, delighting in homemade peach ice cream at an Alabama gas station, and making endless pit stops by cornfields to pee, our laughter echoing across the stalks. Arriving in Destin, I fell hard for its powdery white sands and turquoise Gulf waters, like a slice of the Caribbean. That first year, I shared a full-size bed with Nancy, crammed in a room with another full-sized bed and two other ladies. Angie, my new friend from GNO, plus Sheila and Dea, both from Savannah, joined us, along with others whose names blur all these years later. The house was bursting with chatter and music; the ocean was our backdrop.

That trip became a sacred annual ritual for twenty years even as members of the group shifted. Angie, our unofficial captain, masterminded each trip, booking our stay, assigning who'd bring the necessary supplies, and meticulously splitting expenses. Before each getaway, we'd list conversation topics, ensuring everyone could share their year's highs and lows. We held space for it all—marriages, divorces, dating disasters, pregnancies, stepkids, job changes, promotions, moves, heartbreaks, health struggles, celebrations, and losses. No topic was off-limits, no story too small.

We were a silly bunch, letting loose our cares for just a few days. On the beach, we'd blast music, dancing barefoot in the sand, swapping bikini tops or bottoms for laughs, our antics drawing amused glances from neighbors. We befriended cabana boys and girls working summer gigs, their youthful energy fueling our fun. Most nights, after dinners under string lights, Sheila and I would sneak back to the beach for skinny-dipping under the stars (Ang followed to make sure we weren't too foolish). The cool Gulf water was exhilarating, and our laughter bounced off the waves. We were fearless, giddy, alive.

Over time, our group distilled to four—Nancy, Angie, Sheila, and me. Each year was a treasure, but our twentieth anniversary trip felt divine, a milestone we celebrated with champagne and nostalgia, dreaming we'd be doing this into our eighties. What made our bond particularly special was our openness—we all held different beliefs, political and religious, but never let them divide us. Respect and love trumped all, our history a glue stronger than any disagreement.

Sadly, the trips have ended, as life's tides have pulled us in new directions. But I hold those memories like seashells in a jar—each one shimmering with meaning. Those women were my anchors, loving me through my darkest moments, cheering my successes, and honoring me just for being me. They were my healing, my joy, my proof that friendship can be a beacon. I'm forever grateful for Nancy's laughter and friendship and blessed by my continued connection and friendship with Sheila. Countless moments wove together a sisterhood that will always be etched in my heart. My bond with Angie remains a cornerstone of my life, more than just a friendship—we share a deep, unshakable connection forged over years of living near each other in Atlanta while both of us were far away from our respective families. We were each other's lifelines—always there, no questions asked, dropping everything to lend a hand in a crisis. Our friendship is a bright, steady flame, rooted like an ancient oak, unwavering through life's storms. One of the greatest gifts was being woven into the lives of Angie and her husband Bill's three children. With no kids of my own and my nieces and nephews scattered far from Atlanta, I cherished every moment I spent with them. I loved to have them in my home for a nice dinner or brunch and to cheer for them at sporting events and to share countless other small joys together. Their energy and love were a balm, filling a space in my heart I hadn't realized was wanting.

Settling into a new city, I discovered my tribe—kindred spirits who embraced me without the baggage of my past. This connection became a vital part of my healing journey, offering a fresh start and a sense of belonging that lifted my spirit.

⋮

11

A Season of Growth: Building, Bonding, and Breaking Free

After two years, as the project at ALLTEL stabilized, I craved new horizons. A friend from my New Hampshire days tipped me off about a major business management software company, Pega, opening an Atlanta office. The chance to build something from the ground up was irresistible. I joined to build out the office, quickly bonding with sales lead Chris, a dynamo whose vision matched mine. Together, we hired a stellar team, implementing software that modernized client operations, slashing paper processes with sleek automation. Each successful rollout felt like planting a flag in new territory.

While I was thriving in my career, it became obvious that my marriage wasn't working. In fact, it really hadn't worked from the beginning. We simply didn't share the same goals and values. I struggled with what to do. Divorce was considered taboo in my upbringing, but I couldn't bear the thought of staying married. I sought out and found an amazing therapist, Katherine, who helped me sort through my feelings of guilt and confusion. Eventually my husband and I agreed to part ways. He moved out of state for his job, but I was happy to stay in Atlanta where both friends and my own work remained.

But Atlanta wasn't just work and friends—it was life, raw and vivid. July 29, 1999, is seared into memory: the day of the day trader shooting, Georgia's deadliest mass shooting. And it all happened in the building next door. Believed to be motivated by large financial losses incurred over the prior two months, the gunman went on a shooting spree, killing nine people and injuring thirteen more before committing suicide. Our team was locked down for hours while the killer remained at large, the office thick with tension as we huddled, scouring the web for scraps of news. When the all-clear came, we shuffled to the elevator, grimacing as we saw big black X's on each office and bathroom door that had been searched. Nerves frayed, I pressed the lobby button, and when the doors slid open, we were greeted by the sight of the Georgia Bureau of Investigators, their massive weapons glinting, faces grim, barring our exit. The doors closed, and we descended one more level to the ground floor, where I slipped out to my car, joining a slow crawl of vehicles as each was searched for the fugitive. The next morning, I learned some team-mates had been escorted directly past the crime scene, blood and bodies still visible, this trauma now etched into their minds. I was luckily spared that horror, my gratitude mingled with sorrow. The company rallied, offering support and resources, a lifeline in that dark time.

Soon, though, other challenges arose at work. Sales promises outpaced our software's capabilities, and as a satellite office, we lacked the main office's backing, leaving us stretched thin, constantly apologizing to frustrated clients. The software was riddled with bugs; defects we'd closed reopened like stubborn wounds. I'd face clients' annoyance with honesty, promising to do better, but our team's reliance on the main office's priorities left our requests low on the list. It was a grueling lesson in resilience, but exhaustion set in, and I was ready for the next chapter.

Amid the grind, I found a soul sister in Julie, who'd relocated from Massachusetts. Our Atlanta adventures became legendary, especially our Friday nights at the Tavern, a *Cheers*-like haunt where bartenders knew our names and stories flowed like the drinks. There, I met Lee and Mike, friends who I've cherished now for over twenty-five years, their loyalty a constant. Other dear friends from those nights moved away, and sadly several have since passed, their absence leaving a quiet ache. On Sunday afternoons, I'd return to the Tavern for quieter gatherings, the smaller crowd fostering deeper conversations before a week of travel. Those moments, rich with connection, were a boon I still cherish.

Each step in Atlanta—professional triumphs, personal bonds, and, yes, even the scars—yielded growth, pushing me toward a future I was still discovering, one project, one friendship, one challenge at a time.

⋮

12

A Bold Leap Forward:
Igniting a Consulting Journey

In 1999, a lifeline came from Jenn, a dear friend from my previous company, who urged me to join her at the audit firm **KPMG**. The idea had never even flickered in my mind before. Why would I want to join an audit firm? I recalled the auditors at First NH Bank holed up in conference rooms poring over financial records late into the night. This held no interest for me. I was also paralyzed by the fear that my lack of a college degree would bar the door. But Jenn quickly shared that she was part of a new tech consulting group and that I would be a perfect fit, given my banking and project experience. The market was ablaze, talent in short supply, and my hard-earned experience outshone my educational gaps. To my astonishment, I was hired without a face-to-face meeting (video calls didn't exist then). So after just a few phone calls that left my heart racing with relief and excitement, the future was suddenly wide open.

I'd set a personal goal years earlier: if I didn't hit a certain salary by age thirty, I'd find a way to earn my degree. At twenty-nine, I stepped into what would become a twenty-five-year consulting career, surpassing my salary target just before my thirtieth birth-day—a miraculous gift from the Universe. Fresh off my marriage, I was ready for a seismic shift. The relentless travel the job would entail was a bit daunting but also intriguing, so I figured I would give it five years, eager to dive into the unknown.

I quickly learned that consulting hinges on three pillars: the client, the project, and the location. Rarely did all three align perfectly, but at least one of them was always fantastic. My first project landed me in Pottstown, Pennsylvania, an hour's drive from Philadelphia's airport through rural, rolling hills. The project—a start-up concept for community banking online—was exhilarating, letting me flex my internet banking expertise to guide the client. But the location tested me. That harsh winter brought snowstorms that snarled flights and turned drives into white-knuckled treks, the wind-shield wipers thumping against icy gusts. Still, I thrived, pouring my energy into the work, even as the weekly Monday to Thursday travel wore me down.

My next project, in Silicon Valley for a brokerage firm, was a different beast altogether. The location was filled with high energy—sun-drenched streets, tech-fueled ambition—and the project sparked my curiosity, with a team that clicked like old friends. But the schedule was brutal: early Monday flights out, red-eye returns on Thursdays, my body lurching through time zones as I adjusted to the grind. At first, I felt like a minnow in a vast sea, out of my depth among seasoned consultants. Yet, consulting lit a fire in me. Free from the overblown promises of software companies, I could guide clients toward the right tools without attachment or motive, each success fueling my passion. I found my stride, confidence blooming like a desert flower after rain.

Being in California was a gift. It was my first chance to dive deep into its flourishing offerings. The nearby presence of my brother Steve, who was living in San Francisco at that time, provided an even greater bonus, and I'd sometimes stay over for weekends, our sibling bond a warm anchor. One long weekend, Nancy from Atlanta joined us for a trip to Napa Valley, the rolling vineyards stretching under a golden sun, their rows of grapes heavy with promise. We sipped rich, velvety wines, the flavors bursting as we laughed, the hills a breathtaking backdrop. Another adventure took us to Lake Tahoe in August, its crystal waters framed by snow-capped mountains that stole my breath. We sailed on a catamaran, the boat slicing through the lake's glassy surface, the air crisp with pine. At the hotel casino, we fed nickels into slot machines, chuckling at our small wins. Those trips always began with a drive across the Golden Gate Bridge, its orange towers piercing the morning fog, followed by brunch in Sausalito, where we'd linger over coffee as the mist cleared, before heading north, the road unfolding like a promise.

Our consulting team, split between our clients' offices in Palo Alto and Sacramento, embraced the California spirit. We bonded over baseball games, the crack of bats and roar of crowds knitting us closer. We frequently explored new restaurants, gobbling up salads and sandwiches abundant with avocados for our lunchtime breaks or spicy Thai or fresh sushi for dinners. We wandered new corners of the Bay Area, each outing a spark of joy. On my thirtieth birthday, our project team went out for dinner in San Francisco. The restaurant was full of life; to my surprise, Mayor Willie Brown was there, and when a teammate mentioned my birthday, he broke into song, his voice warm and booming, the room joining in as I blushed, laughter bubbling up.

I loved California's beauty, but the East Coast was calling me back, its familiarity a pull I couldn't ignore. Those months in Silicon Valley, with all their challenges and joys, were a gift, allowing me to forge my consulting career while deepening the bonds—especially with my brother Steve—that carried me forward into the next chapter.

13

A City of Transformation: Triumphs, Trials, and Enduring Lessons

My consulting career took me to extraordinary heights, as I worked with top-tier clients on projects that stretched my skills and horizons. One of my most transformative chapters unfolded in New York City. The city buzzed with even more energy than California—honking taxis, glittering skyscrapers, and a pulse that never slowed. I spent years there, including one pivotal year dedicated to a massive merger integration. That project introduced me to a wealth of people, including Rob, my second husband, his kindness a spark in the whirlwind of work. I was lucky to have a corporate apartment in Chelsea, a cozy respite on the building's eighth floor, which spared me the churn of hotel check-ins. Despite grueling hours, our project team stole moments to explore NYC's magic: cheering at Yankees or Mets games; savoring Broadway shows, their lights and music a fleeting escape; dining at tucked-away restaurants; and getting drinks at our favorite piano bar, Judy's Chelsea. One unforgettable late night after a successful data conversion, we assembled for karaoke, our voices hoarse but jubilant, the room alive with our triumph.

When the project lead at KPMG first pitched the merger integration role to me, I balked. It was a project manager position in finance, and I wasn't a numbers person—my expertise lay in banking systems, not general ledgers or reporting. But she urged me to meet the client, Henry, betting that my project management skills could bridge the gap. Henry took a chance on me, and I dove in, leveraging my banking knowledge alongside the client's subject matter experts. Together, we became a powerhouse. Their operations know-how meshed with my ability to orchestrate complex dress rehearsals, which allowed us to run tests in advance of the live data conversion to prove it would be successful. I crafted detailed scripts, test accounts, and timelines, weaving them into a master conversion playbook for the cutover live event. That project taught me a profound lesson: My expertise could adapt to any challenge, even on unfamiliar terrain. I didn't need to master every detail, just guide the process with clarity and collaboration. The deep dive into ledgers and the complexity of financial, operational, and regulatory reporting armed me with end-to-end banking insights that became a cornerstone for future projects.

9/11

Then came September 11, 2001, a day etched in my soul and the hearts of countless others. That Tuesday morning, I was at Rob's downtown apartment, nursing a bad cold, my head foggy as I lingered in bed. Rob had left early for an 8 a.m. meeting in midtown, the city's hum a distant murmur. The phone's shrill ring broke the quiet—his sister's voice on the answering machine, frantic about a plane and the World Trade Center. Then followed a similar message from another family member. Confused, I opened the window overlooking the Stock Exchange, expecting chaos, but the crowd below was milling around as usual. I flicked on the TV, searching for clarity, when a deafening boom shook the air. Outside, people scattered, their screams piercing the morning. Heart pounding, I raced down three flights to the lobby, where firemen and volunteers were already ushering soot-covered runners in from off the streets, their faces ghostly with ash. The directive was to stay put. I joined others in the building's small gym, where a TV blared the unfolding horror—planes, towers, the Pentagon, Pennsylvania. We huddled together, dozens of strangers bound by disbelief, watching as the world we knew unraveled. One of my friends who'd fled an Amex building by the Hudson stumbled in, his eyes haunted by the carnage he'd escaped, his voice trembling with the weight of what he'd seen.

Hours crawled by. The TV was our only connection to the outside. When news came that ferries were resuming their routes to Brooklyn and New Jersey, some people left, but I knew no one there and so I stayed, since my building had been spared evacuation. Back in Rob's apartment, I found it coated in ash—I'd left the window open in my panic. My cell phone was useless; calls to Rob and others simply failed in the jammed networks. Alone, unsure whether to stay or to flee, fear gnawed at me. Then the phone finally rang—a miracle. It was Rob, his voice a lifeline, reachable only because he'd borrowed a friend's phone with the same 646 area code as his landline. He was in Chelsea with colleagues and friends, near my apartment. He offered to come for me, but with the city in chaos, I insisted on going to him, naively thinking I could walk or catch a taxi. My urge to escape the ash-choked air and be with him overshadowed the fact of my head cold.

Outside, the scene was surreal. Police officers and volunteers guided traffic, their faces etched with resolve, handing out cloths to shield our faces from the dust that hung in the air like a shroud. The kindness of strangers—so unlike New York's usual impersonal hustle—bound us in shared shock. Everyone moved as if in a dream, searching for answers that didn't exist. With no taxis in sight,

I walked north to Chelsea. The city's skyline, set against that bright blue sky, towered majestically amidst the haze of debris and sorrow. When I reached the restaurant where Rob and his friends waited, I was caked in ash, my clothes gray, my throat raw. Seeing him, relief crashed over me like a wave, our embrace a silent celebration that we'd made it through.

Everything changed that day, for millions. I was spared personal loss, but the tragedy struck close. Friends mourned colleagues and loved ones who were gone in an instant. Returning to the office was grim—commutes ballooned from thirty minutes to over an hour, since the trains and subways had been crippled by the devastation. Each day, we walked past the smoldering wreckage, the acrid odor of burnt metal and loss seeping into our clothes, a memory I can't forget. Many teammates sought transfers to other cities; the weight of the environment was too heavy. I stayed, driven to finish the project, with gratitude for my survival a quiet fuel. New York, its people, its scars, and its resilience shaped me, leaving an indelible mark as I moved forward, forever altered by that day and the heartbeat of the city that endured it.

LIFE WITH ROB

In 2002, Rob and I settled into a cozy apartment in Hoboken, New Jersey, a vibrant town buzzing with energy just across the river from New York City, where Rob still worked. I could live anywhere, so I kept my Atlanta home, and we set our sights on eventually moving there together. That year, I was thrilled to meet Rob's family. A widower, he had three grown children who'd long since flown the nest. His eldest daughter lived nearby in New Jersey. His second daughter, along with her own young child, had started fresh in sunny Florida. His son, meanwhile, was wrapping up college in the charming, historic city of Savannah, Georgia.

After a year in Hoboken's lively streets, we packed up and moved to Atlanta in 2003, then tied the knot on a beach in Maui. While I stepped into the role of stepmother and step-grandmother, I mostly focused on simply being Rob's wife, doing my best to blend into his family's lives with care. Over time, I formed unique bonds with each of his children. The arrival of each grandchild filled me with uncontainable joy, their laughter and growth lighting up our lives. Holidays were a whirlwind—tables overflowing with food and the atmosphere filled with lively chatter and the joyful chaos of extended family gatherings—while vacations together wove even more unforgettable memories.

Soon after our wedding, Rob's health took a turn, keeping him from work. It was a heavy blow for him, but my thriving career became our anchor, carrying us through with gratitude and resilience.

⋮

14

The Velvet Hammer: Blending Strength, Heart, and Bold Beginnings

In 2004, almost five years into my consulting career, I earned the nickname "the Velvet Hammer," a title that became a badge of honor. After the NYC merger, I'd spent over two years jetting to Fort Lauderdale on a weekly basis, working with a stellar client there on a transformative project. We were implementing a new system to streamline a tangle of business rules hard-coded in outdated technology, all of it running on old software and hardware so clunky it had become a nightmare to update. My team collaborated with a group of sharp, spirited women, their laughter and camaraderie lighting up our long days. Many of them remain dear friends, our bonds enduring mostly through social media, a testament to the trust we built.

And earning that trust was no small feat. Twice, I faced the gut-wrenching task of having to replace team members sidelined by drinking problems. These delicate situations left me mortified, first with shock, then with resolve. My commitment was unwavering: do right by the client and the team. The client's grace shone through, supporting us as we onboarded replacements, patiently bringing them up to speed. Our hard work paid off with a triumphant implementation, which turned out to be the only success in a program where other parts faltered. Our new system *hummed*. The client's operations became much smoother, and our team stood tall, pride radiating like the Florida sun.

That victory paved the way for pitching the next phase, but it hinged on winning over the client's boss, a newcomer from another division who didn't know me. I poured my energy into crafting a proposal, each slide a promise of progress, to show how we could help them drive greater automation and efficiency. The partner, Mac, and sales lead, Hank, flew to Fort Lauderdale to back me during the pitch, their presence a bolster as we faced the boss's scrutiny. Mid-conversation, he probed my background, my leadership, and—pointedly—whether I was tough enough to wrangle his challenging technology colleagues. He needed someone to champion business needs without buckling under pushback.

Before I could respond, Mac and Hank leapt in, vouching for my reputation as a doer. They'd seen me in action—gentle yet resolute, a listener who could pivot to steely determination. My quiet demeanor sometimes read as meek, but they knew better. Hank, with a grin, declared, "Don't you know? Marcia is the Velvet Hammer!" The room erupted in chuckles, the tension breaking like a wave. The nickname captured my blend of empathy and tenacity, and we eventually won the next phase, a triumph that echoed through my career. "The Velvet Hammer" stuck, becoming a shorthand for my style, helping me secure future proposals as clients saw the same blend of strength and warmth.

I've since urged teammates to embrace their own traits, to craft their personal brand by honing strengths and tweaking weaknesses. Well-meaning bosses had previously nudged me to shift my first impression—urging me to be less quiet, more assertive. I listened but stayed true to myself, refining without reinventing. My success, I believe, stemmed from listening deeply, especially early on, letting clients reveal their needs before I spoke. Peers who rushed in, solutions-first, often missed the mark, their haste a contrast to my patience.

Fort Lauderdale wasn't just about work—it was also a crash course in hurricanes. That stretch of time saw storm after storm, and one client team member became our unofficial meteorologist, pinning National Hurricane Center printouts to her cubicle wall, each a map of possible threats. As I flew home to Atlanta to dodge the approaching storms, I heard tales of hurricane prep: endless lines at grocery stores and gas stations, survival kits stuffed with batteries, water, and canned goods, and the agonizing decision whether to evacuate or hunker down with the shutters up. Years later, when I moved to Florida, I'd learn to live those rituals myself, the lessons of Fort Lauderdale etched in my memory.

Leaving that team after two and a half years was bittersweet, their faces and laughter a part of me. But new challenges called.

NYC AGAIN

Returning to New York City felt like slipping back into a familiar rhythm, the city's cadence—honking cabs, neon lights, and bustling sidewalks—greeting me like an old friend. This time, my client's mission was to help design and implement processes for a bank's branch expansion, a bold pivot from their recent strategy. For years, the bank had been shuttering branches, betting that online banking would be the wave of the future, while slashing real estate costs in the process. But new leadership saw things differently: physical branches, with their personal touch, were vital for attracting and retaining customers. The bank, rusty from its years without opening any new locations, lacked the expertise and bandwidth to pull it off.

Our client, a lone leader in the early days, was tasked with executing this vision from the ground up, and we were there to help him make it real.

Working closely with him taught me lessons that became cornerstones of my career. His voice brimming with passion, he'd share his ideas, and then we'd translate them into detailed plans. Yet our drafts often missed the mark, forcing us back to the drawing board time and again. Frustration simmered until we realized the key: We needed to ask deeper, more probing questions to unearth what he couldn't fully articulate. It was like peeling back layers of an onion, each question revealing a clearer piece of his vision. Once we shifted to this cocreative approach, we clicked, building out processes that captured his ideas with precision.

Initially, another senior manager led the effort, but as the project evolved, I seized the chance to step up. I took the helm, guiding the team with a steady hand. From that point on, the rest of the team and I thrived, helping to successfully build out one of the bank's flagship offices. As so often happens in the trenches of high-stakes projects, my client and I forged a friendship and stayed in touch long after our official work wrapped, a testament to the trust we'd built.

This chapter in New York, much like the city itself, heralded a cherished time of growth. I learned a deeper art of consulting—to listen not just to words but also to all that remains unspoken, to cocreate with clarity, and to lead with confidence. The skyline, glittering under a twilight glow, seemed to mirror my own ascent, each lesson a light guiding me through the rest of my career.

NEW ORLEANS

My next challenge was a pitch for a bank in New Orleans that was seeking to modernize its outdated client processes, starting at the branch level. My banking expertise and knack for business process automation made me a perfect fit. The client, attending a conference in Las Vegas, requested our pitch there, and we poured our hearts into it. The presentation crackled with energy. Our approach and expertise resonated deeply with their needs as we demonstrated how we could help them implement their vision for streamlined operations. Their nods and smiles throughout made a quiet promise. Back in Atlanta, I awaited the verdict, brimming with confidence yet filled with anticipation. When the call came—we'd won—I was thrilled to lead the charge, ready to shape a transformative project in a city still healing from Hurricane Katrina's scars a year later.

We assembled a dynamic team and landed in New Orleans, unsure what to expect in the post-Katrina landscape. For the first few weeks, we worked in an office on the city's outskirts, waiting for downtown space to open. Many of us stayed at the JW Marriott, its sleek lobby a stark contrast to the rest of the city's struggles, though the hotel was desperately understaffed, with workers pulling grueling shifts, their tired smiles at valet or the concierge lounge a testament to their resilience. I met FEMA crews, their hard hats and dusty boots a constant in the lobby, laboring to rebuild the city's fractured infrastructure. One surreal moment came when I spotted Brad Pitt getting out of his vehicle in the motor lobby, his quiet presence a reminder of the celebrities drawn to the city's recovery—his focus on rebuilding homes a whisper of hope.

I quickly fell in love with our client's vision, and their energy was infectious as we aimed to revolutionize the client experience. The client believed in this work, and I was honored to champion it. We crisscrossed the city, visiting branches where tellers and managers shared their ideas, their voices eager, despite the city's wounds. We "shopped" competitor banks, slipping in as customers to spot gaps that we could then leapfrog. We facilitated vendor demos for software and crafted a compelling pitch, backed by bold visuals and a realistic demo showcasing sleek new processes. The road map we built was a beacon of transformation, its business case ironclad. Yet, change this bold unnerved some. But we doubled down, winning over skeptics until the approvals came.

As we visited branches to gather input, we road-tripped beyond New Orleans and further afield into the rest of Louisiana. In the process, I discovered the state's split identity. There was South Louisiana on one hand, steeped in French and Spanish roots, alive with Cajun and Creole culture, including the Mardi Gras parades, folk Catholicism, zydeco rhythms, and dishes like jambalaya that warmed the soul. Then North Louisiana, by contrast, bore more distinct Anglo American and African American influences, with a dedication to crafts like quilting and basketry along with their folk music rooted in gospel and old-time country and hearty food like hot-water cornbread and butter beans. Each branch visit revealed a new facet of the state's heart, enriching our work and my love for its people.

Once we received our green light, we rallied a larger team for the first implementation, and the air was electric with the promise of foundational change. Then, the bank acquired two smaller institutions, ushering in new leadership and sidelining our sponsor—a devastating blow. Funding dried up, and the project paused, a gut-punch to my client and our team. We fought to revive it, pitching the transformation's merits to the new president, but she balked, unwilling to bet on bold change. The bank's slogan, "Banking Made Simple," was our North Star, not just as a tagline but as a call to simplify banking for their clients. Ultimately, our budget went to new signage stripping the slogan away—a move that felt like a betrayal, a safe retreat from risk. That moment crystallized a truth I'd see repeatedly in financial services: Caution often trumps courage, especially in a regulated industry where the potential rewards for risk-taking rarely outweigh the fear of failure.

Despite the project's halt, my time in New Orleans was a treasure. Working with a client who dared to dream big left an indelible mark. The city, just one year post-Katrina, moved with slow but stubborn progress. Families moved from FEMA trailers into rebuilt homes, their front porches flickering with new life. Restaurants and shops reopened, their neon glowing defiantly against the dusk. Early on during the year I spent there, dining options were scarce, but as the city healed, I found ways to savor its soul—the jazz spilling from French Quarter bars, the gumbo rich with spice, the beignets dusted with powdered sugar melting on my tongue. The people's kindness, their resilience woven into every interaction, captivated me. I forged deep friendships with my Cajun clients; our bond was sealed both through shared effort and evenings of laughter over crawfish boils, their accents lilting like music.

My time in New Orleans, a city with such courage and grace, was a chapter I'll always hold close—the people and the project taught me the power of vision, the sting of setbacks, and the beauty of a community rising from ruin. As my career marched on, I carried those lessons forward, grateful for every moment in that soulful, wounded, unforgettable place.

WRAP-UP

For over nine years, I'd been a road warrior with this firm, my life a constant whirlwind of Monday-to-Thursday travel—airport, hotel, client meetings, back home, repeat. I'd thrived on the grind—my suitcase always half-packed, racking up miles and memories. But in the wake of the fallout from the Enron scandal, the consulting arm of KPMG had been forcibly cleaved from its parent company, left to fend for itself and later rebranded as BearingPoint in 2002. Over the years, market conditions and mismanagement bled it dry, and by the time the Lehman Brothers collapse in 2008 sent shockwaves through the industry, rumors of potential buyers had fizzled into grim silence. The financial services division, my home, was particularly hard-hit. While another division found an answer in a rival consulting firm's acquisition, we were left dangling.

Whispers of a buyer surfaced, but it wasn't the rescue we'd hoped for. They wanted to cherry-pick talent, not absorb the whole team. Independence rules, tied to their existing audit relationships, meant some of our client engagements—lucrative and hard-won—would be severed. Out of the Enron scandal, rules were put in place prohibiting audit firms from consulting with the same clients whom they audited. Therefore, those projects would have to end abruptly, leaving those team members stranded on the bench, their futures uncertain. Every day felt like walking a tightrope, wondering who'd get an offer and who'd be left behind. The stress was a living thing, coiling tighter with every vague update from leadership. I'll always remember Frank, our banking leader at the time, whose care was a constant amid the chaos and uncertainty.

Then, finally, an offer landed in my inbox from the cherry-picking firm, PwC. It would be a safe harbor in the storm. But before I could exhale, my phone rang with a call that changed everything. A former boss, his voice brimming with excitement, painted a vivid picture of a new opportunity. He was building a banking practice at a smaller consulting firm, Capco. They were rooted in capital markets but eager to expand. He wanted me—and as many of my colleagues as possible—to help shape it from the ground up. The catch? It was a start-up in every sense, untested in the banking space, with no guarantees for anyone else who might jump ship to join.

I was torn. I retreated to my home office, a notebook in hand, scribbling lists of pros and cons under the glow of a desk lamp. PwC offered stability, a polished reputation, but its independence constraints would clip my wings, limiting the clients I could consult with. The start-up was a blank slate—thrilling but risky, its banking credentials barely a sketch. I wrestled with the choice. I prayed for clarity, a sign. And then, the answer came. Like the feeling of dawn after a long night, I knew. The start-up called to my core, to the part of me that loved building, creating, taking risks. My heart raced at the thought of a fresh challenge, of planting a flag in uncharted territory.

I took the leap, signing on with Capco, without knowing who else, if anyone, would follow. In the subsequent days and weeks, I held my breath, then grinned as familiar names trickled in—colleagues I respected, friends I'd shared late-night brainstorming sessions and drinks with. We were a band of pioneers, stepping into the unknown together.

My first trip to the firm's New York City office provided a jolt of reality. The "office" was a modest space, though alive with the chaotic energy of a true start-up. No direct boss greeted me; I was a free agent for those first few weeks. By sheer luck, a former colleague who'd joined to build out marketing became my office mate, our shared space a lifeline of familiarity amid the whirlwind. We laughed at the bare-bones setup—human resources was still in flux, payroll and other processes required updating, and the local staff raised eyebrows when I explained I wouldn't be relocating to NYC. "Most banking clients are outside the city," I said, watching their puzzled expressions. "That's where we'll be." The HR and operations teams scrambled to adapt, hammering out multistate payroll setups and tax frameworks to support our team's far-flung work.

Undaunted, I dove in, my days a mishmash of action and improvisation. I scoured the small team's existing projects, piecing together what work was already underway. My phone became an extension of my hand as I dialed up former clients and contacts, my voice steady as I shared my new home and probed for their needs. I'd say, "I know you aren't familiar with our company, but you know and trust many of us based on our past work." Each conversation was a spark, a chance to build something real. The office sang with possibility, whiteboards filling with ideas, the air crackling with the thrill of creation. This was no polished machine—it was raw, messy, alive. And I was all in, ready to shape the future, one call, one client, one bold step at a time.

⋮

15

A Blazing Ascent: Building, Battling, and Breaking Barriers

The next seven years at Capco were a wild, exhilarating ride, with the first six standing out as the blazing pinnacle of my career. The founder and CEO was a force of nature—unlike anyone I'd ever met. His vision was a mixture of ambition and audacity, equal parts inspiring and intimidating. He preached a beginner's mind-set, urging us to shed preconceptions and rethink everything from first principles. It was like someone had flung open the windows of my mind, letting in a gust of fresh ideas. He'd started the company years earlier, surrounded by a tight-knit crew of loyalists, and his annual treaty dinners, born at the firm's inception in Aspen, were legendary. These meals were a special time to celebrate the anniversary of the company's launch. The first I attended was in Málaga, Spain, a sun-drenched celebration of our meteoric success. The air palpable with camaraderie, glasses clinking in delight, we toasted to the shared theme "Twenty-Twenty Vision." I'll never forget the electric charge of that night, the feeling that we were building something unstoppable.

As more of my former colleagues trickled in, it was like reuniting a rock band for a world tour, but this time with a bolder, more dynamic sound. The company wasn't without its growing pains—some days, making payroll felt like a high-stakes gamble—but the wins rolled in. I threw myself into building the consumer banking practice, landing my own clients and climbing to senior partner. Each milestone was exhilarating.

The second partner meeting and treaty dinner, held in the golden glow of Sicily, was another unforgettable event. But change was brewing. The founder and CEO hired new North American leadership from the UK to shake things up a bit with the intent to spark new growth, sounding a culture clash that rippled through the team. They were used to centralized banking clients in London; we were navigating a sprawling US landscape where clients demanded local consultants, not remote faces or teams traveling in from elsewhere. The friction was real—some colleagues bristled at the new leadership's style—but I was fortunate to watch, learn, and adapt without being in the spotlight. With no extra budget for new practices, you had to bring passion, conviction, and revenue to the table. That suited me fine; building from the ground up was my sweet spot. I found success through creativity and bold action.

MINNEAPOLIS

The first project I sold with Nick, one of our sales leads and a friend who joined the firm soon after me, was a game changer. At our old firm, we'd been circling this client in Minneapolis for months, hitting dead ends. Undeterred, I reached out again to the tech contacts we'd been nudging, and they pointed me to Rich, a key player on the business side. Convincing Rich we could help wasn't easy—he was skeptical, his arms crossed during our first meeting. But Nick and I were relentless, painting a vivid picture of how we could turbocharge their business goals and smooth over any lingering tech team resistance. When Rich finally signed on, I felt like we'd summited a mountain. But the real climb was just beginning: staffing the project at our lean start-up.

There was no deep bench to draw from, so we got creative. I leaned hard on our recruiting team and pulled in contractors to bridge the gap. It was a high-wire act, but before long we assembled a stellar crew. I can still see the team's first week on-site: It was midwinter, with temps plunging well below zero, and some of our Southern recruits showed up in thin jackets, shivering and wide-eyed in the biting cold. By the next week, when it "soared" to five degrees, they were practically throwing a parade. Yet that first implementation was a home run, cementing our reputation and unlocking years of follow-on work with the bank.

Working with Rich was a masterclass in balance. We became fierce advocates for the business side, but we also had to learn when to ease off the tech teams. As I had experienced in New Orleans, change doesn't land the same for everyone, and sometimes, on the technology side, they just weren't ready for the big ideas. Early on, I noticed "Minnesota nice" was stifling transparency—tech was frustrated when business kept veering to future phases instead of attending to the task at hand. I worked with Rich and the other leaders to build a governance structure that cut through the tension. We set up separate forums for current and future planning, ensuring that both tech and business leaders would cross-pollinate. Decision-making was streamlined: There would be input from all, but a small leadership group voted, with senior leaders breaking any ties. This change wasn't universally loved, but it forced accountability and drove results. I made it my mission to build relationships, ensuring every voice felt heard while keeping our eyes on the prize.

Minneapolis grew on me. Summers were a dream—bright, sunny, perfect for team outings to the new baseball stadium or dinners at restaurants serving up phenomenal cuisine. Winters tested us, but we made it fun, huddling over warm drinks and big ideas. Our team became a tight-knit part of the bank's fabric, eventually supporting a large internet and mobile banking rollout that set a new standard.

One adventure took Nick, me, and Lane—one of my top leads and also a good friend—to Oregon to meet the firm's head of operations. We'd been trying to sync up in Minneapolis but schedules never aligned. After flying in, we shared a delightful dinner the night before our meeting. The next morning, he whisked us to a brunch spot in the Willamette Valley, where business talk quickly gave way to his passion for wine. After the meeting, he insisted we tour the valley, hopping from vineyard to vineyard, savoring silky pinot noirs under a cool, cloudy sky. We capped the day off at his home, where we feasted on pizza and raided his wine cellar—which was housed in his third garage bay, an oenophile's treasure trove. He even handed us a catalog when it came time to pick bottles, spoiling us rotten. Laughing with him and his wife, glasses in hand, felt like we'd stumbled into a movie scene. That day—full of connection, laughter, and unexpected joy—was one for the books.

FIS, OUR NEW PARENT COMPANY

In 2010, a seismic shift rippled through our team of consultants: We were getting a new parent company, Fidelity National Information Services (FIS). Having been promised a surge of investment capabilities, the leadership buzzed with electric enthusiasm, their voices bright with visions of growth and opportunity. But when I heard the name—FIS—my heart didn't leap. Years earlier, FIS had swallowed up financial services tech companies including ALLTEL and Metavante, companies I knew well from my days at Systematics and ALLTEL itself. It wasn't the people I doubted; I could still picture familiar faces, their smiles warm from past collaborations. No, it was the promise of transformation that felt hollow. I couldn't shake the sense that the glittering synergies our leaders were chasing would fizzle like sparks in a storm. Still, we dove headlong into the fray, pouring hours into meetings and brainstorming sessions, hunting for elusive connections that often shimmered just out of reach.

NORTH CAROLINA

My boss at the time invited me to join him for a meeting with his client at a foreign-owned bank. He knew their transformation initiatives were right in my wheelhouse, the kind of challenge I thrived on. The meeting was filled with promise; we left feeling like we'd hit it out of the park. Weeks passed with radio silence, then months later, the puzzle pieces fell into place. The bank was selling its US branch operations to another player but had a bold new plan—to launch a direct bank of their parent company for clients visiting the United States. For foreigners, navigating the American banking system was a maze; without a US credit file, obtaining even a credit card was a pipe dream. This new venture would offer a full suite—credit cards, unsecured loans, and mortgages—tailored to this unique market and seamlessly integrated with the parent bank's processes.

The sales cycle was a frenetic sprint, a high-stakes race condensed into just a few weeks in 2011. Our mission: convince the client we could build this bank from the ground up and execute a full customer and account migration in a breathless nine months. First, we had to rally FIS, our parent company and the project's main software technology partner, to see our value. With persistence, we secured introductions from FIS's account and sales leads, pitching with precision to win over both the client and FIS. When we sealed the deal, I was named program lead, and the responsibility crashed over me like a tidal wave. Those nine months swallowed me whole—a whirlwind of urgency and adrenaline. Yet the audacity of the goal, the sheer thrill of chasing the impossible, was utterly exhilarating.

My role was a tightrope walk bridging the bank's business, operations, and tech teams, wrangling technology ecosystem providers and other consultants, and aligning with the parent company's cautious leadership. My mission was singular: deliver on time, with minimal fallout. I became the glue holding it all together, earning respect by having everyone's back, even when tensions flared. There was no room for bruised egos—we were a team united by a relentless deadline. The bank's staff, many unsure if their jobs would survive the transition, often dragged their feet, their fear manifesting as indifference. Technology providers stumbled over the client's ambitious requirements, and the bank's parent company fretted that the costs would dwarf any returns. Every step felt like a race against the clock, our planning perpetually one beat behind, solutions cobbled together just in time.

The pressure fueled me—it provided an invigorating rush that sharpened my focus. But for others, it was a breaking point. I watched team members buckle and resign, unable to withstand the heat. Each departure was a gut punch; delivering the news to my client felt like confessing a personal failure. Yet I'd look her in the eye, asking for her trust, vowing to find replacements who could keep up. And there were heroes as well—team members who thrived in the chaos, diving into new challenges, learning on the fly, and getting it done. Their tenacity kept us afloat.

We hit roadblocks daily: tech glitches, misaligned priorities, skeptical stakeholders. But we forged ahead, improvising, iterating, deciding fast. We rallied the team around our unyielding deadline, cutting through indecision like a blade. When we finally stood up the new bank and completed the migration, it was a triumph born of sweat and sheer will. The cleanup was a bit painful—loose ends and frayed nerves—but we'd done the impossible. I wouldn't relive those nine months, but I carry the experience like a badge of honor. It became my go-to story for clients: proof that a united team, laser focused on an immovable goal, can move mountains. When you strip away overthinking and accelerate decisions, you don't just meet deadlines—you deliver miracles.

⋮

16

A Pinnacle of Impact: Leading, Innovating, and Uniting

After this triumph, I was soon tapped to lead Banking and Wealth for North America, overseeing a three-hundred-person team with a dozen partners and one of our largest clients. Having previously been side-by-side colleagues with the other partners, I had no idea how they would view me in my leadership role. And yes, my appointment was met with mixed reactions. While most rolled with it based on our history and successes, others were ruffled by their ego. What I quickly came to realize, however, is that everyone, regardless of experience and title, craves leadership and direction. This lesson came as a bit of a surprise.

My Sundays crackled with anticipation for the week ahead. I shook things up, starting with recruiting. I'd noticed that clients were frustrated with some consultants. Despite stellar resumes from top firms, something was off. My HR business partner and I dug into it and realized the issue wasn't credentials; it was fit. We introduced EQ testing in our recruiting process, prioritizing personality and relatability along with experience and credentials. The result? A dramatic uptick in client satisfaction and team performance.

I swapped out drab brown-bag lunches with our team members for engaging TED Talk–style sessions, pushing subject matter experts to hone their storytelling and captivate their audiences. The energy in those rooms was palpable—ideas sparked, and a sense of camaraderie soared. I also fought to bring the entire team together in New York City, securing funding for a rare in-person gathering. For those scattered outside the city, it would be a chance to meet me, along with the rest of their colleagues, and to feel the excitement of our shared mission. That short event was a triumph, as it wove tighter bonds among us all and ignited collaboration that fueled our growth.

My proudest moments were mentoring team members. In spotting their latent potential, I could nudge them toward greatness. I thrived on coaching, never threatened by anyone's success, knowing their wins lifted us all. I was relentless about hiring only the best. The younger generation, my "A team," never ceased to amaze me. They rose fast, mastering client relationships and delivering jaw-dropping work.

Our digital team unveiled a cutting-edge lab, its massive screens transforming workshops into immersive experiences. We collaborated on bold concepts to drag the banking ecosystem—lagging woefully behind its peers—into the modern era. The ideas were there, but the technology wasn't. I didn't shy away from calling this out, even to the leadership of our parent company. My candor paid off; they began to move, and new players emerged, slowly modernizing the banking landscape. Those years were a whirlwind of creation, camaraderie, and impact: a chapter where I didn't just work—I built, inspired, and left a mark.

NEW YORK CITY

I was still living in Atlanta in 2013, so in my capacity as the North American lead for Banking and Wealth, my weeks revolved around the flow of travel, jetting to New York City every Monday. My home base was the downtown Marriott. As I climbed out of the taxi, it felt like climbing into a warm embrace—the bellman flashing a grin, the front desk team calling me by name, the concierge lounge attendants greeting me with delight. Their familiarity was comforting in the whirlwind of my schedule.

That chapter of my career was a high point, a beautiful medley of connection and impact. The office bustled with cooperation. It was a hive of collaboration as teammates worked hard on sales pitches, employee initiatives, and client events. The days sparkled with energy. Along with several other eager colleagues, I poured myself into building our internal women's leadership program, a mission that came alive as I mentored the next generation of young women and spoke at International Women's Day events. We championed causes close to our hearts, supporting charities like Dress for Success, and celebrated together when clients and colleagues were honored at galas such as the American Banker Awards, the Consulting Magazine Awards, Women's Bond Club, and the New York Women's Foundation. Our male colleagues were steadfast allies, amplifying our efforts with unwavering support.

That summer I found myself swept into the heart of a high-stakes sales pursuit, part of a small, determined team that dared to take on a colossal challenge. We were the underdogs—think David squaring off against a lineup of corporate Goliaths. These towering firms were loaded with resources that dwarfed our own, yet we were armed with a game-changing solution, a bold vision that promised to reshape the fortunes of both our company and our potential client. The air in our war room buzzed with adrenaline; whiteboards were scribbled with strategies, and laptops glowed late into the evenings as we crafted a proposal that gleamed with innovation. Against all odds, we clinched the deal. The triumph sent shockwaves through the industry and left us dizzy with the thrill of victory. The moment remains etched in my memory, a once-in-a-lifetime rush, like standing atop a mountain we'd scaled against a howling wind.

The client, a global titan, was in the midst of a seismic shift, divesting chunks of its US operations while navigating a complex transition to integrate local systems into their sprawling global network. They needed a robust team to keep the wheels turning on critical projects for the next few years, to build a bridge that could carry them through the migration. Our solution was audacious: a "re-badging" deal where their employees would join our ranks, donning our company's colors, while continuing to serve the client's projects for as long as needed. It was a delicate dance of logistics and loyalty, a deal that balanced ambition with sensitivity.

I wasn't the architect of this intricate agreement, but I was handed the baton as the point person to lead the transition—a role that felt like steering a ship through a storm. The employees, many of whom had spent decades with the client, faced an upheaval they hadn't chosen. Their world was shifting beneath them, and I could sense the undercurrent of unease. Partnering with my HR business partner (and friend) Kim and a tight-knit crew of colleagues, we dove into crafting a communication plan that would be a comfort for these workers. We huddled together, mapping out every detail with precision. Our plan contained a mix of clarity and empathy—town halls where voices could be heard, one-on-one meetings that could answer individual questions, and messages that glowed with transparency, ensuring the client's goals shone through while honoring the people at the heart of the change. Each step was a path toward trust and alignment, transforming a daunting shift into a shared journey forward.

17

Vulnerability: From Impostor Syndrome to Inspiring Others

At forty-four, sitting in one of my Capco colleague's offices, I felt my heart pound as I prepared to reveal a truth I'd buried for decades: I never finished college, never earned a degree. I was a key figure in our firm, spearheading a major segment and championing women's advancement, yet this secret felt like a shadow trailing me. We were planning an International Women's Day event—the theme was "Make It Happen"—honoring those who'd lifted us up and helped us along the way. As we brainstormed, the conversation turned personal, colleagues sharing stories of their journeys. When my turn came, I hesitated, my throat tight. But something urged me forward. I spoke of my unconventional path—starting with determination and hustle, not a diploma—and named some of the mentors who'd believed in me. The room fell silent, my colleagues' eyes wide with awe. One finally broke the quiet: "Why are we looking for an outside speaker? Your story is incredible. You've overcome so much. You need to share this."

Panic surged. Me, speak? Expose my vulnerability to a room full of colleagues? I imagined ridicule, rejection, whispers of "not good enough." But they pressed, their encouragement unwavering, and I relented, my stomach churning with nerves. Crafting the speech with help from my brother Steve was like unearthing buried treasure. As I poured my journey onto paper, charting every struggle, every triumph, I felt a weight lift, a blissful freedom washing over me. Reflecting on where I'd started—as a young woman leaving a home haunted by religious oppression and finding her way at the age of eighteen, learning to navigate without a degree in a world that prized credentials—brought a clarity and peace I hadn't expected.

On the day of the event, the beautifully decorated room whirred with the anticipation of my colleagues and the other speakers. My voice trembled at first. But as I continued to share my story, from my scrappy beginnings to later heights leading a major segment, the words flowed from my heart. I spoke of the mentors who saw my potential, the late nights hustling to prove my worth, and the quiet fears I'd carried. The room leaned in, some nodding, others teary eyed. When I finished, applause erupted, warm and resounding, a wave of validation.

I braced for backlash, but the outpouring of support was overwhelming—emails, hugs in the hallway, colleagues sharing how my story inspired them to embrace their own unique paths. The shame I'd carried, the nagging belief I wasn't enough, dissolved. I stood taller, free from the burden I'd shouldered for years, proud of my journey and who I'd become.

My track record—years of delivering results, untangling complex problems, and earning trust—shone brighter than any diploma. Beyond raw experience, I'd built a foundation on other forms of education. Over the years I'd earned a banking diploma by studying rigorous courses in Accounting, Principles of Banking, and Law and Banking; taken a weeklong program at Yale School of Management that set my mind ablaze with new frameworks;

and enrolled myself in countless other management and technical courses and seminars, stacking these up like credits toward my own kind of invisible degree. A Harvard alum even nominated me to speak at the Harvard Undergraduate Women in Business convention, where I stood before a packed room, sharing a vivid case study from a massive project I'd led to triumphant completion. My story—woven with career-defining insights and a love for consulting's challenges—sparked nods and applause, a moment that felt like standing in sunlight after years in the shade.

Twenty-five years ago, joining a consulting firm without a degree was nearly unheard-of. A talent shortage and a partner willing to take a chance on my experience had opened the door for me. I was thrilled, but the industry's obsession with credentials loomed large in my mind. Over time, the industry evolved, with many firms loosening their iron grip on degree requirements for partner roles, recognizing the worth of equivalent experience. I cheered the shift, but looking back, I can also now see all the energy I squandered on fear, all those nights spent worrying I'd be unmasked as an imposter. That all changed one International Women's Day, when I stood before a room of colleagues, my voice steady as I laid bare my unconventional journey. The words poured out, raw and true, shattering the chains of doubt I'd carried. I was more than enough—I was legitimate. My journey was a testament to resilience and proof that courage can rewrite the story you tell yourself while lighting a path for others.

SINGULARITY UNIVERSITY

In the spring of 2015, my boss offered me the chance to take a spot at Singularity University's Executive Program in California, held on the storied former NASA campus. The program promised to "reframe perspectives and deepen understanding of technologies shaping the future," inspiring "radically new ways of thinking." I of course jumped at the chance and spent a mind-bending week surrounded by leaders from over forty countries, a mesh of nationalities and ideas. Industry and tech visionaries challenged us to dream bigger than the kind of low-risk, predictable, and stifling incremental 10 percent gains we were all familiar with. We debated moonshots, bold leaps that could redefine industries. I left electrified, my mind fluttering with fresh ways to challenge the status quo. Back at work, I wove those insights into my leadership, sparking bolder strategies for clients and igniting inspiration in my team. That experience wasn't just a program—it was a launchpad for transformation, propelling me to think, lead, and innovate with fearless ambition.

During that time back in New York City, I found a thrill in collaborating with colleagues who brought the concrete jungle to life, none more so than my friend Jeff. He is a force of nature, a maestro of opportunity with a smile that could charm open a locked door. Jeff had an uncanny knack for slipping us into meetings I'd have sworn were impenetrable. Our partnership thrived with friendship and competition, fueled by playful bets that lit a fire under us. We'd huddle together wagering who could drive the biggest sales numbers or pull in the most revenue. Working with him wasn't just a job; it was a fun, living adventure, etched against the backdrop of a city that never slowed down.

HONG KONG

Later in 2015, I embarked on my first adventure to Asia, a continent that once loomed in my mind as a daunting enigma, its unfamiliar languages and cultures swirling in a fog of the unknown. Hesitation had kept me away, but fate intervened when my dear friend and colleague Kim temporarily relocated to our company's Hong Kong office. Her presence there was a beacon, promising guidance through the uncharted. I stepped off the plane into a world electric with possibility, unsure but eager, comforted by the knowledge that Kim would be my compass.

My first night was spent in a boutique hotel on the mainland with few amenities. The next morning, I made a snap decision to flee to a trusted Marriott brand across the way in West Kowloon, where the familiar atmosphere wrapped me in comfort, grounding me in this foreign land. Hong Kong burst into view—streets thrumming with a chaotic symphony of voices, neon signs flickering in a dazzling dance of Cantonese characters, the air thick with the scents of sizzling street food: charred skewers, steaming dumplings, and fragrant noodle broths.

Kim's guidance made the city feel like an open book. We navigated the crowded sidewalks with ease, weaving through a sea of faces—businesspeople in crisp suits, vendors calling out their wares, children darting through the bustle. The city's escalators, snaking up steep hillsides, fascinated me—a pulsing artery of commuters gliding upward, connecting the urban jungle below to the glassy skyscrapers above. Each ride was a window into Hong Kong's heartbeat, a blend of hardiness and grandeur.

One sweltering day, Kim led me on a hike up to Victoria Peak, a climb that tested both my lungs and my resolve. We ascended countless stone steps, the dense vegetation close to the trail, stopping occasionally for a treat or to catch my breath. Reaching the top, it was the view that really rendered me speechless: skyscrapers piercing the clouds, framed by the emerald ripple of Victoria Harbour and distant, mist-shrouded mountains. It was as if the city's heartbeat vibrated beneath us, alive and infinite.

Back in the streets, I learned to trust the hotel valets, who'd scribble my destinations in elegant Chinese characters for the taxi drivers. I'd slide into the back of those iconic red cabs, their seats worn but reliable, feeling a quiet thrill as I zipped through the neon-lit chaos, always safe, always on course. I wandered stunning markets, my fingers brushing over silk scarves and trinkets, each purchase a small victory of confidence. The food was a symphony—crisp, golden dim sum bursting with shrimp, spicy wok-tossed noodles, and creamy egg tarts that melted on my tongue, each bite a love letter to Hong Kong's soul.

Best of all was reconnecting with Kim. Over lunch or late-night chats, we shared stories and laughter, our friendship blooming anew. That trip shattered my fears, proving I could navigate any corner of the world with courage and curiosity. Hong Kong wasn't just a destination—it was a spark, igniting a love for exploration that still burns bright.

⋮

18

A Shifting Tide: Navigating Loss and Seeking New Shores

Five years after our acquisition by FIS, we began to lose our independence. The integration was becoming stifling to those of us who had joined the start-up. FIS is a highly regulated organization, especially given the nature of the services that they provide to financial institutions. Therefore, we became subject to the same rules and regulations ourselves, which made it more difficult, and slow, for our clients to do business with us. Our culture had shifted dramatically. The day the CEO and founder of Capco stepped down in the summer of 2015 felt like the ground shifting beneath us. Then came a blow that hit even harder: my boss moved on. Overnight, the job I'd loved lost its luster. New leaders stepped in, their vision misaligned, my role shrinking, my influence fading like a dimming spotlight. It was one of the darkest stretches of my career, a gut punch of disillusionment.

I stayed another year, soldiering through a major transformation project for a global client, splitting time in Mexico City's chaos. But my heart wasn't in it; I was running on fumes, yearning for an exit package. In hindsight, I'd been "quiet quitting," coasting through that final year, my passion drained. When the exit package finally materialized in August of 2016, it was bittersweet—a golden ticket to freedom laced with the ache of leaving a place that had shaped me. I took four months off, an offer from another tech consulting firm already simmering in the background.

The place had been sacred, not just for the victories I'd notched but also for the countless people who'd made it unforgettable, including those familiar faces who'd come over from my previous firm. While a few loyal friends and supporters stayed on, the office was shaken with turmoil, and many colleagues—my comrades in countless battles—slipped away to new horizons. Yet so many of us remained bonded in an even deeper, fiercer way: My HR business partner Kim and my former team member Kaylin became lifelong friends, and I'd forged connections with a few guy colleagues whom I still consider my brothers today. Together we'd all built something rare—a team that felt like family.

⋮

19

A Soulful Sojourn: Wandering, Healing, and Rediscovery

My first days of post-job freedom were disorienting. It felt like I'd just stepped off a speeding train into silence. No emails, no calls, no meetings, no work laptop reverberating with demands. For the first time, no one needed me. The void was jarring, a shock I hadn't braced for. But soon, I leaned into the liberation, savoring the open road ahead. I ultimately spent four months living a dream I'd never thought would be possible for me outside retirement. It was a glorious, soul-recharging sabbatical, during which I traveled with abandon, each destination a balm for my weary spirit.

TUSCANY

First, in September of 2016, I embarked on a soul-stirring journey to Italy's Tuscan region, a trip that felt like stepping into a living painting. Landing in Florence, I summoned my courage, rented a car, and, despite not speaking a word of Italian, set off for the mountain town of Barga. My nerves jangled as I navigated winding roads, grateful for the blue arrows painted on signs guiding me through the unfamiliar terrain. The GPS stuttered, but the scenery—rolling hills draped in emerald vineyards, golden sunlight filtering through ancient olive groves—kept me enchanted. As dusk settled, I pulled into my hotel, greeted by a warm staff who upgraded me to a room with a balcony. Exhausted from jet lag, I savored a divine dinner—freshly made pasta and a glass of velvety Chianti, all delivered with attentive service—then collapsed into bed, the promise of Tuscany lulling me to sleep.

Midmorning, I flung open the balcony doors to see mist-kissed mountains and a patchwork of vineyards and was hit with a wave of serenity. Distant church bells embroidered the deep quiet. The air was crisp, the sky a brilliant blue, and a profound calm settled over me. I knew I was exactly where I was meant to be. That first day, I surrendered to the moment, lounging by the hotel's pool, the sun warming my skin as I gazed at the rolling hills, their curves soft and timeless.

The next morning's breakfast was a portal—a ripe peach, bursting with juice, transported me back to childhood summers eating fruit from the trees of a member church in Pennsylvania. Its sweetness lingered as I drove forty-five minutes to Lucca, a walled city brimming with charm. Following the concierge's directions, I parked outside the ancient stone walls then stepped beyond them into a world of cobblestone streets, exquisite shops, and centuries-old churches. I wandered, awestruck, before settling in for a meal at an outdoor café. Twirling fresh pasta around my fork, the flavors bright and alive, I felt steeped in the history of the city echoing around me.

Back at the hotel, I claimed a sunny corner by the pool, sinking into the quiet, the landscape cradling my soul. Then, a burst of chatter shattered the peace. A group arrived, dragging chairs together behind me. A kind-eyed man, Larry, asked to borrow the chair beside me. I nodded, mildly annoyed, until I realized three lively couples had set up camp nearby. Sensing my disrupted solitude, they apologized and invited me to join them. Why not? It was a serendipitous choice. The group—two women from Malibu on their honeymoon, another couple from Bend, Oregon, and then Larry and Shelly from Houston—beckoned with a whirlwind of warmth and laughter. Bonded by our shared love of Marriott properties, we swapped stories, their energy infectious. They raved about a nearby winery, urging me to visit.

The next day, I braved a narrow, winding road on my way to Podere Concori, a family-run winery nestled in the hills above the Serchio River. My heart racing, I prayed no car would approach from the opposite direction—there was nowhere to pull over. Upon my eventual (safe) arrival, I found the owners finishing a leisurely Sunday lunch, their laughter echoing through the air. Then Nadia, my guide, led me and two other couples through the vineyard, where we plucked plump, sweet grapes straight from the vines, their juice staining our fingers. The care poured into this organic, biodynamic operation was palpable; the vines were visibly thriving under the family's devotion. We savored a tasting over a lunch of just-picked vegetables and crusty bread, the wine rich and earthy. Meeting the winery's pet donkey was a quirky highlight—and being gently nuzzled was a moment of pure joy.

Then came the unexpected: Nadia offered us a chance to crush grapes. Barefoot, I stepped into a tub of freshly harvested fruit. The cool, squishy texture surprised me as juice began to ooze between my toes. I laughed, stomping gently, feeling like a kid in a dream. Another woman, Maggie from Pennsylvania, joined in—only ladies were allowed—and we bonded over this messy, joyous ritual. The winery, framed by rolling hills and a cloudless sky, was a slice of heaven, its peace wrapping around me like a warm embrace.

Barga's magic continued. Each morning, I'd open my balcony doors to hear distant church bells playing their poetic soundtrack to the misty hills. One evening, Larry rallied our newly bonded crew for a football-watching party in the hotel's cozy library. Though the game ended up not being available after all, we didn't care—stories and laughter flowed, cementing our fleeting friendship. They left the next morning, but I lingered for a hike into Barga. Armed with a map from the concierge, I trekked through the countryside that was bursting with ferns, wildflowers, and babbling streams. Old stone homes with flowerpots swaying on porches dotted the path, interspersed with grapevines and apple and pear trees, all heavy with fruit. Red-and-white trail markers guided me, though I had to retrace my steps a few times, lost in all the beauty. Barga's village, with its narrow streets, ancient churches, and the quiet voice of history, charmed me. I could've stayed forever, but Florence beckoned.

Florence was enchanting, its ancient streets throbbing with life. I wandered, mesmerized by soaring cathedrals, intricate Renaissance facades, and the Arno River glinting under stone bridges. I splurged on buttery leather goods at bustling markets and savored dinners of featherlight pasta, each bite a symphony. One waiter, eyes twinkling, shared tales of his family's olive grove, his pride as rich as the oil he poured. My love for Brunello wine, sparked years ago by my client Rich, led me to hire Cristiano, a Florentine driver, for a day trip to Montalcino, Pienza, and Montepulciano. The drive was a postcard—cypress trees spearing the sky, Tuscan villas nestled in golden hills, vineyards stretching endlessly. Each village was a jewel: Montalcino with its medieval charm, Pienza with its quaint stone streets, and Montepulciano with its sweeping views. I wandered their churches, shops, and piazzas, the air thick with history and peace.

Cristiano arranged a visit to Poggio Rubino, a winery perched on a hill near Montalcino. The views were breathtaking—undulating hills under a sapphire sky. Lunch was a feast of garden-fresh vegetables, crusty bread, and bold Sangiovese wines, their ruby hues catching the light. On the way back to Florence, Cristiano navigated narrow backroads to dodge traffic, his local knowledge a gift. That day, truly spent under the Tuscan sun, was pure magic. Back in Florence, I enjoyed my remaining vacation time exploring hidden cafés, savoring fresh meals, and soaking in the city's timeless glow.

As I boarded my flight home, my heart brimmed with gratitude for the landscapes, the flavors, and the people—Larry, Shelly, Maggie, Tom, Nadia, Cristiano—who'd woven this journey into a tapestry of wonder I'd carry with me forever.

EVEREST BASE CAMP—TREK OF A LIFETIME

Just one week after basking in the glow of Tuscany's golden hills, I began to prepare for the adventure of a lifetime: a trek to Everest Base Camp in the Himalayas. Setting everything up while working would've been unthinkable, but with four months off, I dove into the planning with childlike excitement. I pored over blogs, devouring tips on gear and expectations.

The packing list—gaiters, trekking poles, specialized boots, polarized sunglasses, two types of gloves, a sunhat, a warm hat, a headlamp—was a world apart from my usual routine. REI, North Face, and Arc'teryx became my new best friends, making a small fortune off me with every purchase. My last sleeping bag experience, over twenty years prior on a soggy girls' canoe trip down New Hampshire's Saco River, had been a misery—packing a drenched tent in pouring rain, swarmed by mosquitoes, swearing I'd never camp again. But this was different: There would be a high-tech sleeping bag, compact and cozy, waiting for me on a series of cots in a succession of Himalayan teahouses.

Researching base clothing layers blew my mind. My closet? Useless. But my new down jacket could fold into a tiny ball that doubled as a pillow; it felt like a magic trick. The Gore-Tex jacket and over-pants I picked out were sleek, ready for any weather.

(Thankfully, these wool-free options existed for my sensitive skin, which recoils at even the softest merino.) My daypack, perfectly fitted, would have enough room for water, a camera, snacks, a first-aid kit, and extra layers tailored to each day's conditions. A porter would haul my larger and more hefty duffle, a godsend for the journey ahead.

The medical prep for the trip was less glamorous—five shots, three in one arm, two in the other, all of which were meant to guard against a litany of diseases. My travel doctor also provided me with altitude sickness pills, malaria meds, a SteriPen, and water purification tablets (which, luckily, I never needed). I also packed protein shakes and bars and braced myself for the lack of fresh fruits and vegetables, which I'd soon begin to crave.

The mental and physical prep was another beast entirely. There would be eight total days of trekking, which meant I would spend four to six hours moving daily at a slow, steady pace, before a helicopter would whisk me out again. My Sherpa guide was seasoned and wise, and his team knew well the perils of altitude sickness, especially for athletes who pushed too hard. I trained relentlessly, hiking the North Georgia Mountains, where the Appalachian Trail begins, and even managed to squeeze in some climbs during a late August family trip in the Adirondacks. Each ascent built my confidence as my legs became stronger, and my lungs readier, for the thin Himalayan air.

The six-week journey began with a jolt: a day in New Delhi, India, my first taste of a third-world country. The chaos hit like a tidal wave. There were motorbikes weaving through traffic, entire families balanced precariously on them, as well as vans stuffed beyond capacity, seatbelts a foreign concept. On the streets, children begged, their eyes hollow, while my hotel stood like a fortress, its high walls and armed guards shielding opulent interiors adorned with magnificent paintings, intricate figurines, and cascades of fresh flowers. A city tour laid bare the chasm between wealth and poverty—palaces and slums coexisting in jarring contrast. It broke my heart, a reality so far from my own I struggled to process it.

I was soon on to Kathmandu, Nepal, where the air buzzed with resilience despite scars from a devastating earthquake. Crumbled buildings and heritage sites stood as silent witnesses, yet the people's warmth and spirit shone through. On a sunny day, I wandered colorful markets, the scent of spices mingling with the chatter of vendors, soaking in a culture that was foreign yet welcoming. That evening, over steaming plates of dumplings and fragrant dal, I met my Sherpa guide and fellow trekkers, a diverse crew instantly bonded by our imminent adventure. We did a meticulous gear check, ensuring that I had every necessity for the days ahead.

At dawn, we boarded a small plane to Lukla Airport, with its infamously short runway carved into a mountainside. The heart-stopping descent left me gripping my seat. Safely landed, we fueled up with coffee, eggs, and toast at a tiny teahouse, the Himalayan peaks looming outside. My daypack snug, and my porter trailing with the duffle, we finally set off.

The trail unfolded like a dream—rugged paths winding through emerald valleys, prayer flags fluttering in the breeze, the distant clang of yak bells echoing off snow-capped peaks. Each step felt like a pilgrimage. The culture of Nepal unfolded around me in the crisp air—monasteries perched on cliffs, Sherpas sharing stories of their ancient land. I knew I was here not just to conquer a trek but to immerse myself in beauty, challenge, and a world far beyond my own, my heart swelling with every mile.

As I trudged upward through the Himalayas, a chance encounter with an Australian woman descending the trail stayed with me. Her words, delivered with a sun-weathered smile—"It's about the journey, not the destination"—echoed in my mind. My instinct, honed by years of chasing wins and deadlines, screamed at me to reach the end, to conquer the goal. This time I chose instead to savor each moment, the highs *and* the lows, letting the mountains teach me to slow down.

Each step was a meditation, my trekking poles clicking rhythmically against rocky paths, as my eyes scanned to sidestep yak dung. The terrain was a mercurial dance partner—grueling ascents that burned my lungs gave way to gentle downhill slopes or flat stretches where I could catch my breath, the crisp air sharp in my chest. I moved deliberately, no deadlines pressing on me, pausing when my body demanded it. The Himalayas sang to me. There were roaring rivers carved through emerald valleys, their white foam glinting in the sun, along with children's laughter that spilled from stone villages as I passed, their joy infectious. Then, turning a corner, I'd stop dead, awestruck by vistas that stole my words—deep valleys plunging downward, waterfalls cascading like silver threads, snow-capped peaks piercing the sky. In those moments, peace wove itself around me like a warm wrap.

Teahouses dotted the trail, their wooden benches a haven for weary trekkers. I'd cradle a steaming cup of tea, its warmth soothing my throat, raw from a cold I caught on day one. The dry air and lingering sniffles tested me, but each sip revived my spirit, fueling me for the next leg. Some villages felt tantalizingly close, only to reveal themselves as distant mirages, forcing me to dig deep for one more burst of energy. My Sherpa, a mild-mannered young man, was my anchor, though his "just a little further" could mean fifteen minutes or an hour. One grueling climb up endless stone steps felt like scaling a stairway to the heavens, my legs screaming, until I reached a sunlit teahouse room, my duffle waiting and filled to the brim with warm clothes. Slipping into a fresh fleece, I gazed out at the mountains, feeling victorious.

Other times, frustration crept in. When my porter lagged behind, I'd shiver in the biting cold, clutching hot tea, counting the minutes until my bag arrived. My oxygen levels thankfully held strong, and bottled water and electrolyte powder kept me hydrated, but food was trickier. Early days brought comforting hot soup and unexpected popcorn snacks, but my head cold dulled my appetite and the unfamiliar smells turned my stomach. But determination pushed me through, and the mountain culture humbled me. Up there, electricity was a luxury, internet a myth, and modern toilets a rare find. I marveled at the infrastructure, having been carved into these unforgiving peaks by yaks and human backs. The Nepalese spirit awed me—no complaints, just resilience and kindness. My guide, who didn't know his own birthdate, had never left Nepal, couldn't drive or swim, and lived without email or credit cards. Yet his warmth and contentment challenged my assumptions about what matters. Maslow's pyramid came into sharp focus: air, water, food, clothing, shelter.

My gear—carefully chosen base layers, hats, and gloves—kept me protected, though leaving the warmth of the lodge's toasty stove every night in exchange for a frigid bedroom was always a challenge. I'd huddle in down and fleece, sometimes with a hot water bottle, until my body warmed; some nights I'd wake later drenched in sweat, peeling off layers in the dark.

My health challenges were the worst the day before climbing Kala Patthar. As my illness worsened, I faced the real possibility of missing the summit. Curled in my sleeping bag, appetite gone, I accepted it, releasing the pressure. I had already glimpsed Everest's majesty and for that I was grateful. That surrender worked magic— by evening, I finally felt a craving for an energy bar, a sign of recovery. Ecstatic, I rallied for the climb.

Kala Patthar was a triumph I'll never forget. My Sherpa was my hero, carrying my pack, wiping my runny nose, steadying me on steep descents in the freezing dark, my headlamp's beam slicing through the night. My fingers and toes became numb despite my layers, but reaching the peak as the sun dipped below Everest's silhouette was otherworldly. The sky blazed orange and pink, the mountain's majesty defying words or photos. Back at the lodge, I thawed by the stove, gratitude warming me as much as the fire.

The final trek to Base Camp was a victory lap, the path gentler, my heart light. Arriving at a pile of rocks adorned with prayer flags, I tried to imagine the camp in full swing—tents for summit climbers, weeks of grueling prep. I felt content, my journey complete. Instead of trekking back to Lukla, I splurged on a helicopter ride, soaring over the peaks, their jagged edges glowing in the morning light. Landing in Kathmandu, I savored a hot meal and sank into a soft bed, the perfect end to a journey that reshaped me. The Himalayas didn't just test my body—they taught me to embrace the journey, to find peace in the struggle, and to carry their mighty, wild beauty in my heart forever.

AUSTRALIA AND NEW ZEALAND

After the trek, I flew to New Zealand with a short layover in Sydney, Australia. I didn't have much time to explore, but I savored the chance to unwind, stroll the harbor, and soak in the city's easygoing vibe. One lunch at a cliffside café overlooking the ocean was nothing short of breathtaking. Though I was also surprised to discover how much of the culture still felt frozen in the eighties—charmingly retro, in the best way.

From there, I flew over the Tasman Sea to New Zealand to visit my brother Steve, who had relocated there after meeting and eventually marrying his husband, Pete. The country was pure magic, not only for its jaw-dropping beauty but also thanks to this gift of a family reunion. I spent the first few days at their lodge in Golden Bay, at the top of the South Island. Reconnecting with Steve was, as always, a soothing balm for my soul. With a golden-sand beach just steps from the door, I'd wander along the shore with their dog Meg, letting the rhythm of the waves wash everything else away.

Steve and I then drove south along the wild west coast to their second lodge near Hokitika. The coastline there is another world entirely—rugged black-sand beaches framed by dramatic cliffs and pancake rocks. Swimming was out of the question (the currents sweeping in from Australia are ferocious), but walking those shores felt like stepping into a postcard. I spent a few lazy days savoring Pete's incredible cooking—each meal a small masterpiece. One cloudy morning, we swapped the gray skies for an underground adventure: a scenic train ride through the lush rainforest, followed by a magical exploration of glowworm caves. We wandered beneath thousands of them twinkling, then drifted silently on inner tubes down the subterranean river, surrounded by starlike lights in the darkness.

Next stop: Queenstown, the adventure capital. I'd originally planned to skydive, but cloudy skies unfortunately derailed those plans. Instead, we took a thrilling jet-boat ride down the Shotover River—pure exhilaration. The following day, after a long, delicious lunch at a gorgeous winery, we visited the Kawarau Gorge Suspension Bridge, the world's original bungee site. I'd never had the slightest interest in jumping . . . until I saw the radiant grins on the faces of everyone climbing back up from the canyon. Something clicked. Within minutes I was signed up—and Steve, moments later, followed suit.

Let me tell you: That leap was one of the freest moments of my life. The rush of adrenaline coursed through me for hours afterward, leaving me giddy and alive.

After a quick overnight in Brisbane, it was time to head home. As the plane lifted off, I felt overflowing gratitude—for the laughter shared with Steve and Pete, for the wild beauty of New Zealand, and for the unexpected courage that pushed me off a perfectly good bridge.

Those months weren't just a break—they were a rebirth, a rare time of adventure and reflection that readied me for the next chapter. My anticipation was building as I thought about all the challenges and triumphs to come. This time frame also brought the end of my thirteen-year marriage with Rob. I had been wrestling with this decision for some time; while I remained grateful for the times we shared together, we had drifted apart and were unable to meet each other's needs.

⋮

20

A Vibrant Leap: Embracing New Horizons and Hard Lessons

During my months off, I'd been networking with IBM and ultimately secured an offer that anchored my wanderlust with the promise of a fresh start. I then officially joined the team in January of 2017 full of inspiration, my energy levels high and ready to dive back into work. Just a week or two after I started, I learned that a former colleague and friend would be joining the company as well, and to my delight, he'd be my new boss. After looking into my new client accounts and dissecting financials, I made a compelling pitch on how to refocus our efforts. I set to work after my boss eagerly endorsed and supported my plan of attack.

INDIA AND THE PHILIPPINES

In the summer of 2018, one of my clients at IBM was utilizing our offshore consulting and operational services, which then landed me a rare opportunity: a trip to the Philippines to meet our team there and salute their relentless dedication. Stepping onto Filipino soil for the first time, I was swept into a whirlwind of lively chaos—Manila's streets throbbed with life, a symphony of honking jeepneys, darting motorbikes, and vendors hawking colorful wares under a tropical sun. Yet, amid the frenetic bustle, I was struck by a warmth that radiated from every soul I encountered. My colleagues, with their quick smiles and eager laughter, welcomed me like family, their eyes sparkling with pride in their work. The hotel staff greeted me each morning with genuine cheer, their voices light as if joy were woven into their words. At restaurants, waiters moved with a quiet grace, their kindness as abundant as the steaming plates they served. It wasn't just politeness—it was a deep, unfiltered happiness that seemed to bloom from their core, painting every interaction with a glow I'd never forget.

After that, my journey carried me to India, landing in the bustling sprawl of New Delhi, where the air thrummed with the scent of spices and the clamor of life. Before diving into work, I stole a personal detour to Agra, drawn like a moth to the luminous flame of the Taj Mahal. The palace rose before me, its ivory marble gleaming under the sun, intricate inlays of semiprecious stones catching the light like a thousand tiny stars. I settled onto the same bench where Princess Diana once sat, the cool stone grounding me as I posed for a photo, the monument's majesty stealing my breath. Its domes and minarets seemed to whisper stories of love and loss, each detail a testament to human devotion.

After that brief respite, I plunged into client meetings, first in Hyderabad, then Bengaluru, where the sheer density of humanity was a force of its own, crowds surging like rivers through bustling streets. Sheltered in the opulent cocoon of The Ritz, I was enveloped in luxury, yet the daily commute to the office was a gauntlet. Horns blared, rickshaws wove through traffic like dancers in a chaotic ballet, and the air shimmered with heat and dust. My colleagues, sharp and warm, navigated this world with ease, their resilience humbling me.

As I boarded my flight home, gratitude swelled in my heart like a rising tide. I saw my own life's luxuries—clean water, quiet streets, time to breathe—in vivid contrast to the relentless rhythm of the places I'd been. The journey awakened me, reminded of the fragile gifts I too often took for granted, as my spirit brimmed over with reverence for the beauty and perseverance of the world I'd witnessed.

⋮

21

Morning Stillness, Sacred Whispers: Blessed with Meditation's Joyful Calm

In early 2018, I found myself at a crossroads, wrestling with a soul-draining struggle at IBM. I had joined with a fire in my heart, bursting with innovative ideas to breathe new life into the banking organization, only to watch each one shot down by a leadership team entrenched in fear and rigidity. As a natural maverick, never one to blindly follow orders, I was baffled and frustrated, my spirit bruised by their rejection. "Why hire me if you wanted a yes-person?" I thought, my creativity and inspiration suffocated by insecure leaders. Each day felt like wading through quicksand, my heart heavy with discouragement, my purpose dimmed.

I also came to see that my team lacked the necessary banking and financial services expertise. Intense pressure from leadership led to significant layoffs, drastically reducing my team. And then to top it all off, my boss decided to move on. I was left without mentorship or support, feeling vulnerable and shaken in my confidence.

During this period of turmoil, I clung to a singular solace: my morning walks in nature. One crisp morning, desperate to find a flicker of hope, I paused beneath a canopy of towering pine trees, their emerald needles swaying gently against a serene blue sky. The quiet rustle of leaves and the distant call of a bird stirred something within me, and I experienced a fleeting moment of gratitude that soothed my troubled mind. It was as if nature herself whispered, "Keep going." Those walks became my sanctuary, a sacred pause where the world's weight lifted, if only for a moment, and I could breathe again.

A few days later, I connected with my dear friend Kim, pouring out my frustrations over the phone. Her voice altered as she shared more about how she'd recently discovered meditation through Emily Fletcher, the founder of Ziva Meditation. I'd always been skeptical of meditation—sitting still, chanting mantras, or chasing an elusive calm seemed foreign, even absurd, to my restless spirit. But in my desperation, grasping at straws mentally and emotionally, I was willing to try anything to reclaim my inner peace. I enrolled in Emily's course, and what began as a tentative experiment soon blossomed into a lifeline. Daily meditation wove itself into the fabric of my mornings, a ritual as vital as the sunrise.

At first, the practice felt awkward, my mind a whirlwind of thoughts darting like fireflies in a jar. But gradually, I noticed subtle shifts. On days I skipped my meditation, a quiet unease lingered, as if a piece of my soul were missing. I began to cherish this sacred pause, setting the tone for my day with intention. Instead of reaching for my phone or a hurried coffee, I'd settle into stillness, my breath slowing like a gentle tide, anchoring me as I observed the flurry of my own thoughts without judgment. A simple mantra, like a soft melody, would draw me back to peace, grounding me in the present. Even on days when I had to catch an early flight, I would rise earlier, carving out time to meditate, feeling my spirit fortified, ready to face the day with clarity and grace.

Emily Fletcher's approach resonated deeply with my soul. She taught that meditation isn't about mastering silence or controlling one's thoughts—an intimidating prospect for someone like me, whose mind constantly buzzes with ideas. Instead, she framed meditation as a practice to get good at life, a tool to navigate its chaos with resilience and joy. This truth struck a chord, dissolving my skepticism and inviting me to embrace the practice as a gift, not a chore. Over time, I was even able to open my heart to listen for the divine whispers of God. In those quiet moments, I felt a sacred connection, as if the Universe were speaking softly, guiding me toward a deeper understanding of myself and my place in the world. Meditation became a bridge to the divine, a space where I could surrender my struggles and align with a higher purpose. It continues to be the heartbeat of my mornings, a ritual that centers me in love and presence. It's taught me to dance with life's challenges rather than fight them, to trust in the unfolding of my path.

Then, thankfully, in late 2018, a new opportunity within IBM emerged. A global team wanted a US representative to join them in pursuing a joint venture with an innovative banking tech company. I was all in. I knew one of the founders personally and believed wholeheartedly in the technology. I built out a practice for the Americas with one other outstanding team member and now friend, Tom, supported by the team in London. My mind raced with strategies as we pitched to some of the top global accounts. There were inevitably camps of both the excited and the skeptical, not to mention those who outright doubted the possibilities, which only fueled my passion. I loved every moment of this experience. Here was an amazing opportunity to radically change the banking ecosystem.

After a successful pitch to the CIO of a major global bank, we received feedback that he had never seen such an innovative approach to banking transformation from this organization. We continued to work with him on subsequent efforts to educate his colleagues and pitches to the board.

Over the next couple of years, I worked with a team in Washington, DC, on a cutting-edge pitch for a solution to modernize old government systems and processes for student lending. This would not only increase efficiency and reduce risk but also change the whole process for parents and students alike. I spent time in the Midwest working with a client on an urgently needed banking system transformation. Many members of their team had been with the bank for decades and were starting to retire; the institutional knowledge these folks had acquired needed to be captured, creatively, in order to reduce risk. We crafted a detailed playbook for a banking renovation, working with all the major new technology entrants.

RIO AND SÃO PAULO

In late 2019, while I was still with IBM but right before COVID, I leapt at the chance to consult on a massive banking transformation in South America, thrilled to help lead a workshop in São Paulo with our client and tech partners. Eager to explore a new continent, I landed first in Rio de Janeiro, my heart racing with anticipation. The city hit me like a tidal wave—chaotic, crowded, pulsing with life. I checked into the familiar comfort of a Marriott in Copacabana, its windows framing the iconic beach across the street, a reassuring haven in the urban whirlwind.

Copacabana's shoreline was a bit of a shock. I slipped into my modest bikini, only to feel overdressed amid a sea of sun-bronzed locals. Even older women strutted with confidence in barely-there swimsuits, their ease infectious. The hotel's beach chairs sat tucked back from the water, leaving the prime sandy stretch to locals—a spirited parade of life unfolding before me. As I lounged, soaking up the sun's blaze, the city's clamor enveloped me: samba rhythms blasting from nearby speakers, an Italian airline crew chatting animatedly, and a mixture of other languages swirling in the salty air. It wasn't the tranquil beach escape I'd known elsewhere, but I leaned into the cultural symphony, letting it wash over me.

I ventured to Christ the Redeemer, the statue's outstretched arms towering above Rio, a breathtaking guardian against the skyline. At Sugarloaf Mountain, I stood awestruck, the sweeping vistas of the city's jagged peaks and turquoise bays unfurling below. The people I met emitted warmth, their smiles bridging language gaps.

During this brief visit to Rio de Janeiro, I was captivated by the city's coastal charm—sun-kissed beaches, a laid-back vibe, and the majestic Christ the Redeemer gazing over it all. Then, in São Paulo, I marveled at the highways' impossibly narrow lanes, gratefully leaving the driving to others, and felt the city's frenetic pulse through its towering skyscrapers and bustling streets. Both cities, though distinct, enchanted me with Brazil's vibrant diversity and warmth.

Returning to the United States, I carried a deeper gratitude for the comforts I'd often overlooked, similar to the way I felt after visiting India. The streets back home felt less crowded, the pace calmer, and the sense of safety more pronounced. I was reminded to cherish life's vivid contrasts.

DEEP FRUSTRATION

As the technology I'd championed surged into the mainstream, the company rallied a sprawling global team to steer its course. My heart thrummed with anticipation—I was certain I'd be at the helm, my early contributions having blazed a trail of innovation. I'd amassed a treasure trove of data, forged alliances with key players and competitors, and woven compelling narratives into pitch decks that sparkled with vision. I could already see myself guiding this journey forward, my mind excited with the thrill of what lay ahead.

But then, like a sudden storm cloud blotting out the sun, my role was sidelined. The organization leaned heavily on the solutions I'd crafted, with my data as their compass and my insights as their fuel—yet they shut me out of the leadership circle. The sting was sharp, a blade of betrayal slicing through my pride. Anger flared, hot and fierce, mingling with a deep, aching hurt. I was furious— *pissed off*, if I'm honest—feeling cast aside like a forgotten spark in a fire that was now roaring. Politically, they'd chosen a safer path, one that dimmed my vision for bold change. A mentor who knew the inner workings of the company, offered a bittersweet balm: "Marcia, your ideas are like fine wine—rich and bold, but this company isn't ready to savor them." His words echoed a familiar refrain, one I'd heard across my career and would hear again: My vision always seemed to race ahead, a comet streaking past colleagues and clients who remained content with the safe, the ordinary. I craved transformation—all things new, exhilarating, better—never settling for the mediocre.

Despite the sting, I poured myself into the work for two more years, my commitment unyielding, even in my diminished role. I toiled tirelessly on multiple pursuits, my days a whirlwind of strategy and execution. I scoured the talent pool, recruiting brilliant minds to build a stellar team, their potential a constellation of promise. Yet, deep down, I knew this wasn't my true home—my heart whispered of a place where my vision could soar.

Then COVID crashed into the world like a rogue wave, upending everything. I was grateful to have my job, and for the opportunity to pivot to working from home, but the shift was jarring. I relied heavily on my meditation practice to get me through each day.

⋮

22

The Art of Allowing: Finding Peace in a Pandemic

For over two decades, I was a road warrior, my life a blur of Monday morning flights and Thursday night returns, weaving through airports with a suitcase that felt like an extension of myself. The grind had its perks: Airline miles and hotel points piled up, earning me lifetime platinum status on Delta, with over two million miles flown, and titanium status with Marriott. A couple of years ago, Marriott sent me a jaw-dropping stat—I'd spent the equivalent of over five years in their hotels alone, not counting other chains or corporate apartments. That number hit me like a thunderbolt. I'd mastered dining solo when not with clients or teammates, finding comfort in the rhythm of travel despite the inevitable flight delays, cancellations, and dreaded middle seats. Missing weekday social events stung, but Fridays at home were my sanctuary.

Then COVID stopped me cold. The sudden halt to all the travel was like pulling the plug on my life's soundtrack. I couldn't wrap my head around not boarding a plane—it was my go-to activity for most of my adult life. Now, confined to virtual calls, I felt like a painter stripped of her canvas. Leading a major engagement for a California client I'd never met face-to-face was like trying to build a bridge over a foggy chasm. There were no hallway chats, no shared lunches or dinners to weave the personal threads that make work human. The screen felt cold, the absence of connection a quiet ache.

One of the trips I had planned to celebrate my fiftieth birthday was at a yoga retreat in Costa Rica, but it was canceled the day before departure as the country locked down. My grand plans for globe-trotting to new countries fizzled, and I spent my milestone birthday alone, a quiet shock I hadn't anticipated. But I adapted, trading planes for a road trip to Florida, arriving just in time for a fleeting beach walk before it closed as well. From my balcony, the sea's roar was a soothing balm, though anxiety about all the unknowns of COVID gnawed at me. I cut the trip short, retreating home to safety, navigating a world where "normal" felt like a foreign language.

Watching others grapple with work-from-home life and 24-7 family dynamics made my single life feel less intense. I leaned into virtual happy hours, FaceTiming friends with wine in hand, laughter bridging the distance. One such night in June coincided with the Atlanta riots. I went to bed oblivious, having skipped the news, only to wake Saturday morning to a friend's Facebook video showing a restaurant owner driving through a nearby neighborhood to down-town, filming shattered storefronts, looted mall stores, and chaos I couldn't fathom. I'd long abandoned traditional news outlets, frus-trated by their hype and lack of context, but that day I was glued to my screen, scrolling in disbelief. The violence, the protests, the clash between city and state—it shook me to my core. How could this be justified? What was next? Fear gripped me, exhaustion settling in as I went to bed drained.

Sunday morning, I knew I needed a reset. The news offered no answers, only more noise. I turned to my trusted online bookstore, desperate for a distraction to restore some peace. I stumbled across *The Law of Attraction* by Esther and Jerry Hicks, sparked by a friend's mention of Abraham-Hicks. I dove in, captivated by its concepts, especially the Art of Allowing. The core idea was simple and freeing: I can fully accept myself as I am while allowing others to be exactly who they are, without needing to judge or change them. It was a relief. I didn't need to condemn or try to fix others' actions. If their behavior came from pain or desperation, I could meet it with love and compassion instead of fear.

The book's teachings struck me deeply on another level as well. It encouraged holding a clear, positive intention toward others: recognizing that each person is who they are, fully responsible as the creator of their own life experience and naturally attracting what matches their vibration. Meanwhile, I remain the creator of my own reality, drawing in what aligns with me. Others aren't truly disrupting or ruining my world the way it might seem; they're simply shaping their own. To them, their world might feel perfectly right. Once you truly grasp that this Universe—and our physical experience within it—is infinitely abundant with no limits or shortages, worry fades away. You can allow them to create and attract what's right for them, while you focus on creating and attracting what's right for you.

This perspective was a gift, freeing me from the need to control or understand or be fearful. I could simply let others be.

From that day on, I embraced being an Allower. It brought peace in moments of confusion, in everything from political divides to personal clashes. I didn't need all the facts or the history of someone's pain in order to offer compassion. This shift also deepened my self-love, easing the weight of judgment I'd carried. The riots, the uncertainty, the world's chaos—they didn't vanish, but I found a way to navigate them with grace, focusing on creating my own world, one grounded in peace and possibility.

23

A Coastal Calling: Manifesting My Seaside Sanctuary

For years, I had escaped to the beach in Florida. It was my sanctuary. I was always recharged by the soothing lap of the waves and the glow of Gulf sunsets. The sea's call was undeniable, promising a life where I could wake to the sight of turquoise waters and cloud-streaked skies bridging heaven and earth. But still I stayed in Atlanta for its airport, a necessity for my weekly work travel. Direct flights were nonnegotiable—until COVID flipped the world virtual. Suddenly untethered, I released my longing to the Universe, no strings attached on timing or exact location, though the Gulf's gentle pull, especially around Naples's pristine sands, always outshone the Atlantic's edge. I'd strolled Naples's beaches, mesmerized by their Caribbean-like hues, and vacationed on Anna Maria Island, though its tourist bustle felt too frenetic for a permanent home. I craved paradise with peace.

What was to become my new hometown was, at first, barely a blip on my radar until a few visits revealed its charm: enough culture, a small but lively downtown, and unspoiled beaches just minutes away. On one trip for the holidays in December 2020, I stumbled across a development under construction. The only lot that caught my eye was already pending, so I shrugged it off, not fully sold on the area anyway. But the next day, the Universe whispered: I learned that the buyer had backed out. A spark ignited. I talked with the saleswoman, my intuition on high: *This is it.* That weekend, I flew back, toured the lot again, and felt an unshakable certainty. The home style that would fit on the lot even provided the perfect layout for entertaining, something that brings me pure joy. As I finalized the contract in the sales office, I noticed a line of hopeful buyers outside, all of whom were silently wishing I'd falter. Walking away, I felt guided, grateful for divine timing, thrilled with anticipation.

Building my home took nearly a year, slowed by COVID's grip on supply chains and labor. Still, I savored every trip to my future home city, diving into the design process. At the builder's design center, I handpicked light cabinets, the perfect flooring, and sleek fixtures. I wanted a breezy Florida aesthetic, a stark departure from my Atlanta home. Designing the pool was a thrill, my nerves eased by the designer's steady hand as we crafted a backyard oasis. I reached out to Cristy, my Atlanta designer, who eagerly took on the project. Working from floor plans, she wove her magic again. We scoured Atlanta's rug mart for just the right carpets, hunted for statement lighting, and curated furniture that felt like me. Her creativity transformed a daunting task into a seamless, delightful collaboration.

Every piece of the move—every choice, every chance—fell into place serendipitously. I know it was no accident; it was God's perfect timing, orchestrating a dream I'd held for years.

⋮

24

A New Path Ignited: Chasing Vision, Embracing Risk

Over my five years at IBM, my phone buzzed with recruiters pitching new horizons, each call a fleeting spark of possibility. Yet none ignited a fire strong enough to pull me from my path—I wasn't ready to leap without a vision that set my soul ablaze. In the spring of 2021, two giants, Deloitte and Accenture, reached out, stirring a flicker of curiosity. Deloitte, a prestigious audit and consulting firm held promise. I genuinely enjoyed meeting with the countless sets of interviewers. But it eventually loomed like a fortress of rules: mandatory retirement at sixty-two, a grueling decadelong climb for partnership perks, and invasive financial disclosures probing into my family's private affairs. It felt like a gilded cage, not a calling.

Accenture I'd always viewed with skepticism. Many of its employees, fresh from college with little real-world experience, couldn't hold a candle to my seasoned industry expertise and the trusted teammates I brought to every challenge: that was the competitive edge I'd wielded at countless other firms. But this time, something shifted. A potential boss's candid voice cut through my doubts, his honesty as refreshing as a cool breeze. He admitted that senior hires often struggled to last beyond two years, yet his assurance of support, not to mention his need for my specific expertise, lit a spark. I could see it—a chance to build something extraordinary. The vision took root in my mind. Meanwhile, Deloitte's responses turned sharp, their arrogance flaring like a warning flag in the wind when I hinted that I was considering going with Accenture. I made my choice, embracing the risk of a shorter tenure. I'd long dreamed of pivoting in my fifties or sixties, stepping away from financial services to chase a new chapter, and this felt like the right leap.

My decision crystallized around two truths: I couldn't commit another decade to consulting's relentless grind, and this Accenture team, brimming with potential, was worth joining. I accepted the offer, my heart racing as I set a start date just weeks away. But first, I finally made my escape to Costa Rica's lush embrace. There I could decompress and prepare myself to once again step into the unknown.

:

25

A Turning Point: Releasing Pain, Embracing Freedom

In October of 2021, on my final day at a transformative healing retreat in Costa Rica, I stood at the edge of a profound shift, though I didn't yet know it. I'd spent ten glorious days rejuvenating in the jungle, feeling the stress melt away from every aching joint and muscle. My one-room cabin had served as a peaceful oasis, warm and comfortable, while the soft breezes whispering through the window would gently caress my skin, soothing my nerves. The morning yoga had been refreshing to my tense limbs, each stretch releasing a sigh of relief from my body, my muscles loosening, becoming more supple with every pose.

Listening to the howler monkeys expressing their desire to mate, their calls vibrating through the air, had made me smile and feel a tickle of joy in my chest. Dining on clean, delicious, organic food, grown and prepared with so much love, had not only nourished my body but also warmed my soul, filling me with a sense of health and vitality as the flavors exploded in my mouth.

Meeting and communing with new friends who shared the same

desire to take a break from life's struggles and reset, I had felt a comforting warmth of companionship, my heart lightening with each shared laugh and story. Hiking around the jungle on dirt roads, the earth beneath my feet firm yet forgiving, had led me to stunning views of the ocean in all its majesty. The sight had taken my breath away, my pulse quickening with awe.

Walking barefoot on black-sand beaches, the grains cool and slightly gritty against my soles, had helped me feel rooted, grounded, as if the earth itself was drawing out the tension from my feet. Floating in the gentle waves of the Pacific, I had become one with the vastness of the sea, the water buoying my body, the salt cleansing my skin, and the rhythmic motion of the waves lulling me into a state of tranquility.

Daily treatments from gifted healers had been transformative; each touch on each pressure point had seemed to erase tension from my body, exhausted as it was from both work and life. The pain ebbed away, replaced by a tingling sensation of relief. My body had begun to feel lighter, more alive, as if I was shedding layers of stress with each session.

After wrapping up my five years with IBM, I was mentally and physically worn out. It wasn't the experience I had hoped for. I didn't feel fulfilled. I didn't feel like I had achieved the success that I wanted. I didn't feel supported and recognized for all the work and energy and new ideas that I had brought to the table.

On the last day of my retreat, I impulsively decided (at least, I considered it impulsive at the time) to undergo one more treatment, oblivious to the profound impact it would have and how it would transform my life. I had never experienced a Reiki treatment before. Essentially, it's an energy cleansing and healing experience. I shut my eyes, clueless about what even to anticipate. I oscillated between skepticism—*This is kind of odd, what the heck am I doing here?*—and an attempt at openness. During the treatment, I didn't sense much of anything but chose to accept this.

As the session neared its end, the extremely kind and nearly glowing therapist gazed at me and declared, "Marcia, I sense a blockage in your body, perhaps something you're clinging to, something you need to release. Maybe you need to dance more, love more, to be free. Does that resonate with you?" Oh boy, she struck a chord there. I burst into tears, feeling vulnerable and terrified yet not unsafe, rather enveloped by this astonishing feeling of being truly seen and heard. I felt profoundly understood without many words having been spoken. I had this instant validation that I was indeed stuck, harboring so much suffering.

I would later reread *Living Untethered* by Michael Singer, and in this book he speaks of these blocks as Samskaras. Every painful incident from our past that we don't release gets stored in the body. And since it was stored with pain, it releases as pain. Eckhart Tolle in *The Power of Now* describes this as "emotional pain-body." I hadn't previously explored this notion in any depth—of past pain having a physical impact on our bodies and overall health. I have since come to realize the connection in a very real and intense way.

I departed from that retreat feeling invigorated, rejuvenated, and resolute in my determination to muster the courage to delve deeper and discover a way to release this blockage. I didn't realize it then, but it would take another two and a half years to achieve the freedom and peace I yearned for, to shed the weight of my past and reclaim my true self. But, indeed, I would eventually share my stories of healing, finding immense joy, peace, and clarity about my identity, my gifts, and my purpose in this beautiful, abundant world.

⋮

26

A Final Leap of Faith: Embracing Change and Choosing Love

joined Accenture in December of 2021, right at the same time my home in Florida was slated for completion—a serendipitous alignment. The transition was electric, a double helix of change weaving together. Despite the virtual onboarding, never meeting many colleagues in person, I felt a warmth settle in my chest. This consultancy, alive with possibility, felt like a homecoming—a place where my ideas could finally take root. My spirit felt like it was soaring as I stepped into this exciting new chapter. For the first year, I worked mostly virtually, a blessing that allowed me to be home for the endless stream of contractors and delivery services required for my new home. I was grateful for the flexibility.

I was stunned to hear, however, that the role I thought I'd been promised during my interview process would be different than how it had been pitched to me. I quickly began to see the challenges of not having grown up in the company, of not knowing the cultural history, not having long relationships, and not knowing how to navigate the system. While the company offered support with integration, it wasn't enough. I couldn't break into the leadership circle. I was an outsider. I was the stepchild.

Not to mention I had the distinct impression that the depth of my thirty-plus years of experience was being diminished by people with vastly less expertise. I felt I couldn't do my job or be successful. I was boxed out of access to certain clients, and all of a sudden, other colleagues appeared out of the woodwork, claiming they knew my content as well as or even better than me, yet without the depth of knowledge I brought.

I was angry and disappointed, even though I had been warned. For some reason I thought I could excel and would have the support I needed to be successful. Regardless, I kept on trying. I quickly realized we had a huge uphill battle and that most clients didn't see us as offering the services I came to provide. I worked on countless pitches, refreshing content and bringing in new ideas and angles. Once again, I found myself back in the fine wine story: The industry just wasn't ready for my ideas from this organization, nor were the account teams I worked with. My efforts were often met with resistance, leaving me with feelings of deep frustration.

And, quite frankly, there was no budget for investment either. Earnings dropped significantly during this time. I felt grateful to escape the impact of some downsizing thanks to the support I had from my boss. Some colleagues at my same level only made it to the one-year mark.

However, one silver lining in joining this organization was a partnership with the recruiting firm that had placed me, who offered specialized tests to analyze strengths, behaviors, and strategies to ease my transition. Initially, I scoffed at the idea. My skepticism was evident—how could this possibly help? I was entrenched in a situation that seemed unchangeable, resigned to just dealing with it, heavy with the burden of adaptation.

But, boy, I had never been more wrong. I took the tests and then met an amazing woman, Jill. As we pored over the results, I experienced more aha moments with her than I had had in a long time. I realized so many things about myself, such as how I had given up my power and how I was still wrestling with or allowing past issues to block my path. But the biggest revelation came when she guided me toward actually detaching from the situation. She offered up a better approach that would not only help me see the situation differently and more broadly but would also equip me with more effective tools for my own empowerment.

Jill challenged me, her eyes sparkling with intensity, to regard everyone with love and compassion. She also shared another interesting perspective. In her view, there are three phases of life—Victim, Warrior, and Messenger. When we are born, we are dependent upon our parents for everything to sustain and protect us; essentially, we are powerless and helpless. Many people stay in Victim mode and can't get past it, blaming others for their situation, remaining unable to break free. Those who move on from this state feel a need to grow up, then set out to create and live the life they want with independence; they recognize that it's time to prove themselves to the world. Eventually, a small group of others will release themselves from needing to be the Warrior and will graduate into Messenger mode. With this shift comes a desire to help others, perhaps stepping back from the limelight, reshaping what achievement means.

I felt a pang of sadness when reflecting upon the fact that, while I was primarily still in Warrior mode, and at times had even tasted the beginnings of my Messenger mode, I had temporarily regressed to Victim mode. I traced this back to my seventh year at Capco. Ugh, that was embarrassing. Why did I give up my power? Why did I blame others for my negative situations? I had felt slighted and unsupported. I hadn't recognized at the time that I simply needed to view those challenges as life experiences, that I could always choose to move forward to regain my power.

THE FINAL CHAPTER IN MY CONSULTING CAREER

Over the previous eight-plus years of my career, I had achieved numerous successes. But I came to see there was another, different outcome emerging from those often painful years: I had been actively manifesting a break from the confines of my oppressive religious upbringing, aiming to push my spiritual growth to new heights. I didn't even fully grasp what that meant at the time. Now, looking back, it's clear how each situation and experience, both positive and negative, shaped my understanding. Gary Zukav's perspective has stayed with me like a quiet compass: Every moment that hurts, no matter how sharp or heavy, arrives carrying a hidden gift. It's an invitation to grow, to see more clearly, and to choose love over fear in a place I couldn't before.

I used to separate my career and work life from my spiritual life, a division I now find puzzling. After all, I'm living one life where these aspects are deeply interwoven, especially given the countless hours I spent at work. For years, I actively sought spiritual growth, constantly questioning and searching for answers. Those answers and experiences poured in from every corner of my life—sometimes met with a quiet nod of recognition, other times they stirred up confusion or pain. In those cases, I had to ask myself, "Did I truly invite this situation or experience? What was I meant to learn from it?"

At times, I got cocky, feeling a sense of self-righteousness. I'd think of my career, "I earned this, I did this, I have the experience, I did my time," then would become filled with frustration when I realized it was never enough. This mind-set clashed with the humility and openness required for spiritual progression, leading to moments where I struggled internally, trying to reconcile the ego's demands with my soul's journey. Eventually I would understand that each experience was part of the plan.

A MIRACLE IN DISGUISE—BE CAREFUL WHAT YOU
MANIFEST BECAUSE THE UNIVERSE WILL DELIVER

As of October 2023, I was four months into supporting a major program with Accenture. I had been with the company for just shy of two years at that point. I was caught in a relentless whirlwind, shuttling between my home and the client's site like a weary traveler on an endless loop. Each week, I'd brace myself for the grind of air travel, boarding packed Sunday flights with a long layover in Atlanta. This was exactly why I had remained living in Atlanta for so many years; I could get a direct flight almost anywhere from the city's airport. In these moments, I was grateful I could at least find refuge in the familiarity of Delta's Sky Club, often catching my favorite NFL games on my iPad as I waited for the next flight. The journey was a drain, sapping my energy before I even stepped foot in the client's door.

On Monday mornings, I'd shake off the fog of travel and dive back into the project, a high-stakes dance of deadlines and deliverables. Then come Thursday night or Friday morning, I'd board another flight, grateful to be headed to the fleeting sanctuary of my own home. I'd carve out a few precious hours to escape to the beach on Sunday mornings, where the salty breeze and the gentle crash of waves against the shore washed away the week's chaos. Barefoot in the sand, I'd let the sun warm my skin as the horizon stretched before me, wide and endless. These precious moments offered a much-needed reset before the cycle began all over again.

My social life was left on pause, the faint echo of past dinners and remembered laughter with friends replaced by hurried texts and promises of "soon." Yet, despite the grind, the work itself was a joy. Engaging with the client's team—bright, driven, and occasionally quirky—was invigorating.

On the last day of October in 2023, I was in a large conference room with my colleagues when my boss pinged me in the late afternoon, inquiring if I had a moment to connect. I snatched my laptop and dashed down to a small, private office, clueless about the subject. He didn't beat around the bush and said bluntly, "Your time is up. There's nothing more I can do. Your last day is December 1." The news blindsided me, leaving me in shock. I was fully billable, and my sales numbers would go a long way toward meeting my goals for the coming year. My boss was apologetic that the company didn't support the investment needed. He said he still believed in me, my capabilities, and my experience, acknowledging that both he and the company had let me down.

I mumbled some form of gratitude but still felt engulfed by shame and a sense of failure. Why was this happening to me? What would my team think? What would my client think? And why in hell didn't he wait to tell me until I was back at my hotel? Mortified, I gathered my composure, wiped away my tears, and returned to collect my belongings before retreating to my hotel room.

Later, I connected with our human resources lead, who outlined the details of my exit package. I was pleasantly surprised and began to shift my perspective. Then, it hit me like a thunderbolt: I had manifested this! There was no cause for shame or embarrassment. Who cared what anyone else was going to think? I had always known that, at some point in my fifties or sixties, I would want a change. I wasn't sure what that change would look like, but I knew that despite my successful career in financial services consulting, I didn't want to pursue it indefinitely. So now, approaching my two-year mark with the company, it became glaringly obvious that this was the moment to embark on something new. What an incredible opportunity! I hadn't specified how, when, or where the change would come; I'd just released my intentions into the Universe.

Later that evening, as I was toasting my future with champagne, the senior project lead reached out, inquiring if I'd be interested in staying until the project's conclusion. Why not? I could salvage some dignity with both my client and the team. This would grant me time to contemplate my next chapter while still drawing a salary for another few months. I could conclude my tenure on a triumphant note. Life was indeed good and continued to work out perfectly.

RETURNING TO LOVE AMONGST LIFE'S CHALLENGING EXPERIENCES

And then, a couple of weeks later, I hit a snag in the form of an unpleasant situation with a team member. To exacerbate matters, I was overruled in my attempt to manage the conflict. I was livid. It was like, "Are you kidding? I agree to stay, and now I'm dealing with this? Why am I even here?" Utterly distraught, I decided to ride out the storm, not to rock the boat, but it sapped every ounce of my energy. This ordeal monopolized far too many of my waking thoughts. I was genuinely at a loss, wedged between a rock and a hard place, with little support.

For Christmas 2023, I escaped for a trip back to Rome. I was mentally and physically drained and dreaded the thought of being home alone or joining any family or friends. I had originally booked a trip to Israel, which I was very excited about, but ended up cancelling due to the unrest that had escalated into war. So, while I relished being back on the streets of Rome, soaking in the sights and the mesmerizing Christmas lights and indulging in some exquisite Italian cuisine, I was still miserable and lonely. The gloom wouldn't lift; I was still seething over the work situation, unable to see beyond it or reframe my perspective. I was stuck in a complete "woe is me" mind-set.

On the flight home after Christmas, I was scrolling through my online book library when I rediscovered *The Law of Attraction* by Esther and Jerry Hicks. Revisiting the first few chapters was exactly the spark I needed to lift me out of my funk. After acknowledging, painfully, that I was choosing to linger on negativity, I consciously shifted my thoughts in a new direction.

Returning to my client's site in early January with a changed perception and renewed energy, I chose to extend compassion to everyone I had felt had wronged me. The book's teachings made it clear that whatever I give my attention to starts to become part of my experience—without exception. I realized I had fed the situation far too much negative focus, which only made it grow stronger in my reality. I also moved my mindset away from simply putting up with the difficult behavior and toward truly allowing it. The difference was profound: Tolerating something still carries negative emotion inside, while genuine allowing brings a sense of freedom because it releases that resistance and negative feeling entirely.

Too many times, I'd allowed my expectations to be shattered by the outcomes of certain situations, but I've since learned to view these moments differently. I see now that I'd expected certain people to conform to the roles I'd assigned them. When they didn't, it disturbed me, and I chose to suffer. This was a profound lesson for me—recognizing how much choice we have in our suffering. It's counterintuitive to our cultural conditioning. We think we can control situations or people, but we really only have control over our own thoughts and perceptions. This is why we hear so many inspiring stories from heroes who've faced immense loss, persecution, or tragedy and learned to see their circumstances differently, to rise above. You can choose door number one—to wallow in suffering—or choose door number two—to reframe your perspective, turning instead to love.

⋮

27

A Call for Transformation: Embracing the Divine Feminine in a Fear-Driven World

For most of my career, I'd kept my head down, driven by a few simple mantras: excel at my craft, deliver results, and keep pushing forward. I learned to navigate corporate politics well enough to get by—I was never one for kissing the ring. Yet I watched in awe as colleagues mastered the game, marveling at their finesse in maneuvering power dynamics, a skill I respected but couldn't fully embrace. It didn't light me up. My competitive streak burned bright, but not if it entailed crushing others. I was motivated to win deals so I could solve clients' problems. I always savored the satisfaction of impact over conquest. The financial rewards were sweet as well, no doubt, fueling a life I cherished, but the joy came from the work itself, not the posturing.

When I was at Capco in 2014, my boss once sat me down for a candid heart-to-heart about my communication style. He'd been nudging me to speak up more in his leadership meetings, where the air often crackled with loud, sometimes abrasive voices. I wasn't shy, but I had no desire to shout over the noise or to morph into someone

I wasn't. I pushed back, urging him to see the differences in how his team communicated and to set some ground rules that didn't reward the loudest people in the room. To his credit, he listened, open to my perspective. But he also shared how his mentor had drilled an opposite approach into him—survival of the most vocal. That conversation was an eye-opener about the benefits of inclusion: It's not about forcing everyone into the same mold but creating space for every voice, not just the ones that boom. I also subtly adapted my own strategy, making a point to connect one-on-one with colleagues more often before meetings, when I could share my ideas in quieter settings that would allow me to be heard without competing in a verbal cage match.

GENDER, BOUNDARIES, AND CORPORATE CULTURE

Countless times over the course of my career, I was the only woman in the room. This was simply the reality in financial services and consulting, where the grueling lifestyle often deterred women, especially those seeking to start families. We tried tirelessly to support women, assuring them that, with our backing, they could thrive as consultants. But the pressure was real—many felt they couldn't give their all while simultaneously balancing the demands of a family, fearing they'd fall short. Some left for industry roles, hoping for relief, only to find themselves back in the same trap: Without boundaries in place, work will always demand more. Luckily, I'd learned early on that saying no was a superpower, not just at work but in my personal life as well. It's not about disappointing others or risking exclusion; it's about owning your limits. Companies and bosses don't set those boundaries—you do.

Conflict, especially the shouting kind, never sat right with me, especially when it was paired with other traits like comparison, judgment, and arrogance. In the corporate world, sidestepping that whole fleet of behaviors could paint you as weak, so I'd learned to accept them as par for the course, but never felt good about it. Over time, I saw them for what they were: fear dressed up as strength. This conditioning, centuries deep and often male-dominated, of course wasn't just a male issue. Women, myself included, had absorbed it, feeling forced to play the game in order to survive.

I worked at two major firms led by female CEOs and was initially thrilled about it, believing this to be an amazing milestone. But the shine on their leadership faded when revenues dipped. I heard that one of them turned ruthless after poor earnings calls and tore into underperformers. I witnessed the other firsthand post-COVID, when the profit boom fizzled. In a virtual meeting, she berated hundreds of us leaders, her voice dripping with blame, demanding we "try harder." I was mortified to be part of that company. Her fear-driven tirade didn't inspire me—it attempted to drain me, stifle my creativity, and sap my drive. I had to dig deep to rise above it. Yet I knew deep down that the corporate world's norms didn't have to be my truth. But not everyone can do that. Many people will even take that contentious energy home with them, where it rubs off on family and friends.

WORK-LIFE BALANCE

We often frame work-life balance as a time issue, seeking to address it with flexible hours, ample vacation, or generous parental leave. That's part of it, but it misses the deeper truth. When pressure mounts and energy sags due to yet another reorg, missed revenue targets, paltry raises, or stalled promotions, the toll isn't just temporal. It seeps into our souls. Even if we try to shield our families from it all, the frustration certainly festers. Some will vent to loved ones, while some may instead try to bottle it up, becoming a simmering pressure cooker. Others may double down, logging more hours, chasing a fix that never comes. Solving this crisis is going to take more than just clocking out early. At a much deeper level, it's about releasing the fear-based, ego-driven energy we carry—whether that's comparison, defensiveness, or arrogance—before it poisons both our work and home lives.

Imagine replacing all that negativity with love-based traits, with teamwork, listening, collaboration, and leadership rooted in confidence, intention, and humility. Picture a team pouring positive energy into a pitch, a deliverable, or a bold vision for change—not in an attempt to outshine anyone else but to create something extraordinary together. There is transformative potential here, a truly radical answer to the crisis of work-life balance. But corporate incentives don't reward these traits. I dare to ask: What's the harm in flipping the script? Why not try a love-based approach? I'd be willing to bet that the outcomes improve—more wins, more revenue.

I hold deep respect for the women CEOs I mentioned previously and the countless other trailblazing women I've worked with in the corporate world. They navigated systems that told them love was woo-woo, weakness by any other name. The imperative was clear: If you can't beat them, join them. Before leaving consulting, I had a candid chat with a client—a senior woman, brilliant and kind—about her former colleagues, tough-as-nails women I'd seen as overly aggressive, even harsh. Her perspective stopped me cold. She told me she was grateful for their ferocity; their refusal to yield had carved a path for her. Those mavericks, shattering glass ceilings, had to be abrasive to be heard. It's a bitter truth: Progress often demanded these women play the game harder than anyone.

But does it still have to be this way? I believe there's a better path. We got DEI wrong—not the intent, but the execution. As a white woman, I know my barriers were fewer than others' and I strove to never lean into victimhood, though, despite my advantages, I still sometimes gave away my power. Yet DEI often pushed forced hires, placing good people in roles they weren't ready for. We should've instead focused on embracing the Divine Feminine—all things nurturing, intuitive, and collaborative—in both genders while also honoring the Divine Masculine's strength and drive. We desperately need to reframe our conceptions of traditional work life, moving away from ego's grip—with all its fear, competition, and judgment—and toward love, connection, and purpose.

I was born in the 1970s, when women still couldn't open bank accounts without a man's signature. So yes, progress has been made in my life-time, but it's not enough. I'm eternally grateful for the clients, colleagues, bosses, partners, and suppliers in financial services who shaped my journey. Yet the relentless demands, outdated culture, and fear-based imperatives—"Win at all costs!" "Prove your worth!" "Never falter!"—exacted a heavy toll on my mind, body, and spirit. After leaving consulting, it took nearly a year for me to decompress and unravel the damage so that I could begin to reconnect with what matters. Yes, some pressures are inevitable, but I know there's a better way.

⋮

28

Velvet Hammer's Current: Weaving Strength and Heart into Leadership

As I shared previously, I was called the Velvet Hammer. The nickname landed with a mix of pride and a playful sting. The "hammer" part? It was probably a gentler jab than harsher labels could have been, but it captured my essence: I got things done, relentlessly, with a blend of kindness and steel. Raised by parents who instilled a fierce work ethic, I learned early to aim high and deliver. My expectations were skyward, not just for myself but for my teams as well. Most rose to the challenge, their potential igniting like sparks catching fire. But some faltered, and I had little patience for laziness, arrogance, or half-hearted efforts. My reputation was forged through my ability to deliver projects on time, on budget, with quality that shone like polished glass. Clients trusted me, and that trust was my currency, built on countless late nights, truth telling, and meticulous plans.

Yet, beyond the wins, my true joy was unlocking others' potential. When I found out one of my dear friends and former colleagues reached senior partner at her firm, my heart swelled, bursting with pride as if it were my own victory. I'd seen her brilliance early, even when she doubted herself, and I'd nudged her—gently, persistently—to see it too. I'd tell her, "You're capable of more than you think. You are ready for the next level." She'd brush my comments off, deflecting them, but then would rise every time, her work ethic and talent carrying her to new heights. She did the heavy lifting, but I like to think my belief in her lit the path. Countless others followed suit, no matter if they were junior analysts or mid- and senior-level managers. Each one of them had been full of genuine possibility. Watching them all blossom was my career's greatest thrill, outshining even the biggest client wins.

Inevitably, some team members clashed with my high standards, especially when their missteps would spark my frustration. I'd privately pace my office, with papers strewn across the desk, wondering why they couldn't deliver. But I eventually learned to shift my approach, to teach rather than judge. I'd sit them down, my initial buzz fading, and would say to them, "Tell me if you don't know something. It's okay. We'll figure it out together." I had no tolerance for coasting or bravado, but if they were honest—vulnerable—I'd pour my energy into helping them bridge their own gaps. "Go research," I'd urge. "Bring me two or three options, tell me what you think, and why." They'd return, eyes nervous but eager, presenting solutions we'd refine together. I took the risks with them, guiding them until they stood steady on their own.

Inclusion was paramount for me. Even the greenest team members joined client meetings, their notepads ready, soaking in the room's energy. On my last major project, I noticed a young analyst—brilliant, with a degree from a prestigious university, her documents pristine, her slides a work of art. But when I was present, she shrank, her voice diminishing to silence. One afternoon, I pulled her aside in a quiet conference room, the city skyline gleaming beyond the glass.

"Your voice matters," I said. "You're learning this client as fast as any of us. You have the right to speak up." Her eyes widened, hesitant, but over weeks, I watched her transform. In a packed meeting, her hand shot up. Her insights were predictably sharp, but even more impressive was her confidence blooming like a desert flower after rain. My heart sang.

Despite my best attempts, not everyone on my teams thrived. Some weren't cut out for consulting's grind, and that was okay. I'd give them a fair shot, but when it was clear the fit was wrong, I'd have the tough talk. In a softly lit office, I'd explain, "This isn't your path; it's time to part ways." Some left with relief, others with resentment. But many later thanked me after they'd found their true calling and flourished elsewhere, whether in industry, marketing, nonprofits, or start-ups. The hardest cases were those who hid behind bluster, winging it with arrogance to mask gaps. I'd confront them, the air tense, voices rising in heated exchanges. Some came around, their gratitude quiet but real; others never forgave me. And that's okay.

Being the Velvet Hammer meant balancing strength with heart—I knew how to drive results, yes, but I also knew how to lift others up to become their own best selves. Each success, each transformed colleague who I celebrated on the journey of my career helped me to forge a legacy of impact and care that I'll carry forever.

In that spirit, I'd like to offer a couple bold lessons to live by, principles that will allow anyone to forge a path with strength and heart:

1. Lead with uncompromising standards, but lift others up.

Push for greatness in yourself and others, but pair rigorous expectations with genuine support. Believe in people's potential and nudge them past self-doubt, then watch them soar—your leadership can be the spark that changes their trajectory.

2. Embrace tough calls with courage and compassion.

Don't shy away from difficult decisions—especially when it comes to correcting someone's course or even letting someone go. Approach them with clear-eyed truth and empathy, knowing that tough love can guide others to where they're meant to be, even if it stings in the moment.

⋮

29

A Soulful Dawn: Embracing Purpose and Divine Inspiration

It was April 2024, finally the end of my project and the grand finale of my twenty-five-year consulting career. I was feeling a mixture of relief and pride as the final project concluded in unprecedented success.

I decided to take a few months off to explore what I wanted to do next, the excitement of new possibilities sending a burst of energy through me. I met up with my close friends Kim and Kaylin in Miami for an extended weekend. We had a ball as usual, my cheeks sore from smiling, my heart racing with the thrill of being surrounded by love and encouragement. The physical touch of hugs and the warmth of shared stories all recharged my spirit.

Then, I was off to Costa Rica for another retreat, this time with Emily Fletcher, the amazing founder of Ziva, the woman from whom I had learned to meditate. The anticipation caused butterflies to flutter in my stomach.

I had been on Ziva's mailing list for years and followed Emily on social media with interest. But when an email about a Sacred

Secret retreat hosted by Emily and her team at the end of April in Costa Rica landed in my inbox, I hesitated, procrastinating on my application. Yet the feeling persisted: This was something I needed to do. Despite my skepticism, and the cost, my curiosity was piqued. Beyond meditation and manifestation, the program also included something called Pleasure Prayer, a concept that clashed with my conservative upbringing. Not knowing what to expect, I finally mustered the courage to apply, feeling both anticipation and apprehension. Emily and her team quickly accepted my application and welcomed me to the upcoming program.

This retreat marked one of several pivotal moments in my life, actively transforming my existence, all in perfect timing. Initially, I'd thought I would be facing a two-month gap between the end of my project and the start of the retreat that would potentially leave me adrift, unsure of how to fill my time. But then, miraculously, my project was extended, so the gap then shrunk to almost nothing. I knew the Universe was conspiring in my favor there, and I was filled with relief.

One of the retreat's requests was to bring an item representing something you wished to either release or embrace in your future, or both. I chose to bring a symbol that resonated deeply with me—an open heart pendant. I knew this was the dawn of something new, and I wanted to arrive there ready to absorb, to learn, with my heart wide open. The thought of this sent a shiver of excitement down my spine, my pulse quickening at the potential. Holding the pendant, I felt a surge of warmth, embodying my desire to embrace this next chapter with openness. I was eager to explore possibilities about my purpose, to envision my next chapter, including my future life partner, all while my breath steadied with anticipation and my eyes glistened with hope.

I touched down at the airport in Costa Rica, my eyes scanning the crowd to meet up with other retreat attendees for the shuttle ride. I noticed that I had unwanted feelings of judginess starting to surface. Who were these people I'd be sharing the next four days with? What had I gotten myself into? I met a few of the other participants, and we headed to the small café in the airport where we managed to get a few seats and a bit of lunch, waiting for others to join us, exchanging pleasantries. On the bus, I attempted a few tentative conversations, but doubt gnawed at me. How was this going to play out?

Upon arrival at the retreat center, I was hot and weary from the long wait at the airport and the subsequent bus ride, but after a quick shower and a change into fresh clothes, I felt rejuvenated, my energy levels surging. Now I was more open to meeting everyone. As I mingled, I connected with a few wonderful souls, including Emily herself, whose kind, energetic but down-to-earth demeanor washed away my reservations. Warmth spread through me with each smile she offered. Emily has this uplifting presence and grace that is hard to describe; her energy is a combination of high vibration and calmness. My perspective began to shift, the tension in my shoulders easing as I reminded myself to keep an open heart. With this realization, excitement continued to bubble up inside me. I was committed to making these days count. My heart beat with the new-found rhythm of anticipation.

After an informal meet and greet and some dinner, we gathered for the opening puja ceremony, a time for prayers and offerings. Emily set the stage for the next few days by patiently answering questions. She introduced her team, and then the attendees all shared a bit of who we were and why we were there. When the ceremony ended, we headed to our rooms, simultaneously exhausted from the travel day and excited for the morning.

CONNECTING THE DOTS FROM MY PREVIOUS TRIP TO COSTA RICA

The first major ceremony began at the crack of dawn the next morning. As I stepped into the room dubbed the "Center of Joy" and was greeted by some of the most amazing humans I'd ever met, a wave of peace washed over me and my heart settled into a comforting rhythm. I felt I was exactly where I needed to be. The space was a beautiful, safe haven, and I instantly felt at home. This would be a sound ceremony, with the option to partake in plant medicine. I had never ventured into such territory before, but I had heard stories of others' life-changing experiences, so I was full of curiosity.

Just seven minutes into the ceremony, after Emily's mesmerizing opening and the soothing, enveloping sounds of the instruments, I lay down beneath a cozy blanket, and the medicine began to work its magic. I saw the most radiant colors and ethereal images, my body feeling as if it were gently floating, weightless. A brilliant white light enveloped me, stretching from the crown of my head to the tips of my toes, giving me a sensation of freedom. My limbs felt unburdened and my mind, body, and soul aligned. Coming down from this high, I shared my revelations with another participant in the room, my voice trembling with joy and my eyes wide with wonder. I felt an overwhelming sense of liberation and peace, believing I could now tackle the blockages the Reiki therapist had identified years before—the deep-seated Samskaras that had pained me over the last half-century. I felt incredibly blessed; that ceremony alone justified the entire trip to Costa Rica.

Yet the event only continued to get better from there, not just the sharing with the other attendees but the continuous releasing and surrendering as well. Emily's approach is threefold: Visualize what you want and what you would love to have or experience; Alchemize anything in its way (get into the rage or sorrow and give voice to the pain while refusing to suffer with it); and then Magnetize what is already there. The Magnetize sessions also included sacred time for breathwork and Pleasure Prayer so that we could get to a place where we felt so good in our bodies that we could then envision our dreams as already fulfilled. While this was a new concept to me and most others, I came to fully understand the importance of it. We so often just focus on our minds, and sometimes on our hearts, while giving little focus to our bodies and how we feel in them. Our bodies can give off negative energy because of places where a more healthy flow has been blocked. Releasing that negativity and coming to a place of pleasure aligns both our mind and our heart's desires.

We also talked about learning to develop a relationship with the Future Me so that we can see more clearly what we have healed from our pasts, what we have let go of, and where and how we spend our time. Looking back from that Future Me, we can determine what changes we have made, how we have sculpted and architected our future, and how we have turned up the dial on creativity and our power. Ultimately we can see how we have learned to fully experience divine bliss, appreciating every situation as a gift.

During one of the Alchemize sessions, I realized that, at that particular moment, I didn't have the need to release anything that was holding me down. With Emily's prompting, I chose instead to weep for the generations that came before me. This contemplation started a pivotal change in thinking about what past generations have endured, enabling me to begin looking at their experiences and behaviors from a place of compassion rather than annoyance or judgment. I was starting to see so much more clearly the culture, the pressure, the expectations, and the history that had been prevalent for centuries. I could see not only all that they had overcome and what progress was made but also what issues they weren't able to fix. I had often found myself frustrated previously that more changes hadn't been made and more questions hadn't been asked (especially since I'm the type of person who questions everything, especially if it is foreign to me). I began to realize that many people just went with the flow, especially when they found themselves in nonconfrontational or controlling families and cultures.

It wasn't long before I was able to release the judginess that shamefully had crept in again at the airport. I could finally see everyone's beautiful spirits. We bonded, danced and cried together, shared meals that warmed our hearts, and cheered each other on with genuine love. We found common ground despite our differences, realizing we were all experiencing similar feelings of suffering, loss, pain, joy, excitement, and love.

I left that retreat not just inspired but fundamentally changed, a new person with a new perspective so profound it was beyond words. My body felt light, my mind open, my spirit joyous, and I was brimming with hope, love, and possibilities, unshackled from past burdens and stories. I was connected to time and space in an unprecedented way. I was able to think about my past, present, and future selves completely differently.

One of the retreat's greatest gifts was a voluntary integration period. There would be a virtual gathering that kept our community connected going forward. Knowing we'd face highs and lows as we returned to familiar routines, Emily understood the power of sustained connection after all the emotional intensity of the retreat. So for the next two months, we were paired with a partner to share daily dreams via WhatsApp. Each morning, we'd set an intention for the day, and before bed we'd reflect on it: Had our dream manifested, was it unfolding, or had unexpected miracles been sparked along the way? This practice was exactly what I needed as I stepped into my next chapter. In the way it offered a balance of structure and freedom, it was a refreshing shift from the corporate rigidity I'd known for the past thirty-five years.

ALL ABOUT INSPIRATION

Back in Florida, I was elated just to be at home without any major agenda. I could feel my body relaxing, my mind unburdening itself. During the first month, I had an explosion of ideas, my brain ablaze with possibilities. What would my next chapter look like? Who was I here to serve? What was my path forward? I opened my heart wide, allowing ideas to cascade and build upon one another, my breath quickening with each new thought. I remained open to everything, my senses heightened.

I had a significant revelation: I didn't have to abandon financial services consulting if I didn't want to. I didn't have to remove myself from a context where I still felt comfortable and confident; I just needed to reframe it in a way that felt empowering, that allowed me to stay in my power. Still, there was this pull, this deep yearning for something different, stirring deep down within me.

I quickly established an invigorating new daily routine. I made sure that each day would include something mental, spiritual, physical, and *fun*. Thanks to this, my body felt more alive, my spirit more connected.

I started journaling daily. The pen flew over the pages as if it had a life of its own. I also devoured books—I reread Michael Singer's *Living Untethered* and then his *The Surrender Experiment*. My heart pounded with each insight, finding something on every page to stir my soul. I consciously embarked on this work to cleanse my heart, digging deep to remove the reasons for my stored Samskaras, confronting why my heart wanted to close in the first place. This work sparked a new chapter of inspiration and creativity that I was unaccustomed to. I not only felt an intense desire to probe further into how my purpose was to play out but also a responsibility to use my gifts as God intended.

Despite my desires, fear still gnawed at me. Am I worthy? How could I write a book, start a business, speak, coach? These thoughts made my palms sweaty and my heart race. So, I kept exploring, learning, pushing these fears aside.

I immersed myself in books by my favorite spiritual authors, battling impostor syndrome head-on. I found comfort in the universal truth that everyone who starts something new starts terrified. I thought of Rosa, a coach I met at Emily's retreat who is now a dear friend, who shared the observation, "When your purpose is bigger than your fears, you will move forward." This encouragement lightened my load and helped my breathing to steady as I realized I had a story to share; in fact, I had an obligation to share it if it could aid others. I reconnected with my purpose and my gifts, aiming to help others find more joy in this chaotic world.

I also read books by Pam Grout, an amazing author I first discovered in the summer of 2023. Her messages and call to action in *Living Big* really strengthened me. She writes about how most of us stay unaware of our own greatness and the powerful truth that the divine pulse flows right through us. That realization hit home. I knew it was time to stop holding myself back, let go of my fears, embrace what I was born for, and start living big.

I started reconnecting with God in a new, profound way, not the way I'd been taught. Instead, I reconnected with a loving Creator who wanted me to live and love expansively. I examined Nature and all living beings with fresh eyes, choosing to see everything differently, even snakes, which made me chuckle. (Living in Florida, this is a necessity, though, I'll admit, I once called my neighbor in a panic to remove a snake from my lanai.) Michael Singer's metaphor of neither clinging to butterflies nor resisting snakes resonated with me, as my mind opened to this new perspective. His teaching challenged me to see beyond my fear. Could I release my resistance to snakes, to see their purpose, their place in nature? Why do I cherish the butterfly's grace but recoil from the snake's sleek power? Each creature, no matter if it expresses itself with the delicate flutter of wings or the silent glide of scales, is a stroke of the Divine's brush. So when I pause, startled by a snake's sudden appearance on my path, I now take a breath and step back. *God made this creature*, I remind myself. *Let it be.* In those moments, my resistance melts and peace floods in like a warm tide, washing away the fear. I still haven't mastered this completely—I continue to flinch sometimes—but I'm learning to honor every living thing, to see the beauty in what once terrified me.

Of course, this message runs deeper than butterflies and snakes. It's a mirror reflecting the ways I cling to or resist life itself. Where am I holding onto past fears like heavy stones in my pockets, weighing me down? What grievances do I nurse, what old hurts or slights do I replay in my mind, letting them steal the light of the present? The Law of Attraction rings in the background, reminding me of the truth I've come to know: What I resist persists and grows stronger with every ounce of negative energy I pour into it.

I was on a quest for peace, and for love, seeking divine help to open my heart to all of God's creations, even the ones with difficult personalities. I was granted a vision to focus on a person's spirit, beyond physical form, which was wildly liberating, and my heart swelled with this realization. We can only physically see a person's outsides, but looking deeper spiritually shows the Creator's perfection in all of us. Living into this truth was grueling, my heart sometimes tightening with resistance. I had to remind myself, every time I came across a challenging situation or personality, that this is my spiritual assignment, that I had sought this out. Well, of course, as I've noted previously, it's important to be careful what you seek out, because the Universe does deliver.

Towards the end of that month, nervousness began to creep in, my stomach knotting up with fear. How could I truly move forward? What would come next? And then, I encountered a powerful quote from Abraham-Hicks in my Instagram feed: "I don't create through action; I create through vibration. And then my vibration calls action from me." Yes, of course! This mirrored what we practiced at the Ziva Sacred Secret retreat in Costa Rica.

So I reconnected with some of the tools and practices we had learned, feeling so deeply inspired to honor my gifts and purpose at this point in my life. I knew I needed a name for the business I wanted to launch. I wrote down a list of possibilities, checked available internet domain names, and then shared my list with a few friends to solicit their thoughts. On the last day of the month, my new business, SoulFullJoy, was born. My heart was pounding, still open and full of inspiration, as I sought guidance on how and who to serve in my next chapter.

TEN THINGS I WISH I HAD KNOWN

As I closed out this chapter of my life, I began to reflect on the prior years of my amazing career, feeling grateful for the opportunities and experiences that shaped me.

Upon reflection, I have identified ten things I wish I had known and applied more consistently throughout my career. I share them here in the hope that it may help those of you who are still in the thick of your own careers.

1. Your title is not who you are.

While in the corporate world a specific title can be important, it does not define you as a person and you do not need to feel overly attached to it. Yes, I was a partner at a prestigious consulting firm. Yes, consulting is what I did for a living. Yes, that was amazing. But when I was suddenly no longer associated with that role, I had to dig deep into the essence of who I am.

So take the time to do that throughout your career. Stay true to who you are outside of work. Each of us was created with unique gifts and we are meant to live big, beautiful lives. For me, at the core, life is about loving each other—yes, even in the corporate world. So take more time to encourage, collaborate, and cheer on others; that will certainly help you find more joy in the journey. Explore your gifts and use them to their full extent.

2. Stay in your power.

There were many times throughout my career when I recognized that I was in my power. I knew I was in a good place emotionally and was feeling confident and successful and was absolutely loving every minute (well, *most* minutes) of my work. Unfortunately, there were other times when my self-confidence dipped, and I ebbed into impostor syndrome. These times were largely when I had specific expectations about certain outcomes, then, for whatever reason, bosses or colleagues shattered them: I did not get the role, the title, the deal, or the kind of collaboration from teammates that I thought I deserved. So I would start to question myself. While I did not think at the time that I was giving away my power, that is exactly what happened. I slipped back into victim mode.

When this happens—and it happens to all of us—my best advice is to simply acknowledge it and then move on. Don't take it personally. It is a momentary frustration. It will pass and there will be another opportunity. So do whatever it takes to get back in your power. Do not suffer or let negativity consume you. Get out of victim mode and back into warrior mode as quickly as possible. You are worthy.

3. There is no need to defend yourself.

This one is interesting, as most of us feel compelled to do this in one form or another. It is the logical thing to do when questioned. But ironically, and there is a subtle nuance, it is actually the wrong thing to do in that circumstance. I have learned that defending myself comes from the ego and never leads to a positive experience. Rather, explaining a position, or providing further details or rationale, without sounding defensive provides a much more positive experience for both parties. Staying unattached to the reaction of the other party, especially when they do not agree with you, is much more satisfying. Learning to witness or observe situations without attachment brings so much more peace. And then, be willing to admit you are wrong if it comes to that.

4. You only need your own approval.

From an early age, I quickly learned to crave approval and recognition. This tendency carried over into the workplace naturally. If I did not get the approval I was seeking, or if someone else "less worthy" received more, it was frustrating to me. The pursuit of approval consumed my energy and time way more than I needed it to.

If you look outside yourself for approval, you will always be disappointed. You are the only one in the world who needs to recognize and approve of you. The ego likes to make us think differently, but it is so much nicer when our focus is internal as opposed to external.

5. Let grievances go quickly.

Too many times I held on to the fact that someone did something to me. If they went behind my back, took credit, talked over me, blamed me, or excluded me, it was so easy and seemingly justifiable to fixate on what happened and then continue to replay it like a broken record. But this takes away from the present moment. We may talk about work-life balance, but even when we are home not working, it's completely possible that we're focused on these kinds of negative experiences, which are actively taking away from our family time or personal downtime.

It is just not worth it. Negative energy piles up quickly. I have held on to some of it for years. So, I urge you to forgive and let go. The freedom and peace outweigh the need to be right.

6. Comparison is about fear.

It is easy to do—compare yourself to this person or that person to justify your own capabilities and experiences. Yet this comes from the ego and a place of fear.

The reality is that comparison is not helpful and wastes precious time and energy. Be confident and humble in your abilities, and opportunities to shine your own light will always come through.

7. There is more to any situation than just the facts.

From an early age I was taught that the most important thing was to work hard and gather all the facts. I later found myself shocked when I would do my research and assemble all the facts, only for someone else to use it against me for their own gain. Quite frankly I could never understand why it happened. Even when I knew I was in the right, it still did not matter. I also saw colleagues bold enough to talk about subjects that they knew little about, often misrepresenting the facts, who then for whatever reason received the deal, the promotion, the recognition.

I can see now that when I focused on the facts without enough human connection—without relating, without stories and imagery, without the emotion or the feeling in a presentation, whether written or verbal—that was often not enough to bridge the gap. As humans, we crave connection and need more than just facts. So remember to always find the emotional or energetic point of connection in the material that you've been researching and preparing; it will often make all the difference.

8. Apply "the Art of Allowing" often.

How many times over the years have I been annoyed with teammates, bosses, and even clients? Maybe I did not like their approach, or how they handled certain situations, or sometimes even their personalities. (There was always someone who really rubbed me the wrong way!) But I now recognize, thanks to Abraham-Hicks, the difference between tolerating and allowing. Allowing does not feel negative emotion, but tolerating does.

So, do your best to choose to see those you are surrounded by through the lens of love. See the Spirit and the light that is in everyone, beyond their physical personality. It makes the day so much brighter.

9. Incorporate high-vibrational methods that enable greater inspiration.

So many times I approached the creation of deliverables and presentations as yet another task on a checklist. It was like I was thinking, "What can we dust off and reuse? How quickly can we create and get this out the door?" It's true that time pressure from colleagues and clients is always there.

Yet, I encourage you to take the time you need to feel good and inspired. Learn to recognize how you and your teams are feeling in your bodies and notice where your energy is. Use tools and techniques to get into a good-feeling place; maybe you want to go out into nature for a bit or do some breathwork or simply take a step back, envisioning the end product and how it will make the client or team member feel. *Then* start the work. So often we do not think there is time for these kinds of exercises, or maybe it all feels a little woo-woo. But you know that when you are overtired and overworked, the low energy you are working from does not yield the same results.

10. If you are not choosing love, you are choosing fear.

I spent too much time being driven by the ego. I was pushed around by my need to be right, my need to win, my need to be the best. The list goes on. It always felt like those were necessary and inevitable parts of what it took to be successful, so therefore I assumed it was justifiable.

There is a better path. If it is not love, it is fear. Yes, even in the corporate world. We typically refrain from using the word "love" in that context, but the reality is that fear has no problem showing up in so many ways. It overshines all the goodness. For example, the minute that our numbers are missed, we are compelled to find the problem and blame someone for it. Our behavior then changes. We lose inspiration or, worse, become apathetic. But when we choose love, the teamwork, the collaboration, the listening, the innovation, and the confidence all show up with different and undeniably improved results.

⋮

Part III

Embracing Wholeness:
A Tapestry of Healing and Connection

Returning to love's warm embrace, healing woven with forgiveness's grace,
Answers bloom where once shadows danced, elusive dreams now held in trance.
With grateful heart, I honor Source, a radiant light on my soul's course.
A path to wholeness, sacred and bright, unfolds in holiness, bathed in light.

Living bold, with love's grand fire, miracles spark, lifting me higher.
Cherishing life's earthly weave, each thread a gift, I now believe.
Seeing Spirit's glow in every frame, each soul alight with divine flame.
A peace beyond all knowing flows, serene and deep, where stillness grows.

Anchored in the Now, I choose love's call, releasing fear to rise above all.
Feeling every pulse, no judgment near, just open heart, raw and sincere.
Surrendering soft, I let burdens fall, heavenly bliss hums through my soul's thrall.

Compassion blooms for all Creation's span, a love that holds each heart and hand
Claiming gifts the Divine has sown, blessings bright in my spirit known.
Casting off old beliefs that bind, I free my soul, my truth aligned.
In unity, we shine as One, belonging whole 'neath love's eternal sun.

Decades ago, I set foot on a winding, often shadowed path of healing, a journey that has woven itself into the very fabric of my existence and will thread through every moment of my earthly life. The unanswered questions that once looked like heavy storm clouds on the horizon have dissolved, their mysteries unraveled under the gentle light of clarity. I hold the brilliant truth of my life's purpose, a light that glows steadily within me, illuminating the way forward.

My heart brims with gratitude, a warm tide that surges through me as I stand in this moment, marveling at the landscape of my life—lush with growth, dotted with hard-won triumphs, and softened by the quiet beauty of truths and lessons learned. The air around me is alive with possibility, each breath a reminder to stay present, to root myself in the now. I seek to honor the gifts I've been given: the strength forged in struggle, the wisdom carved from reflection, and the love that has bloomed in unexpected places.

As I turn my gaze to the next chapter of my life, I feel stirrings of inspiration and am eager for what lies beyond the bend. My spirit remains open, listening for the soft whispers of guidance—intuitive nudges that point me toward what I must still release. With every step, I am committed to fulfilling my purpose, as I move forward into the exciting unknown.

30

The Gift of Sensitivity: Welcoming My HSP Trait

'd always known I responded to the world around me with more sensitivity than most; my emotions had always been a tidal wave that could swell and crash without warning. Family, friends, and culture often reminded me of it, their well-meaning advice to "toughen up" or "stop feeling so much" leaving me confused and ashamed. I craved to be heard, understood, but a void lingered, its cause elusive. As a child, I'd flee to teachers for comfort when we watched movies like *Oliver Twist*, my heart aching for the characters' pain, unable to untangle fiction from reality. Growing up without a TV or movie exposure made those stories hit even harder, my reactions to them raw and unfiltered. Cartoons? Those at least felt fake, leaving me cold.

Society taught me to suppress it all—be still, be quiet, bury the feelings. But my sensitivity wasn't just emotional. Farm visits with my family in New York and Connecticut were sensory assaults; the pungent smell of horse and cow manure in barns overwhelmed me, leaving me gasping while my siblings seemed unfazed. I felt foolish, out of place. One Sunday, forced into an itchy polyester dress, blue with white polka dots, for church, I squirmed in discomfort, the fabric prickling my skin. Yet my pleas were brushed off as mere complaints. Even now, I crave the comfort of soft, gentle clothes—a need that has never faded.

My body amplified every extreme. I'd burn with heat, my face and body aflame, or would shiver uncontrollably, chilled to the bone. As I shared previously, living in the Cottage at Fairwood with a wood-burning furnace made it worse—in the cooler months, vents blasted scorching heat, then the rooms would fade to icy cold by morning, leaving me shivering, even under several layers. Hunger also hit like a storm, my stomach roaring, turning me hangry and miserable. After eating, I'd feel stuffed, uncomfortable. I later learned my carb-heavy childhood diet—homemade bread, oatmeal, muffins, and the snickerdoodles or molasses crinkles that filled the cookie jar—lacked the macro balance my body craved, which only amplified those swings. No one saw my reactions as valid; I was just "dramatic."

Losses hit me hardest. When a close cousin, my budding best friend, moved away at twelve, I was gutted, her absence a gaping wound. I struggled to make friends at school or in my insular community, leaving me adrift with emotions too big to handle. Later in life, after I'd moved to Atlanta, I found that I loved the city's transient energy. I welcomed meeting other newcomers who were also eager for connection, but then their departures in my twenties and thirties left me reeling, feeling abandoned. Marrying into a loud, boisterous Italian family was a thrill—so different from my reserved upbringing—but their off-the-cuff remarks stung deeply. My tears, triggered by hurt, were met with eye rolls, reinforcing my "overly sensitive" label. At the time, I lacked psychological tools that would allow me to let their words slide, so I instead retreated to shame. I would eventually learn how to see things in a different light and control my reactions more effectively.

My senses are often on high alert. I'm easily startled. My nerves are jangled when my eyes become watery from the wind or sun, when a single hair on my face begins to drive me to distraction, when loud noises like sirens or bright lights or strong smells overwhelm me. Water has always been my solace. Rivers, lakes, the sea, even a backyard fountain in my Atlanta home feel like sanctuary to me, washing away my stress. Childhood camping trips by lakes in Maine or walks to the streams of Chesterfield Gorge near Fairwood brought me a profound peace and the kind of deep quiet I could sink into. Later, vacations to the Caribbean, Hawaii, or Florida were all about the waves' soothing sounds and the sun's warmth, all of it recharging my spirit.

Music was another comforting outlet. Growing up, hymns and Christian piano music felt flat, uninspiring. But school bus rides introduced me to rock radio. Hearing Pat Benatar, Sting, and The Rolling Stones ignited a spark. When some church members eventually called the school and asked them to ban the use of the radio on the bus, those silent rides were torture. But a cassette player with headphones became my rebellion. U2's anthems resonated deep in my soul. I've since danced at their concerts, lost in emotion. I was lifted by the music I heard at school dances or blaring from an eighth-grade classroom (Def Leppard!) or even during solo dance parties; it all connected me to the musicians' raw feeling. Secretly, I still dream of a second life as a rock singer, pouring my heart into song and rhythm.

As an introvert who learned to play extrovert for the sake of my career, I needed quiet to recharge. Shallow small talk at business conventions or parties drains me; I always vow never to return. Deep, meaningful conversations, one-on-one or with a small group, are my fuel. So my sensitivities often felt like a burden, especially at work, where tears or emotions were taboo, signaling weakness, while loud outbursts were routinely shrugged off. I felt alone, angry at myself for lacking control, and convinced no one cared or understood. The message I received was "just keep it under control."

Then social media introduced me to the idea of empaths and highly sensitive people (HSPs). I brushed it off as fluff until curiosity led me to more research on it. A subsequent call with my psychotherapist niece confirmed it was real, and she pointed me to Elaine Aron's book, *The Highly Sensitive Person*. Reading that in July 2019 lit me up with a flare of recognition. Learning that being highly sensitive was a legitimate trait—not a flaw to be fixed—felt like unearthing a buried treasure. In devouring the text, I learned that 18 percent of people have HSP traits, which means they process everything more deeply, observe and reflect before acting, and experience heightened emotional and sensory responses. Carl Jung had explored the notion, then Aron's research in the 1990s validated it. My life snapped into focus—I wasn't broken, just wired differently.

The relief was profound. My sensitivities weren't flaws after all. They were traits that let me process faster, intuit answers, and connect deeply with nature, music, and ideas. When I encountered Aron's descriptions, particularly her points that a life lived in close contact with the unconscious tends to be richer and more fulfilling, and that highly sensitive people often have a deeper, more soulful and spiritual orientation, I felt my essence mirrored in them. I was able to reframe my feelings, embracing them without shame. Now, if I felt irritation at others' behavior? I could let it go, understanding why I felt such heightened awareness. I was free. I'd successfully untangled my sensitivity from social awkwardness and the religious oppression of my childhood.

Upon further reflection, I find it highly probable that my early intuition that something wasn't right with The Kingdom was all thanks to these sensitivities that I experience. I recently came across the written response I'd received from my father in my early twenties after I'd sent him a letter sharing the impact of my strict childhood upbringing:

> I, on behalf of the church, am facing up to the fact that some church policies and attitudes of leaders have been very damaging to sensitive spirits in particular and perhaps to everyone to some degree. I mention this because I am becoming increasingly aware of how many hurting people there are because of this style of ministry. And whatever problems you may be dealing with I recognize that you have been impacted by these things. Some, at least, of the symptoms you describe and the feelings you have suffered are no doubt directly attributable to the feeling of oppression that has come from the church ministry. Mom and I now realize that we were agents of this, even if unintentionally.

Reading that letter at twenty-three stirred a complex mix of emotions—yes, there was relief at my parents' acknowledgment of the damage that had been done, yet there was also a lingering sense that it came a bit too late. I write about this not out of resentment; I know they were navigating parenthood while steeped in deep-seated cultural and religious beliefs that had shaped their own choices. Their regret was heartfelt, their commitment to supporting my healing journey undeniable. Rather, my words here aim to illuminate the path I took through my own childhood wounds, offering insights from my personal recovery to help others. Through the process of healing, I've gained a deeper understanding of the broader societal forces—especially the centuries-old patriarchal oppression woven into religion and corporate life—that extend far beyond my personal story.

Now, I am learning to live with a fierce, unapologetic vibrancy, my body swaying to the rhythm of life itself. In the glow of my lanai or the heart of my kitchen, I crank up the music and let it set me free. The raw electric pulse of AC/DC's guitars ignites my veins, while U2's soaring anthems lift my spirit to the stars. Pink's fiery defiance sparks a rebel yell within, and Def Leppard's glossy riffs pull me into a whirlwind of nostalgia. Leonard Cohen's smoky, soulful verses wrap me in a velvet embrace, each note a meditation. Every genre, every beat—be it a thunderous rock anthem or a tender ballad—pours through me like a river. Arms flung wide, I dance with abandon, the music weaving through my soul, a vivid celebration of being utterly, joyfully alive.

My heart expresses its emotions boldly, and when the weight of overwhelm, frustration, or fear surges within, I let the tears flow freely, each one a sacred offering to my truth. They stream down my cheeks, warm and unashamed, cleansing my soul like a summer rain.

I marvel at nature's brilliance and experience it as my sanctuary—I stand in awe beneath the boundless, sapphire-blue sky, its depth pulling me into a contemplation of infinity. Lush green trees sway like wise sentinels, their leaves whispering secrets of resilience, while flowers—pops of crimson, violet, and gold—dance in the warm breeze. The earthy perfume of fresh basil or rosemary, plucked from my herb garden, fills my senses, grounding me in the moment. I rejoice in awe as the full moon casts a silver glow across the night, when stars twinkle like scattered diamonds, and my spirits lift as serene sunsets paint the horizon in hues of coral and lavender, each one a quiet promise of renewal.

I lose myself in the rhythm of poetry and prose, words weaving tapestries of meaning that wrap around my heart. In my kitchen, I pour love into every dish, chopping vegetables and stirring fragrant sauces, crafting fresh meals for loved ones gathered in my kitchen. In moments of stillness, I sit quietly, the world fading as peace floods through me—a warm, golden tide that soothes my mind, body, and spirit, leaving me weightless yet whole. My sensitivity, once a shadow

I hid from, is now my strength, a sacred gift that lets me live and love with fierce abandon. No longer dimming my light, I shine as I am—bold, open, and gloriously alive.

⋮

Breaking Free: Shattering the Box
of Limiting Beliefs

Forged in youth's tender, pliable clay,
Conditioned deep where shadows hold sway.
We're taught to toil, to wrestle, to strive,
Clawing through life just to survive.

"Shun the risks," they warn, "or fall to despair,
Failure lurks where bold dreams dare."
Life's painted harsh, a grueling climb,
Privilege gleams for others' time.

Unworthy, we're told, unfit to rise,
Our capabilities dimmed by doubting eyes.
"Stay in the lines," their voices confine,
No hues of wonder past boundaries' design.

Imagination, a childish spark,
Labeled foolish, left to the dark.
"Grow up," they urge, with a stern decree,
Caging the spirit that longs to be free.

Yet beneath this weight, an ember glows,
A joyful beat where wild dreams flow.
Unshackled, I see through the rigid lore,
My soul's bright colors will soar evermore.

How many times have you found yourself standing at the edge of a dream, only to shrink back, whispering to yourself, "I can't"? The reasons pile up like stones: "It's just who I am." "Resources are scarce." "I don't know the right people." "I don't have enough money." "My upbringing held me back." "I'm not smart enough, strong enough, talented enough." I've wrestled with these limiting beliefs for years, tracing their roots like a detective hunting clues. When did I stop believing I could do anything? Did I ever truly hold that boundless faith? When did I build a box around my potential, its walls invisible but unyielding? Yet, at eighteen, I left home with just $90 in my pocket—a measly sum that barely covered a week's necessities. The world was massive, uncertain, but I wasn't daunted. I trusted that I could figure it out, fueled by a conviction that hard work would carve a path to success, whatever that "success" might be.

I love watching parents or mentors ignite that spark in young children and seeing their eyes go wide with possibility. "The world's yours," they say. "Want to be a rock star? Go for it. An artist? You've got this." Their belief is a warm glow, unshaken by doubt. I live for those moments when I can fan that flame in others, young or old, helping them see the potential that lies within. We all need to reclaim that childlike audacity, the unfiltered belief that anything is possible. Sure, some dreams face hard limits—if you stand at five foot two, you're not likely to dunk in the NBA—but most barriers aren't so clear-cut. They're stories we tell ourselves, scripts we've memorized without questioning.

As I previously mentioned, one of my career highlights was at Capco in 2009 when I joined to help build out the banking practice. The founder and CEO was relentless in his commitment to creating something big and amazing. He continuously challenged us to embrace a beginner's mind-set. My colleagues often scoffed at the boldness of his vision, likely fearful that the task at hand wasn't achievable and so figuring there was no need to set themselves up for failure. But I thrived on this inspiration. Yes, I too wanted to reach for the stars. It felt way better than settling for mediocrity. Essentially, it was a challenge to forget the past, to rise above the limiting beliefs we all carry from previous failures. Who wouldn't want to think and act boldly? Well, that certainly was how I found the most success in my professional life. Beginner's mind wasn't just a buzzword; it was a key that unlocked my potential, reminding me that the only true box around me was the one I'd built myself. Breaking free felt like flying.

HALF MARATHON

In 2016, in my mid-forties, I found myself in one of those quiet, soul-searching moments that had punctuated my life. Sitting on my Atlanta patio, the soft trickle of the backyard fountain grounding me, I probed the edges of my self-imposed limits. This time, my body was the target—specifically, my belief that I couldn't run. I'd been a daily walker forever, my feet tracing familiar paths through leafy neighborhoods, but running? That was for others—lithe, athletic types, not a pear-shaped woman like me. I'd slapped a label on myself early on: not an athlete. Growing up, that label felt cemented. My brothers played school and community sports—baseball, basketball—while I cheered from the sidelines, basking in the outlet I was denied. Girls in my community couldn't wear the required athletic shorts, so I just watched instead of playing, my dress a silent barrier.

At home in Fairwood, I experienced flashes of joy when kicking a ball, swinging a bat, or tossing a football with my brothers and cousins. Those moments created a sense of freedom, especially since all the girls were in dresses anyway and no one was singled out. But I never excelled at these games, carrying the weight of "not good enough" into adulthood. I told myself runners were built differently; their bodies were sleek, not like mine.

Yet, that spring morning so many decades later, a spark of defiance flickered. What if I tried? What was the worst-case scenario here? At least I'd fail quietly, with no one the wiser. So, I laced up my sneakers, heart pounding, and set out to run a mile. The air was crisp, birds were chirping, and my breath was ragged but steady. I did it—not fast, not gracefully, but I ran a mile. The rush was electric, a surge of empowerment that lit me up. If I could do one, why not two? Then three. At three miles, I felt it—the fabled runner's high, a euphoric wave that made my body feel like it was soaring. Suddenly, I understood why people loved this. The pain of those first miles was a gate, not a wall, and I'd pushed through.

Emboldened, I set a wilder goal: to run a half marathon in Nashville the next spring. Long Sunday runs became my ritual, each new mile a pinch-me moment. My playlist pumped through my earbuds, propelling me forward as I marveled at my own audacity. By the time I aced my twelve-mile training run, I felt invincible, my body strong, my spirit soaring. I wasn't chasing speed, just the promise I'd made to myself: to finish the race.

During my training, I turned to massage and stretching for relief, and in a stroke of serendipity, I met Erin, a gifted practitioner with her own thriving business rooted in myofascial stretch techniques. Her skilled hands worked magic, unraveling the knots in my weary muscles with a blend of expertise and intuition. Beyond the soothing relief, a deeper gift emerged—we clicked instantly, our conversations flowing as easily as a warm breeze. Erin became a fast friend, an answer to my quiet prayers for richer connections in my life, transforming routine sessions into moments of healing and heartfelt camaraderie.

Race day finally arrived. It was a brilliant, sunny morning in Nashville, the air alive with anticipation. I'd trained solo, music my only companion, but I expected that the live bands along the route and the camaraderie of other runners would buoy me. But reality had other plans. The heat was relentless, which made my sweaty shirt cling to my skin. And the hills—they were brutal, rolling monsters I hadn't trained for, my preparation woefully lacking. My feet swelled, each step a jolt of pain as I wove through slower runners. The final two miles were brutal; I mostly walked, grimacing, the finish line a distant mirage. When I finally crossed it, exhausted but unbroken, a wave of triumph washed over me. I'd done it—I'd conquered a challenge that I had once deemed impossible. Through the sound of the crowd's cheers, feeling the weight of the medal around my neck and the ache in my legs—I knew this was a victory carved from pure will.

I haven't run a race since, and I don't feel the urge to. Not because I can't—I know I could—but because the fire to prove something has burned out. That half marathon wasn't just a race; it was a sledgehammer to my limiting beliefs, shattering the box I'd built around myself. I'd dared to dream bigger than my doubts, and the freedom of that moment still shines through me, a reminder that I'm capable of more than I ever imagined.

CREATIVITY

For years, I carried a heavy, invisible chain—a limiting belief that whispered I wasn't creative enough. In my mind, creativity was a dazzling realm reserved for singers with voices that soared like birds, composers who could weave symphonies from thin air, artists capable of splashing bold colors across canvases, writers spinning worlds from words, or actors breathing life into stories on stage. My thirty-plus years in financial services? Nothing creative there; that was all just implementing new processes and procedures, hardly the stuff of wild imagination. Or so I'd thought. But looking back, I now see it differently. My mind had been a quiet forge, sparking with ideas that lit up boardrooms. I'd crafted innovative solutions for clients, each one birthed by a small burst of originality. These efforts didn't fit my narrow definition of creativity back then, but they glowed with an ingenuity specific to my chosen field all the same.

For many years I'd had a desire to write a book, to share my story. Yet as I began seriously thinking about putting pen to paper in the spring of 2024, doubt curled around me like a heavy mist, obscuring the path ahead. I'd scratched out poems here and there over the years, raw emotions spilling onto tattered scraps of paper, but a book? The idea towered like a forbidding forest, with gnarled branches woven into shadows, fierce and untamed. Could I ever carve my way through to its wild heart? Even now, as my fingers fly across the keyboard, a feeling of uncertainty quivers beneath the surface of my mind, a quiet echo of that old, gnawing fear.

What shifted the ground beneath me was diving into Pam Grout's books. Her words leapt off the page like a resounding drumbeat. She emphasized a truth that reverberated in my core: Everyone stumbles through doubts and fears, especially at the start of something new. The first book an author writes, the first stroke a painter makes with her brush, the first chord a musician strums—it's all raw, unpolished, trembling with vulnerability. Pam reminds us that even The Beatles, legends in their prime, once fumbled through off-key notes in smoky, dimly lit venues. Pam's assurance cut through my haze, her encouragement a lighthouse beam. We each carry a story, unique as a fingerprint, and our life path is sacred. Why not let it spill onto the page, where it might spark hope or inspiration in even one other soul? That idea took root, blooming like a wildflower in cracked earth, urging me to write, to create, to trust that my story—my own forest of experiences—emits a light worth sharing. Fear melted away the moment I surrendered just enough, letting my blazing purpose burn through the shadows of doubt that had long clung to me.

I'm calling out to you—yes, YOU—to torch whatever fears are holding you back. If your heart races at the thought of writing your story, splashing your art across a canvas, crafting poems that sing, or even just leaving the corporate world to start your own business, then answer that call. Your gifts aren't just talents—they're your legacy, a fire bestowed upon you. You are fiercely worthy.

SIX STEPS TO UNLEASH YOUR FIRE

Step 1: Uncover Your Spark—What do you burn to achieve, and why?

Dive deep into your soul and pinpoint what sets your heart ablaze. Is it a dream that makes your pulse race, a vision that floods you with joy and electric inspiration? If it makes you feel alive, chase it with everything you've got.

Step 2: Torch the Fear—Face it, name it, let it go.

Fear whispers that you're not enough, but you are. Dig into the roots of that doubt—what's holding you back, and why? Confront it head-on, then release it like smoke into the wind. Does your purpose now roar louder than your fear? If so, let it win.

Step 3: Leap into Action—Take that first bold step.

Don't overthink—just start. Take one daring step, feel the rush, and see where it leads. Does it still light you up? Keep moving. The journey is alive with possibility.

Step 4: Fuel Your Fire—Learn, absorb, grow.

Immerse yourself in knowledge. Devour books, soak up stories, and let others' journeys ignite your own. Every page you turn fans the flames of your dream.

Step 5: Charge Forward—Push through fear's return.

Fear will creep back, knocking at your resolve. Acknowledge it, then shove it aside. Pick your dream back up when you're ready, and keep charging toward the summit. You've got this.

Step 6: Revel in Your Triumphs—Celebrate every victory.

Shout your wins from the rooftops, no matter how small they seem. Every step forward is a blazing testament to your resolve. You are worthy.

⋮

32

The Wanderer's Awakening: Travels That Transformed Me

Each new state, each foreign shore I tread,
My soul unfurls, my awareness spreads.
Through bustling streets and whispering plains,
I see humankind in a glowing, shifting frame.
No longer bound by my small, familiar sphere,
I'm cracked open wide, the world's force near.

Each journey shifts the lens within my core,
Transforming me, opening unseen doors.
From my little world, I'm forever set free,
To marvel at landscapes where ancient spirits dwell.
No frame can hold the awe they impart,
These sacred terrains that awaken my heart.

Growing up in a sleepy country town of fewer than two thousand souls, where a single traffic light blinked lazily at the main crossroads, the wider world felt like a distant dream. My childhood was framed by fields and woods and quiet air, all of it far from the action of urban life. So, stepping into bustling cities as an adult was like plunging into a sparkling, chaotic painting—skyscrapers piercing the sky, horns blaring, neon lights flickering in a frenetic dance. For me, having an HSP trait, the energy was a double-edged sword: electrifying yet overwhelming, a sensory overload that could leave me frazzled. Though I had visited Boston numerous times in my youth, returning there in my early twenties ignited my hunger for the energy and diversity missing in those quiet towns.

To stay anchored in bustling cities, I learned to seek out pockets of nature to stay grounded—anywhere I could take a quiet walk along a riverbank or hear the rustle of leaves in a wooded park or the gentle lap of water against the shore. I spent several years traveling weekly to New York City, and I'd often stay at the Marriott Downtown so I could rise early to stroll along the nearby Hudson River. The water's steady flow was a balm, its shimmer catching the morning light, calming my spirit before the day's whirlwind began.

My first trip to Europe, to a partner retreat in Málaga, Spain, at the age of thirty-nine, was an awakening that cracked my world wide open. As the plane descended, I glimpsed the Mediterranean's turquoise expanse, and my heart skipped. Stepping onto Spanish soil, I was hit with a sensory feast: the tang of salty air, the chatter of a language I couldn't parse, the dazzling colors of markets spilling over with fresh olives and citrus. The history—soaked into ancient stone streets—and the customs, from leisurely tapas lunches to late-night laughter, were mesmerizingly different yet achingly beautiful. I wandered Málaga's sun-drenched plazas, awestruck, wondering why it had taken me so long to cross the Atlantic.

I'd traveled before—to the Caribbean's and Mexico's turquoise beaches, as well as Canada's crisp landscapes—but Europe felt like a new universe. The idea of it had once seemed daunting, foreign in the truest sense, especially in places where English wasn't the default. I'd never been adept at languages, but I found navigation surprisingly intuitive—universal signs, familiar images in airports, and the kindness of strangers bridged the gap. I left Málaga on a high, my soul thirsty for more.

That trip sparked a hunger to see the world, to peel back its layers and challenge my assumptions. Travel became a mirror, revealing both the flaws and the beauty we often overlook in the United States—our polluted food system, our quick judgments of other cultures, our naïveté about the world's complexity, and yet also its remarkable human spirit. I wish everyone could step into the flow of daily life in another country, to feel the humility and wonder of being an outsider, to see how small our differences truly are against the backdrop of shared humanity.

A year after that first trip to Spain, I returned to Europe for another partner meeting, this time in Sicily, at a luxurious resort perched above the Tyrrhenian Sea. The water sparkled like a sheet of sapphires, stretching to the horizon, and dinners at a nearby winery were a sensory explosion—tables laden with massive Parmesan rinds, their nutty aroma mingling with the sweet tang of local wines.

Before the meeting, my then-husband Rob and I toured Rome, and the city stole my breath. We roamed its ancient streets, the Colosseum's weathered stones whispering stories of gladiators, the Pantheon's dome defying time. The Vatican dazzled with its gilded opulence yet left me uneasy with its ostentatious weight. Our hotel, a short stroll from the Spanish Steps, was a perfect base—cobblestone alleys led to bustling piazzas, fragrant with espresso and fresh-baked pastries. Every meal was a delight: plates piled with pasta, eggplant dishes so divine and gelato so creamy they felt downright sinful. Rome's chaos and charm wove their way into my heart. That trip initiated a love affair with Italy I'd reignite again and again, each visit revealing new charms—Tuscany's hillsides and Florence's art, Lake Como's glassy waters cradled by emerald mountains, Milan's quiet blending of sleek modernity with timeless grace. Each discovery only deepened my craving to come back again to explore more of Italy's boundless allure.

Travel didn't just show me the world; it reshaped me, teaching me to embrace the unknown, to find peace in nature's quiet, and to carry the beauty of every place I've been deep within my soul.

FURTHER EUROPEAN TRAVELS

In late 2018, I began a new tradition of crisscrossing Europe's enchanting landscapes alongside two extraordinary souls, Kim and Kaylin, who share my wanderlust. Finding travel companions whose interests sync with mine—curious, open, and ready to soak in every moment—is a rare treasure, and with the two of them, every journey opens my eyes and heart alike.

ROME AGAIN

Our first escapade together was a spontaneous post-Thanksgiving jaunt to Rome, sparked by a last-minute invite from Kim. She was already planning to go with a couple of her friends, and I leapt at the chance, coaxing Kaylin to join us. From the moment we landed, our connection was effortless, like old friends picking up where we left off. Rome greeted us with overcast, cloud-streaked skies and gentle rain, its cobblestone streets glistening under the twinkle of Christmas lights strung across ancient alleys. Kaylin and I shared a trusted Marriott hotel, and each morning we'd make our way to a nearby café, the air thick with the aroma of freshly made cappuccinos and buttery croissants still warm from the oven. We'd linger over breakfast, savoring the frothy coffee and flaking pastries, reminiscing about the previous day's adventures with the hum of the city waking up around us.

Once we met up with Kim and her crew, the day would unfurl with a delicious lack of urgency. We wandered Rome's labyrinthine streets, letting whim be our guide—no rigid itineraries, just the joy of discovery. We'd pause for leisurely lunches at trattorias tucked down side streets, where ruby-red wine flowed freely, loosening our stories and sparking peals of laughter that echoed off ancient stone walls. Some afternoons, we'd duck into charming shops, fingering soft leather purses or marveling at hand-painted canvases, each a tiny piece of Rome's soul.

Every step felt effortless, each moment a joyful time in shared adventure. The rain might've dampened our shoes, but it never touched our spirits. Rome, with its blend of timeless majesty and festive glow, was the perfect backdrop for a trip that felt like pure magic—proof that the right companions can turn a getaway into a memory that sparkles long after the journey ends.

PORTUGAL AND FRANCE

Several years after our Roman adventure, post-COVID wanderlust pulled us first to Portugal and then on to France, a journey that unfolded with highs and unexpected twists. My trip began with a snag—a missed connection in Atlanta after a maddening delay from Florida. Frustrated, I leaned on the familiar comfort of the Delta Sky Club, pleading with the attendants to reroute me anywhere in Europe, trusting I'd find a way to Faro, Portugal. Their magic secured me a flight to Paris's Charles de Gaulle airport, but exhaustion dulled my instincts. Rushing to make a tight connection to Faro from the Orly airport, I made a rookie mistake, bypassing the trusted taxi line for the first driver who beckoned—a choice I'd soon regret. Halfway to Orly, his demeanor shifted, a sly edge creeping into his voice. At Orly, he demanded an outrageous fare, payable only in cash. With no choice, I let him trail me to an ATM, my heart sinking as I handed over the money. Yet, as I boarded my flight to Faro, gratitude eclipsed frustration. I recalled my learnings on the Art of Allowing. Instead of resentment, I chose compassion for a man trapped in a life of deceit, his con a fleeting shadow on my journey.

In Faro, at Portugal's southern tip, I met up with Kim, such a delight after my crazy trip. After a refreshing shower and change of clothes, we wandered the streets to find a delightful café for dinner and drinks, reconnecting with joy. Kaylin and another friend joined us the next day, settling into our cozy Airbnb perched on the beach's edge. The sand here wasn't the powdery white of Florida's gulf, but it sparkled under the sun, the Atlantic's waves a rhythmic lullaby during our daily strolls. Mornings began with coffee from a local café a short distance away, the sea breeze carrying the briny tang of salt and adventure. We boarded the ferry and wandered into Faro's old city, its cobblestone alleys lined with pastel buildings glowing in the golden light. Dinners were a pleasant surprise, all so affordable we'd gape at the bill, chuckling in disbelief at the tastiness of the food and wine compared with the price. One afternoon, we braved paddleboarding in the bay, my first attempt. The current tugged fiercely, waves slapping our boards, and we surrendered quickly. We paddled to shore, salty and sun warmed, grateful to be back on land.

Another day, we laced up for a walk along the Algarve's rugged coastline, where dramatic cliffs plunged into turquoise waters. Our hilly climb gifted us with vistas that stole our breath—crashing waves, jagged rock formations, and an endless horizon that felt like the world's edge. By midday, we came across a charming café perched precariously over the sea. We sank into wicker chairs at the tables draped in checkered cloth, savoring chilled glasses of crisp rosé, the wine's blush mirroring the flush on our cheeks. Refreshed by the local cuisine, we wandered into a nearby village, its narrow streets alive with color and chatter. Shops brimmed with treasures: hand-painted ceramics glazed in oceanic hues, intricately woven baskets smelling faintly of straw, and delicate lace shawls that caught the light.

Our Uber ride back to Faro was a thrill in itself—our driver regaled us with tales of Portugal's history and his own mischievous youth. He zipped along the hilly roads with fearless glee as we held on for dear life. The day was a treat as it ran the gamut from experiencing nature's grandeur to forging meaningful human connections to feeling the pure joy of exploration.

After Faro, Kaylin, our other friend, and I flew into Lisbon for a whirlwind visit that set our senses ablaze. The city's golden light bathed its hilly streets, where pastel buildings leaned into each other like old friends. We plunged into Lisbon's tasty food scene, savoring every bite, and indulged in a shopping spree focused on designer bags, the tax-free allure fueling our excitement.

Then, we jetted to Paris, a city I'd once dreamed of exploring hand in hand with a romantic partner but now was glad to enjoy in the company of friends. I was determined to drink in its magic no matter what. The summer heat was fierce, a shimmering haze rising from the cobblestones, but Paris dazzled nonetheless. One morning, while sipping rich and frothy cappuccinos, we sank our teeth into croissants from a delightful café—the golden, buttery layers flaked onto my lap, their warmth an epiphany that redefined pastry forever. Another afternoon, I escaped from the heat by ducking into the Ritz hotel where Princess Diana's fate had turned, and sat there savoring a glass of champagne, grateful to be alive. The Parisians I met, far from the stereotypes, were warm and witty, their rapid-fire French a melody that set the scene as we sat at sidewalk cafés, savoring French cuisine and delicious wine.

To dodge the heat, we zipped through the city on tuk-tuks, their drivers doubling as guides, pointing out hidden courtyards and quirky statues. Notre-Dame was majestic, its spire still cloaked in scaffolding, a phoenix mid-rebirth, its gothic arches whispering centuries of stories. Our final night was pure enchantment—a sunset cruise on the Seine, the river's surface a mirror of rose and gold. After getting a bit lost but finally making it aboard, we sipped chilled champagne, the Eiffel Tower rising ahead, its iron lattice twinkling against the dusk. As the boat glided along, Paris unfolded like a love letter around us, bridges arching gracefully, its lights a constellation of dreams. This journey—through Portugal's sunlit shores and

France's romantic heart—was a vivid celebration of resilience, connection, and the joy of simply being there.

GREECE

In the fall of 2023, Greece beckoned, and I eagerly packed my bags for the adventure, ready to join Kim and her partner Chris there. My journey was to begin with a drive to Tampa's airport. From there, I would meet up with Kaylin at JFK Airport for our flight to Athens. But the Universe had other plans. Just as I was about to leave, Kaylin called, her voice crackling with urgency—her connecting flight to JFK was grounded by a storm sweeping the Northeast. Undeterred, she'd snagged a flight to Connecticut and arranged a car service to JFK. Moments later, though, my own flight to JFK was canceled, stranding me in Florida. I settled in for the night, anticipation simmering, and caught a new flight the next day, finally touching down in Athens a day behind schedule.

Upon arrival, I took a quick shower at our hotel, the cool water washing away travel's fatigue. Kaylin and I then stepped into the city's alluring charm and wandered to a nearby café, its tables spilling onto the sidewalk, where we savored frothy cappuccinos and fluffy eggs accompanied by a bowl of fresh fruit. Fueled and ready, we set out for the Acropolis, its ancient stones glowing under a fierce September sun. The climb left us sweaty, our breath catching not just from the heat but from the jaw-dropping vista as well—marble columns standing like sentinels against a sapphire sky, Athens sprawling below in a mosaic of white rooftops and bustling streets. We descended into the Plaka district, settling at a shaded café where cobblestones gleamed and bougainvillea spilled over walls. Sipping crisp Greek rosé, its hue like a summer sunset, we savored plates of tangy tzatziki and grilled octopus, the flavors bright and briny, each bite a celebration of this ancient land.

Next, we flew to Naxos to reunite with Kim and her partner Chris, checking into a charming Airbnb nestled in the island's rolling hills. I had actually first met Chris during my time at Capco years before, so it was an easy reunion. That evening, we joined them for a night of revelry—clinking glasses of chilled rosé, feasting on spanakopita and fresh seafood, and dancing under strings of fairy lights in a taverna alive with music. Our laughter echoed into the night, rekindling our bond.

The next morning, I was beyond grateful that Kaylin and Kim kindly located a dentist for me for an emergency visit. Kaylin even patiently accompanied me while the Greek dentist fixed me up temporarily, an experience I will never forget. The dentist did his best, but the language barrier was real. The outcome was frustrating, but I rallied despite some pain, grateful for the distraction of friends. Later we all piled into a rented four-wheeler with Chris at the helm. Our tires kicked up plenty of dust as we roared toward a seaside café they'd discovered earlier. A salty breeze cooled our skin as we sipped more rosé, its chill a perfect foil to the heat of the sun, and we savored appetizers of fresh tuna and a delightful charcuterie platter piled high with cheeses, meats, crackers, and other delights.

The following day was pure magic: We chartered a boat to explore Greece's fabled waters. The vessel sliced through turquoise waves, the horizon endless and shimmering. We anchored near hidden coves, diving into crystal depths where fish darted like living jewels, the cool water a blissful escape from the heat. Laughter rang out as we lounged on the deck, the sun painting our skin golden, the sea's rhythm rocking us into a state of pure joy—one of my favorite days, etched in my memory.

Kim and Chris's pleas later rallied us onto a ferry bound for Mykonos, so we could raise a glass for his birthday at their cliffside hotel. The stunning vistas showed us the Aegean in a thousand shades of blue beneath a blazing sun. The rest of the island thrummed with life—whitewashed buildings sparkled like pearls against rugged, sun-scorched hills, while vibrant villages and beaches burst with radiant charm. After a delectable breakfast, coffee flowing like the sea itself, we claimed a cabana with a front-row view of the deep, shimmering waves, toasting Chris as promised with crisp rosé. Laughter erupted freely as we swapped stories, and as our chatter splintered into side conversations, Chris, with his irresistible British charm, playfully corralled us back into a lively communal exchange. I think my cheeks might still ache a bit from the joy of that unforgettable day, every moment glowing with warmth and connection.

From Mykonos, Kaylin and I hopped another ferry to Santorini, settling into an Airbnb carved into a cliffside cave, its whitewashed walls cool against the heat. Hauling our suitcases up the island's iconic stairways was a workout, our laughter echoing as we navigated the zigzagging steps. The effort was worth it—the views were breathtaking, with pastel sunsets igniting the caldera, painting the sky in hues of coral, lavender, and gold, the white-domed villages cascading toward the sea like a dream. We sipped Assyrtiko wine on our terrace, its minerality crisp and bright, and lost ourselves in the island's magic, each vista a postcard come to life.

Our final stop was a brief jaunt to Amsterdam, a stark contrast to Greece's sun-soaked glow. Rain pattered on the city's canals, their waters reflecting gabled houses and neon signs in a soft, silvery haze. We wandered the cobblestone streets, umbrellas bobbing, warmed by the locals' hearty friendliness, their accents like a melody. The Anne Frank House was a sobering pilgrimage, its cramped attic rooms a haunting testament to resilience, leaving us hushed and reflective. After savoring Dutch crepes at a cozy café, the powdered sugar dusting our noses, we continued to explore the streets, appreciating each moment together.

Another unforgettable trip etched in the books, we flew home, our hearts brimming with memories of Greece's radiant seas and

Amsterdam's rainy embrace, blessed by the connections, discovery, and joy that would linger long after we landed.

MILAN, LAKE COMO, SWITZERLAND, AND SPAIN

About a year after our Greek odyssey, Kaylin and I aligned once more with Kim and Chris, this time ultimately pointing ourselves toward the windswept shores of southern Spain, where Chris would be indulging his passion for kite surfing in Tarifa. However, eager to tick another country off our respective bucket lists, Kaylin and I wanted to weave a jaunt to Switzerland into our itinerary before joining them.

So we crafted a journey for ourselves that encompassed shimmering lakes, alpine peaks, and sun-soaked beaches. Our planning had to be meticulous—we spent hours researching train schedules and ferry routes, as well as temperatures in each destination in order to be mindful of the diverse climates we'd be crossing. Masters of minimalist travel, we managed to pack only a single rollaboard each. Kaylin's introduction of clever packing cubes helped turn my suitcase into a marvel of efficiency, every outfit and essential neatly tucked into place. Airbnbs with washers and dryers would also prove to be a boon, allowing us to keep our compact wardrobes fresh throughout the journey.

But first, our adventure began in Italy's north. We landed in Milan after a swift overnight, which was blissfully free of the transatlantic travel snafus that had plagued past trips. After checking into our chic hotel, we strolled through Milan's bustling heart, the air alive with the clatter of espresso cups and the hum of stylish locals. At a lovely trattoria, we savored a lunch of creamy burrata and ripe tomatoes drizzled with balsamic, the flavors bursting like summer itself. That evening, our concierge steered us to a hidden gem of a restaurant tucked down a quiet cobblestone street, its facade draped in ivy. Candlelight flickered across exposed brick walls as we feasted on tenderloin, the tender meat melting under our forks, paired with a velvety Barolo that warmed us from within.

The next morning, after a final amble past the Duomo's soaring spires, we navigated to Milan's bustling train station, my first foray into Europe's legendary rail system. I'd heard tales of its efficiency compared to the United States' patchy network, and with Kaylin by my side, the experience felt like a breeze. Tickets in hand, we boarded a sleek train bound for Lake Como, the carriage humming softly as it sliced through rolling hills. At Varenna, we hopped onto a ferry to Bellagio, and the ride was pure enchantment—emerald waters rippling under a cerulean sky, villas with terracotta roofs peeking through lush greenery, their reflections dancing on the lake's glassy surface. Our Airbnb, complete with jaw-dropping views, delivered on its promise: wide windows framed the lake's serene expanse, and we could see sailboats bobbing like toys in the distance.

In Bellagio, we surrendered to la dolce vita, wandering the steep, flower-lined alleys where bougainvillea spilled over stone walls. Mornings began with cappuccinos and authentic European croissants—golden, buttery, and impossibly flaky, made with simple ingredients that shamed their American cousins. Lunches and dinners were feasts of wood-fired pizzas with blistered crusts, silky tagliatelle slicked with ragù, and crusty bread dipped in peppery olive oil, always paired with crisp local wines that sparkled on the tongue. One rainy day only amplified the charm—we dashed between boutiques, raindrops glistening on our hair, unearthing treasures: vibrant silk scarves, buttery leather purses, and handcrafted shoes that felt like wearable art. Another day, we hired Mario, a young boat captain with a twinkle in his eye, to whisk us across Como's azure waters. The breeze whipped through our hair as we marveled at the coastline's pastel villas and craggy cliffs, the lake's beauty a living postcard that left us breathless.

Another day, a ferry strike scuttled our plans to explore other nearby towns, but Bellagio's magic held us happily captive, its charm more than enough for this leg of the trip. Our journey to Switzerland, however, became a whirlwind of improvisation. From Bellagio, we ferried across the lake, hoping to hire a car service to Lugano's train station. But the narrow, twisting roads deterred most drivers, leaving us no choice but to board a local bus. The driver, a maestro of the hairpin turns, navigated with fearless precision, the scenery flashing by—vineyards clinging to slopes, distant peaks dusted with snow. A language mix-up had us hopping off too early, but Kaylin's sharp eyes spotted a taxi, and the driver whisked us to Lugano's station just in time. The train to Spiez was a dream—plush seats, panoramic windows framing postcard-perfect views of alpine meadows and glittering lakes. Upon arrival, we strolled to our Airbnb overlooking the Thunersee, flinging open the windows to let the crisp mountain air rush in. The lake shimmered like a sapphire, nestled amongst the Swiss Alps' majestic peaks, their snow-capped crowns glowing in the twilight. Dinner in the local village café warmed us with steaming potato soup and chicken cordon bleu, its golden crust encasing gooey cheese and savory ham, each bite a hug from Switzerland's heart.

The next dawn, we rose early for a journey up to Jungfraujoch, the "Top of Europe." The train chugged upward, carving through tunnels and past glaciers that gleamed like frozen rivers. At the summit, we stood awestruck, surrounded by a sea of snow and ice, the wind carrying the scent of ancient frost. The view—peaks piercing the clouds, valleys cradling emerald lakes—was a soul-stirring spectacle that felt like touching the divine. That afternoon, we descended to Interlaken, ducking into a rustic Swiss restaurant where we dipped crusty bread and pickled vegetables into a bubbling pot of fondue, a combination of nutty Gruyère and Emmental, a creamy delight that warmed us against the rainy chill.

The next morning, a train whisked us on to Zurich, its sleek skyline a contrast to the mountains we'd left behind. Once there, Kaylin and I wandered through the city's cobbled streets and along its shimmering lake, our laughter and chatter weaving effortlessly through the crisp alpine air. As late afternoon painted the sky in hues of gold, a strange haze clouded my left eye, flecked with a flurry of new floaters darting like tiny shadows. We opted for a cozy evening in, savoring room service in our separate rooms, content with the quiet. But curiosity gnawed at me, and I dove into Google, scouring the internet for answers about my eye. The consensus was stark: Get it checked, urgently. Kaylin, ever my steadfast companion, was by my side as we navigated the city again the next morning.

The first clinic we found lacked the ability to probe my retina, so Kaylin, quick and resourceful, tracked down an emergency center that could squeeze me in. Their machines hummed and glowed, revealing a tear in my retina—a jagged fault line in my vision. A referral and a tense taxi ride later, we arrived at a bustling hospital. The waiting room was crammed with emergencies, each story more urgent than mine, and time stretched into a restless blur. Finally, the doctor confirmed the diagnosis: Laser treatment would seal the tear. I sat frozen, heart pounding, as the young doctor worked with precision, the laser's faint pings—over a hundred—echoing like tiny sparks, welding the tear back together. Relief washed over me; of all places that we had traveled, Zurich's innovative care was a quiet miracle. I was reminded again that God does watch over and care for me in mysterious ways.

From Switzerland's alpine embrace, we jetted to Málaga, Spain and then on to Tarifa on the southern coast. Reuniting with Chris and Kim and then meeting some of their other friends was like listening to a favorite song—warm, familiar, electric. We watched Chris carve the waves with his kite sail, a dance of wind and water, while we savored plates of delicious tapas and glasses of rosé. The days brimmed with connection, laughter spilling over like the Spanish sun.

When Kaylin and I had planned our itinerary, we'd hatched a plan to hop a ferry from Tarifa to Morocco—a fleeting chance to check another continent off our bucket lists. But when we arrived in Tarifa, Chris, with his dry British wit, called us mad. He warned us about the dicey ferry terminals, recent border control chaos, rampant theft, and tempestuously churning seas. His words sank in, and we swapped our ferry dreams for a taxi back to Málaga, grateful for his advice. From there, a train whisked us on into Madrid's lively atmosphere, where we'd soak up our final days before flying home. Though Morocco had eluded us, we caught a tantalizing glimpse of Africa's rugged coastline from Tarifa, a fleeting tease of the adventure that awaited another day. It was another unforgettable journey, forever etched in our hearts.

These European travel experiences bring to mind a handful of cherished life lessons:

1. Embrace adaptability as your superpower.

Life's twists and turns are inevitable, but adaptability transforms them into adventures. Embrace the unexpected, trust your instincts, and lean on companions to navigate the unknown—every detour can lead to magic.

2. Cultivate gratitude for life's quiet miracles.

Look for the quiet miracles—supportive friends, timely interventions, or moments of beauty—that guide you through life's uncertainties. Gratitude turns fleeting moments into lasting treasures, reminding you that you're never alone on the journey.

3. Cherish connection as the heart of experience.

Prioritize the people who make your heart sing. Shared experiences, no matter how grand or how simple, create deep connections that live beyond the return home from any destination. Invest in relationships—they're the true souvenirs of a life well lived.

⋮

33

Mesmerized by Nature: My Favorite Places of Awe and Tranquility

Through pine and birch, I wander deep,
Where towering giants in majesty sweep.
Birds weave their songs, a melodious stream,
A gentle brook glides, polishing stones in a dream.
Earth's rich scent rises, Mother's warm breath,
Sunlight caresses my face, soft as a wreath.
In stillness, my soul softens, reborn and renewed.

By ocean's edge, I stand, entranced,
Where waves roar fierce, in turquoise expanse.
Barefoot, I tread on sands silken and white,
Floating in swells, weightless, alight.
Sea's briny perfume drifts, wild and free,
Sunset ignites, a blaze of fiery glee.
In stillness, my heart softens, reborn and renewed.

Through neighborhood paths, I stroll with delight,
Butterflies twirl, their wings catching light.
Alligators lounge where pond's edges gleam,
Skies unfurl blue, a boundless, rich dream.
A cardinal flares, crimson bold in the tree,
Purple blooms sway, delicate, wild, and free.
In stillness, my spirit softens, reborn and renewed.

Ever since I was a child, the outdoors has been my sanctuary, a counterpoint to the cool comfort of my home, where crisp sheets and a soft bed cocoon me at night. But the call of nature—its massiveness, its quiet power—has always pulled me. For as long as I can remember, daily walks have been my saving grace, a ritual that sets my soul free. Whether I'm wandering the shaded trails of New England's woods with my family, where sunlight filters through towering pines and leaves crunch underfoot, or tracing the powdery white sands of Florida's beaches near my home, the rhythm of my steps unlocks my mind. The world fades, and my thoughts unfurl—sometimes sparking deep inspiration, other times soothing sadness, anger, or unease. In Atlanta, I'd roam my neighborhood's hilly streets, drawn to parks where water features murmured, their gentle ripples a balm. Each walk left me recharged, ready to dive into a project or face the workday with fresh energy.

Evenings, too, belong to the outdoors. In Atlanta, my tiny backyard was my happy place, tucked away from the city's bustle. A small fountain bubbled at its heart, its soft gurgle drowning out distant highway drones and siren wails, casting a spell of tranquility. I'd sit there, watching the squirrels playfully dance across the fence, letting the day's weight slip away. Now, living in Florida, I've found a new oasis—an outdoor living space encased in a protective cage that mostly keeps out flies and curious critters, save for the occasional gecko, a tiny, harmless guest perched on my chair's arm, its eyes glinting like little jewels. My home backs onto a preserve, a lush expanse of palm trees, stunning old oak, and tangled Florida foliage. The pool's water features—two water bowls cascading like a fountain—create a chorus of soothing sound, weaving peace into the evening air. I sink into my chair as the sky turns to dusk and feel utterly at home.

Memories of childhood camping trips come flooding back, vivid as snapshots. Those summer escapes were all my family could afford, but they were magic. We'd pile into the van, headed for a lakeside campsite where we'd pitch our big green tent, its canvas walls flapping in the breeze. I loved the ritual—driving stakes into the earth, the smell of pine and damp soil, the anticipation of nights under the stars. We'd gather sticks, their rough bark scraping our hands, to roast marshmallows over a crackling fire, the flames dancing as golden goo dripped onto the logs. Evenings or rainy days meant Monopoly marathons or Scrabble showdowns. But my favorite moments were solitary, slipping away to wander wooded paths or perch on a smooth rock by a stream, mesmerized by the water's gentle flow, its surface catching the light like liquid glass. Those quiet interludes, with only the rustle of leaves and the stream's soft song, filled me with a peace that lingered long after we packed up the tent.

Whether it's a neighborhood stroll, a twilight pause in my backyard haven, or a day at the beach lulled by waves, nature remains my reset, my muse, my space to breathe. It's where I find clarity, inspiration, and the courage to move forward—one step at a time—when sadness, confusion, or anger clouds my heart.

I've learned that nature's embrace offers both a sanctuary for healing and a mirror for growth, teaching us all to find peace and wisdom in its timeless rhythms. In that spirit, I offer these encouragements to get out there and enjoy some time in nature yourself.

1. Nature is a healing refuge.

Immersing yourself in nature—whether through woodland walks, moments by a stream, or time in a backyard oasis—can soothe emotional turmoil, spark inspiration, and provide mental clarity, offering a universal sanctuary for finding peace.

2. Nature is a mirror for inner growth.

Engaging with the natural world invites you to reflect on your own growth, as its rhythms—trees reaching skyward, waves carving shores—mirror the resilience and unfolding of your spirit, guiding you toward deeper self-awareness.

⋮

34

Fresh Flavors and Dance-Floor Delights: Cooking Up Joyful Connections

As a kid, I eagerly seized every chance to help with baking. One of my favorite tasks was chopping tart frozen cranberries and zesting oranges for our Christmas cranberry-orange bread. The moment that loaf emerged from the oven, its citrusy warmth filled the house with holiday magic. Pies—especially blueberry bursting with the tastes of summer and pumpkin spiced with fall—and cookies were my playground. But these days, aside from whipping up the occasional loaf of banana bread, my whisk stays on the shelf. Baking's rules and sugar-heavy results no longer spark the same joy; my heart now leans toward healthier, freer flavors.

Cooking, though? That's where I come alive. No meticulous measuring cups, just a pinch of this, a dash of that—pure improvisation. I'm hooked on the alchemy of fresh ingredients, handpicked to dance on my palate. Cooking shows are my guilty pleasure, each episode a masterclass in bold flavor combos and clever techniques that I can't wait to riff on.

Fresh herbs truly spark my creativity in the kitchen, whether that's basil's sweet perfume, cilantro's bright zing, mint's cool whisper, or rosemary's earthy hum. I'm no chef, but I've learned to wield them as best as I can, blending their magic with the sharp kick of peppers, ginger, garlic, and the subtle snap of green onions, striking a balance that teases the palate without stealing the show. My mango salsa? It bursts with tropical sweetness and a spicy edge, the perfect partner for flaky fresh halibut or golden-crisp crab cakes, turning every bite into a little celebration of flavor.

There's something meditative about chopping veggies or prepping herbs, my knife slicing through stress as much as ingredients. After a grueling work week crisscrossing the country, I'd hit the Friday market, hunting for treasures—seasonally ripe produce, just-caught seafood, and a bouquet of flowers to brighten my table. Those hauls turned into effortless meals, bursting with color and taste, sometimes even artfully assembled for a no-fuss feast.

When I first met my former in-laws, their holiday spread was more "meh" than memorable—his sweet elderly mom, bless her, just couldn't muster the Italian feasts he reminisced about. I saw my chance and jumped in, scouring recipes to recreate that old-school magic along with some inspiration of my own. The first time I served up a feast, the table erupted in grins and requests for second helpings. Nothing beats that high—watching people savor the food you have prepared, hearing their chatter fade as they all dig in. At chaotic family gatherings, the kitchen became my refuge. Plotting a multidish Thanksgiving extravaganza, timing each course to perfection, gave me the perfect excuse to dodge small talk and bask in the calm of creation.

Living in Florida's endless summer now has reshaped my palate—I gravitate to all things lighter, brighter, fresher. I've fine-tuned my recipes over the years, but I'm always chasing that next great dish.

Entertaining is my love language. Whether it's a cozy dinner for friends and loved ones, or a lively gathering with my signature charcuterie board and handcrafted appetizers, my home transforms into a warm, inviting stage. Each dish is a chance to spark joy, forge bonds, and create memories that linger long after the last bite. I keep grand bashes to a minimum—big crowds can drown out the connection I crave. Instead, I'm infamous for spontaneous dance parties, twirling across my kitchen floor or swaying on the lanai, letting music weave us together in moments of pure, unscripted bliss. I've learned to take the time to do the things I love and then outsource the rest where I can.

I feel strongly that two primary philosophies have helped me find my voice in the kitchen over the years. First, I truly view cooking as both creative expression and stress relief. The act of cooking, with its improvisational freedom and tactile engagement, serves as a powerful outlet for creativity and a way to unwind from life's stresses. Cooking can be a meditative and fulfilling practice. I encourage everyone to explore their own creative passions as a means of finding balance and personal satisfaction.

Second, food and entertaining can provide an intimate means of fostering connection. Preparing and sharing food, whether through a festive family feast or a spontaneous gathering with a charcuterie board, fosters deep human connections and creates lasting memories. For me, cooking and entertaining brings people together. When paired with moments like spontaneous dance parties, these intentional, heartfelt gestures, even simple ones, can strengthen relationships and build moments of joy and community.

35

Friendships: Savoring Life's Seasons of Connection

Although I often struggled with friendships in my early years, since then, my life has become rich with friendships, each connection a blessing on my life's journey. From childhood cousins who doubled as my first playmates to the countless bonds forged in the crucible of work assignments, from the serendipity of social encounters to family members who have become cherished friends, these relationships have all painted my world with joy.

Some friendships endure despite years of silence, their memories aglow with warmth. Reconnecting after long gaps feels like unearthing buried treasure—time may have weathered us, but the spark remains. Two such gems are Jess and Lisa, friends from my teens and early twenties. After I moved to Atlanta, our contact faded to yearly Christmas cards, a faint whisper of connection. Then, during a work trip to Boston in my forties, they joined me for a reunion that crackled with delight, laughter spilling over like wine at a long-awaited feast. Every few years, we rekindle that flame, each gathering a testament to bonds that defy time's erosion.

I've marveled, too, at reunions with cousins and other dear friends, awestruck by how the years have sculpted us into new shapes while our shared roots hold firm. I'm deeply grateful for the enduring friendships with my former stepfamily, although our get-togethers are less frequent than before.

But not all friendships last, and their endings sometimes carry a quiet sting, an ache we're rarely taught to navigate. Unlike romantic breakups, with their fiery confrontations or tear-streaked farewells, friendships often dissolve in whispers, leaving a bruise that throbs in silence. The saying "people enter your life for a reason, a season, or a lifetime" sounds tidy, but when a friend fades without explanation, the wound cuts deep. I've stood on both sides of that divide: the one who drifted away, leaving pain in my wake, and the one left staring at an unanswered text, the silence roaring like a storm in my ears.

The loss of those friendships stung, like a sudden frost sweeping through a sunlit garden. I mourned the music of their voices, the warmth of their presence. But clutching that grief, letting it fester, robbed me of the present's light. Eckhart Tolle's *The Power of Now* became my compass, teaching me that grief is human, but grudges are chains. Forgiveness—of others and of myself—became my key, not to erase the hurt but to let peace settle like embers after a fire. Tolle's wisdom on boundaries struck me like lightning. If I set boundaries with anger, they breed pain, but if I set them with clarity and remain rooted in the truth of what serves me in present time, they offer freedom. Looking back, I recall how I once fled friendships in a haze of frustration, especially when someone's actions would skip and replay in my mind like a scratched vinyl record. But simply cutting ties didn't banish my anger—the anger continued to shadow me. Now, I have learned to draw boundaries with a steady purpose, like tracing a line in the sand under a clear sky, my heart unburdened and light.

I've learned that a crowded circle isn't the goal. Some friends are meant for a season, their presence a brilliant flare, bright but fleeting. Letting go isn't forgetting; it's standing in the now, heart open, ready for new connections while honoring the echoes of friendships past. Each, whether a reason or a season, has shaped me, their laughter and lessons etched into my bones, illuminating the path forward.

My current community in Florida has sparked a joy I never anticipated. These friendships have bloomed like wildflowers. At our neighborhood's lively "Bahama Bar," I found soul siblings in Rene and Kim, kindred spirits whose bond feels like destiny. Other neighbors too have grown into friends, our shared spaces and spirited community events igniting meaningful connections. Our "Fri-Yay Fundays" with the paddling and kayak crew are bursts of pure delight—gliding across shimmering waters, trading stories as the sun dances on the waves, chasing fleeting glimpses of dolphins and manatees. Beyond the neighborhood, unexpected connections, such as the one I found with my now dear friend Chelsea, have blossomed into heartwarming friendships, anchoring me with every shared laugh and adventure. Each moment whispers, *You're home.*

⋮

36

Unleashing Boundless Love: Finding Joy in a Childless Path

Though I never bore my own, my heart has always swelled for the children in my life. Their wide-eyed wonder and unfiltered joy fill me with a warmth that feels like sunlight breaking through clouds. I love diving into their world—sprawling on the floor, giggling through silly games, or curling up with a picture book and watching their faces light up as I read, their laughter a melody. Babies, oh, babies—they're my burst of light. Their soft, velvety skin with that sweet, powdery scent, their innocent coos as they nestle in my arms—it's like holding a tiny miracle, my heart brimming with tenderness and awe.

Despite this, I never felt the fierce pull toward motherhood that others describe. Fear held me back—though not of children, but of myself. I worried I'd either swing too far from my own strict upbringing, overcompensating with leniency, or worse, mirror its control, stifling my child's spirit. I needed to learn love's depths—its patience, its freedom—before I could pass it on. Reflecting now, I see my path was meant to unfold this way, childless but rich with connection. I kept the possibility of adoption in my heart, even past childbearing years, a quiet option I never closed off. But I've found peace, trusting life's design for me.

I'm also blessed with several nieces and nephews, each a bright star in my sky. Though miles apart, being Auntie Marsh is a role I cherish. I've watched them grow—from toddling first steps to striding into adulthood—cheering at their milestones often from afar, my heart swelling with pride. Now, as a Great-Auntie to two precious little ones who call me Auntie Marshie, I'm smitten anew. It's such a treat to watch their personalities developing. I marvel at my niece's mothering abilities; she's patient, fanning the flame of her children's curious little minds, exposing them to nature with reverence and awe. I often remind myself to emulate the gift of childlike freedom and unreserved joy that shines through their faces and actions.

During my years in Atlanta, I formed a special bond with three incredible kids—children of Ang and her husband Bill who lived in a neighboring city. I held each as a newborn, their warmth in my arms a memory etched in my soul. Watching them blossom felt like witnessing magic. They each developed in their own unique way, going from shy dreamers to survivors of their teenage years and then on to finding their passions. They'll always hold a sacred place in my life.

During my marriage to Rob, his children and grandchildren stole my heart, and I loved them as fiercely as if they were my own. Stepping into the stepmother role was a delicate dance, especially since I was actually so close to his kids' age that our connection was almost more like a sisterhood. I moved through it with love, sometimes stumbling, but always striving to show up fully. I cherished their milestones—cradling grandkids for their first baths, their tiny, slippery bodies warm in my arms. Family vacations were a mixture of joy and chaos: beach days alive with sandcastles and sunburns, one trip cut short by hurricane winds and the faint tremor of an earthquake. In a lakeside cabin, a storm cut our power, but the kids' triumphant cheers over their first caught fish lit up the darkness. Holiday gatherings, countless and sparkling, filled my heart—Christmas lights twinkling like stars, Thanksgiving tables laden with turkey and trimmings, birthday candles flickering as we sang, voices joyfully off-key. Each moment is a cherished gem, a treasure of watching them grow into their own. When Rob and I parted, the kids' question pierced me: "Will we still see my Marcia?" Thanks to Rob's grace, the answer was a resounding yes. Their presence remains a gift I hold with endless gratitude, woven forever into my life's story.

In my loneliest moments, I questioned my choice. The quiet of an empty house could amplify doubts, whispering, *What if?* Friends sometimes chalked it up to my career's demands, the road-warrior life of consulting. Maybe. I could've found a local job and balanced motherhood if I'd chosen it. But when I married Rob, who was open to having more kids, I'd already leaned toward a different path. His illness cemented it—I became the sole breadwinner, my focus necessarily on work. Yet, each time doubt crept in, peace returned like a tide. Love, I've learned, isn't bound by blood. It's in the nieces and nephews who call me Auntie, the friends' children who light up my home, the step-grandkids who still claim me as theirs. My life is full, not despite my choices, but because of them—a thriving mix of connection, built on love's boundless reach.

For those like me who don't have the longing, or for those who are unable to conceive, just know that there are other joys in life that, while they don't fully replace, can offer delight.

I've learned that love transcends biology, weaving a rich tapestry of chosen family bonds. Trusting my unique path has brought a profound peace, proving that fulfillment lies in honoring what feels true. And in the unfiltered joy of children, I find a spark to stay playful and curious, their wonder reminding me to embrace life's simple delights, one moment at a time.

37

Bound by Love: Grateful for Sibling Connections and Brotherly Bonds

'm the lucky middle child in a colorful family quilt—stitched between an older sister and brother and a younger brother and sister. Growing up, I didn't feel tightly bonded to my siblings. I'd poke at my brothers, tossing teasing words or inventing mischievous antics to provoke them, these sparks of mischief a bid for their attention in disguise. But somehow, of course, I was the one who'd end up in hot water, their laughter or scolding leaving me sulking. Still, glimmers of joy flicker in my memory—shared moments now softened by time, like old photos tucked in a drawer.

WENDY: A BEACON OF CARE

Wendy, my older sister by four years, shines like a steady lighthouse. A kind, hardworking nurse, she sailed through our strict upbringing with a calm I envied, never seeming as rattled by the rules that chafed me. A straight-A student, she set a bar so high that teachers sighed when I didn't quite reach it. We weren't cut from the same cloth, but her caring always found me. One Christmas, she surprised me with a bike, its shiny frame a symbol of her thoughtfulness. I'd barge into her room, full of chatter, and though I must've driven her up the wall, she never shooed me away. I still smile thinking of us as kids, fresh from our first funeral, when I innocently asked her who the "lady in the bed" was; her patient answer was a quiet gift.

When I was scraping by in my early days, Wendy's small sums of money given to me from out of her modest nurse's paycheck glowed with her generosity. She later wove a beautiful life with her husband, raising two incredible kids. After a brief chapter in Atlanta, they settled in Dallas, where I enjoyed visiting their family for many holidays.

Later in her life, Wendy faced her own storms that shook her world, forcing her to pause and unravel the beliefs we'd been raised with. In her forties, she was ready to confront the religious and cultural hooks that had never snagged her before and handled it with a grace that made my heart swell with pride. She later shared with me, humbly, that she finally understood all the questions that I'd wrestled with as a kid. That moment stitched us closer together. I know she'd move mountains for me, and I'd do the same.

ROG: A STEADY FLAME

Childhood memories of Rog, my big brother by two and a half years, burn bright, like a campfire on a crisp night. Growing up, he was all in on both sports and school. He was a whirlwind of focus who also dodged trouble with ease. We weren't thick as thieves back then—our paths diverged like trails in a forest—but I always felt the quiet warmth of his care. He built his family young, tying his heart to them with a love that glowed fierce and steady. We didn't see each other often in those early years of his parenthood; our visits were like rare sparks flying from a fire. But over the last decade, those embers have grown into a steady blaze.

Rog is a rock—a devoted dad, and now grandpa, whose gentle kindness wraps his family like a soft flannel blanket. I marvel at the fierce love in his eyes, a lion's heart paired with a tender touch. A hard worker with a soul tethered to nature, he chases life's pulse through long bike rides that cut through rolling hills, runs that weave past whispering pines, and winter skiing or snowshoeing that carve paths through the snow-covered hills.

In the past years, our bond has deepened, like roots stretching further into rich soil. We share late-night talks, unraveling the twists of career shifts, relationships, and the weight of our strict upbringing. Getting to know him as an adult has been a gift, like discovering a hidden meadow bursting with color. He's kind, always loving, his heart a wide-open door. Visiting him and his family feels like stepping into a warm hearth; when he comes to my place, it's like the arrival of sunlight breaking through clouds. While we both love the wild—me drawn to the ocean's rhythmic crash, him to the mountains' rugged embrace—he thrives better than I do in the bite of cold weather when frost sharpens the air.

Rog is never more than a text or call away, his friendship steady and loving, his deep care a blessing. His genuine heart lights up my world, and I'm endlessly grateful for the brother who's become one of my closest allies.

STEVE: MY ANCHOR IN A SEA OF STARS

I've never had a single "best" girlfriend, but instead, a constellation of incredible women who've lit up my life—some from childhood and others from my Atlanta days, work adventures, or my new community. Some friendships were like shooting stars, dazzling for a season before fading with distance or changing paths. I still cherish them, knowing we could reconnect and pick up right where we left off, hearts in sync. But through every tide, one person has been my unshakable anchor: my brother Steve.

Steve is my safe harbor, the one I can bare my soul to without fear. He listens with an open heart, supports without judgment, and loves with a warmth that feels like a sun-soaked afternoon. I often wonder how I'd have navigated life without him—thankfully, I've never had to find out.

Our time together is a kaleidoscope of joy. We've danced at concerts under neon lights, cheered at baseball games, hiked trails where the earth hummed beneath our feet, kayaked through shimmering waters, and explored cities bursting with life. We've sipped wine at vineyards, leapt from bungee platforms with hearts racing, lazed for hours on sandy beaches, battled it out in croquet matches, and twirled through dance floors. Countless meals and bottles of wine have fueled our endless conversations, each moment a thread weaving us closer.

One Saturday morning, I was lounging on my couch, still waking up to the day, when Steve called. "I have something to tell you," he said, his voice steady. I leaned in, curious. "I'm coming out. I'm gay." The words hit like a lightning bolt. I hadn't seen it coming—he was just about to turn thirty. My mind raced, hoping I'd never said anything hurtful about anyone's identity. I hadn't, he assured me, his chuckle easing the moment. But my heart ached: How had he carried this truth for all these years in our rigid family and church? He brushed it off with a laugh, saying it wasn't a big deal—though, by the way, he'd loved watching the male skaters during the Olympics. He'd known since he was six, he said, a truth tucked quietly in his heart.

I remembered him dating a stunning woman in his early twenties. When I asked what that was like, he said he'd tried to love women, could've made it work, but his heart didn't spark for them— not like it would for a man. I was floored that I hadn't suspected.

Steve, with his warm, masculine energy, didn't fit any stereotype I might've imagined. I was just grateful he was stepping into his truth, shedding the weight of secrecy.

Steve is a burst of light—gregarious, kind, making everyone he meets feel like they're glowing. After moving to San Francisco, he then wandered to Seattle near our brother Rog and spent a few months in Arizona before anchoring in Alaska for years. One winter, he jetted to New Zealand and met Pete, his now-husband. The only downside? Steve would eventually move to New Zealand for good. But my joy for him—and for myself in gaining Pete as a bonus brother—outweighed the distance.

Steve and I vowed to see each other yearly, the burden greater on him than me, and until COVID, we did. He'd cross oceans to visit the States, meeting me in Hawaii's turquoise embrace, at my homes in Atlanta and Florida, in California's golden glow, on Mexico's sandy beaches, or in the midst of New York's electric hum. Other times, we'd rendezvous in Maine, Vermont, or Iowa to see family. But in his company, each trip was a new adventure.

I'll never forget traveling to New Zealand for Steve and Pete's commitment ceremony. It was pure magic, held at their lodge in Golden Bay, where the beach stretched like a silver ribbon under a springtime sky and red roses blazed along the property, a fiery backdrop to their love. Rog had flown in to join us as well, and we danced under the stars, celebrating their unbreakable bond. When New Zealand's laws later allowed same-sex marriage, I initially questioned why it mattered—my old-school roots clung to the idea of marriage as a man-woman bond. But Steve and Pete's perspective opened my eyes. It wasn't just about legalities like medical decisions; it was about honoring their love with the same dignity. They deserved that, and I cheered for it.

Though I wish I could see Steve and Pete more, our love nevertheless blooms across the miles. I've returned to New Zealand three times, each visit a whirlwind of laughter and connection. Steve's my translator when Kiwi slang leaves me puzzled, his grin lighting the way. He's my rock, my brother, my forever friend, and his heart keeps mine shining, no matter the distance.

ROSIE: A RAY OF RESILIENCE

Rose, my little sister who is nine years younger, sparkles like a firecracker, bursting with life. Way back when, upon learning Mom was pregnant again, our house buzzed with excitement, like a hive humming with anticipation. I can still see myself at that time, folding soft cloth diapers for baby Rosie, her tiny giggles filling the air like music. She was always a bundle of joy—sweet, outgoing, a sunbeam in human form. But my memories of her early years are more like scattered snapshots, blurred at the edges. As she grew, I became caught in my own storm, questioning everything, lost in the swirl of my own thoughts. With our age gap, it's almost like Rosie danced through her youth as an only child, a solitary planet in her own orbit.

Rosie's life has been a canvas of highs and lows, painted with courage. She became pregnant young, too young to feel ready to raise a child. With grace, she chose an open adoption, a gift that kept our niece woven into the fabric of our family from the start. A few years later she gave birth to another beautiful baby girl. Then, one Thanksgiving, a phone call shattered our world: Rosie's six-month-old daughter had passed from SIDS. The news hit like a tidal wave, leaving us gasping in its wake. My heart aches for her, for the unfathomable grief she still carries, a shadow that lingers in her quiet moments.

Yet Rosie's spirit is a phoenix. Years later, she found the love of her life, a partner who lights up her world. Together, they're raising a beautiful daughter, a girl who sparkles like her mother. Rosie holds a tender, unshakable place in my heart, her resilience a flame that warms me. I care for her deeply, forever awed by the way she rises, shining through every storm.

Sibling bonds, like the roots of a mighty tree, may need time to grow deep, but now their strength can weather any storm. Cherish the moments—big or small—that tie you to those who share your history. Your special people may not always be close in distance, but their love, laughter, and shared stories can light your path, reminding you that family is a quilt of connection, stitched with resilience and grace.

⋮

38

From Fear's Chains to Love's Embrace: My Soul's Path to Healing

At twenty-five, having just moved to Atlanta and curious about the soul of the South, I slipped into the pews of a few local churches, hoping to find a spiritual home that resonated more than the rigid doctrines of The Kingdom, within which I'd been raised. The music in these churches was alive—guitars strumming upbeat contemporary melodies, voices rising in joyful harmony under the glow of stained glass. For a moment, I would feel a spark of inspiration, a pull toward something new. But then the sermons roared in—Baptist preachers thundering about hellfire and brimstone in a way that reminded me of sermons I'd heard in The Kingdom, their words heavy with fear. My body tensed, recoiling as if stung. The hypocrisy stung too: Sunday services felt like a social checkbox, an hour-long ritual before people dusted off their faith and returned to their lives unchanged. Disillusioned, I kept searching.

In those early Atlanta years, I found an anchor in Katherine, my therapist, whose steady presence guided me through the wreckage of my brief but difficult first marriage. More than that, she helped me unravel the knots of my past from my upbringing in The Kingdom, knots I later understood as post-cult trauma syndrome, a form of PTSD. Her office, with its soft lighting and comfy chairs, became a sanctuary where I began to peel back layers of fear. Slowly, I discovered not just who I was beneath the conditioning but also why I was here and what it meant to live freely. Each session felt like shedding a heavy coat, the weight of old beliefs falling away as I stepped into a lighter, truer version of myself.

Years later, in my forties, I faced another lingering shadow: Fairwood, the place where I'd grown up, steeped in the oppressive grip of The Kingdom. I'd visited once in my thirties, driving up from New York with Rob to show him where I was raised. The long, winding driveway stretched before me like a portal to another life, and as I approached, anxiety clamped my chest. The air felt thick with old memories—control, fear, isolation. I didn't even step out of the car, just drove through, the landscape foreign and unwelcoming. It was no home, just a relic of a life I'd left behind.

But in my forties, I knew I had to return, this time alone, to confront it fully. I flew into Manchester airport, rented a car, and drove toward Fairwood under a brilliant blue sky, the sun casting golden rays across rolling New Hampshire hills. Memories flickered—childhood games, strict rules, the weight of expectation—but they didn't grip me. As I pulled into the driveway, Fairwood appeared diminished, its once-imposing buildings now small, weathered, and faded. The power it held over me was gone, dissolved like mist. I drove past the lake where we used to swim, its surface sparkling in the sunlight, and felt a quiet relief. Good memories surfaced, soft and untainted, and I left with closure, the oppression finally buried . . . or so I thought.

But Fairwood wasn't done with me yet. In October 2019, I returned for a relative's funeral, and the journey tested me. On the flight to New Hampshire, a delayed connection cost me my upgraded seat, and I found myself wedged in a middle seat at the back of the plane. The discomfort was trivial, but it cracked something open. Sobs poured out, uncontrollable, as waves of anxiety about returning to Fairwood and seeing so many people from my past crashed over me. It wasn't about the seat—it was the dread of facing that place again, its echoes still lingering in my bones. I thought I had closure from my last visit, but something stirred up in me again. I couldn't name it.

The next morning, I met my niece for breakfast at a cozy café, the smell of coffee and a plate of eggs over avocado toast grounding me. Her warmth and our shared camaraderie wrapped me in courage, steadying my heart for the day ahead. The funeral, though, was a marathon—a three-hour religious service that felt like a time warp back to The Kingdom's rigid dogma. Stories and sermons swirled, disconnected from my own truth, and I sat there practicing the art of witnessing without judgment, refusing to let the ego flare or make anyone wrong. Afterward, I lingered briefly, reconnecting with family and old friends under the shadow of Fairwood's faded halls. Their faces were a bittersweet gift, but the air still felt heavy, and I couldn't wait to escape.

Later, over dinner with my brother Rog, who had also attended and shared similar reactions, we spilled the day's emotions, the conversation easing the weight. We debriefed, laughed, and made sense of it all. The next morning, I drove to the airport under a soft dawn light, the road stretching ahead like a promise of peace, my heart finally at rest. I've learned that it's okay when triggers from my past surface and that it's more important to remember not to stay discouraged or weighed down by them. I now have the tools to face them head-on and then move forward.

SPIRITUAL TEACHERS

Over the years, I've stumbled upon and been drawn to a variety of healers and spiritual teachers whose words weren't shackled by dogma. Their teachings—gentle, expansive, rooted in love—lit a fire in my soul, offering the clarity I'd been chasing. I know this has been God answering my cries. Many times, I felt the presence of angels or Spirit. I felt comforted and loved, cradled and safe, rejoicing. Each encounter—through books, talks, or quiet moments of reflection—felt like a step toward peace, their voices soothing the jagged edges of my past.

Yet, beneath the inspiration, a restless searching stirred. I was chasing something elusive—a final release from the heavy chains of the patriarchal, oppressive religion I'd been raised in, a path to true spiritual freedom. I couldn't name it or picture it. It was like trying to grasp a dream upon waking. Looking back, I see now that fear still lingered, woven into my bones by the well-meaning family and church members who introduced me to a God I couldn't understand—a God who seemed to emanate judgment, ready to punish. The idea of a Creator who crafted us only to demand endless repentance for our humanity felt like a knot I could never untie. It clashed with the stirrings of my soul, leaving me adrift.

In my quest, I began to reshape the Divine in my mind, letting go of the stern "God" of my childhood. Instead, I leaned into softer names—Spirit, Source, Universe—each one a gentle exhale, distancing me from the weight of old memories. These names felt expansive, like a wide-open sky over a sunlit field, free of the thunderclouds of guilt and sacrifice. Still, the past clung to me, its echoes whispering doubts even as I sought clarity.

In 2014, a new light appeared in my life in the form of Gabrielle Bernstein, a spiritual teacher whose soulful energy and grounded wisdom pulled me in. Her books became companions, their pages dog-eared and underlined, brimming with messages that felt like they were written just for me. Through her, I had my first glimpse of the teachings of *A Course in Miracles*, a spiritual metaphysical text transcribed in the 1970s. However, I didn't dive into the *Course* itself at the time; I barely knew its depth. But Gabby's interpretations, threaded through as they were with themes of returning to love and choosing love over fear, were just what I craved.

The exercises, affirmations, and meditations from her book *Miracles Now* became my daily rituals, like morning coffee for my soul. The subtitle of the book indicated what I ultimately found within: *108 Life-Changing Tools for Less Stress, More Flow, and Finding Your True Purpose.* As I began to incorporate these tools into my life, I found that they made my days much more peaceful. Some of them helped me relieve stress in the moment of a challenge at work or to find a better way to react to difficult personalities. Others encouraged me simply to sit cross-legged on the couch in my bedroom, while sunlight streamed through the window, repeating her affirmations. These practices steadied me. They helped guide me through the chaos of daily life and offered a framework that softened the still tight grip of my upbringing. Even now, those tools remain anchors, helping me navigate moments of doubt or fear. Gabby is indeed a gifted spiritual teacher who has touched my soul.

I first came across Michael Singer a few years after he wrote his first book, *The Untethered Soul: The Journey Beyond Yourself.* I was fascinated by the information, but it was a lot to take in. I resonated with so much of it, as he is a phenomenal writer who shares his conclusions about life based on his own journey. He clearly articulates the differences between our mind, our heart, our body, and the ego. He prompts us to pay attention to what is going on inside, what we are perceiving, and how we react to external events, urging us to remember that there is a more peaceful way to live. I keep coming back to *The Untethered Soul,* and as I reread it each time, I have additional ahas that are life-transforming. He is one of the first authors I'd come across who could cite references from the Bible and the message of Christ in a context that made perfect sense to me.

And then when *Living Untethered: Beyond the Human Predicament* came out in 2022, my eyes were opened in an even more dramatic way. He explains the way that creation and evolution align to both science and principles in the Bible, something that I really didn't understand previously. Quite frankly, thanks to my upbringing, I had no idea what to believe about creation and evolution. We were taught to believe that evolution was an evil, man-made phenomenon that went against our Creator. And since most anything scientific goes over my head, these ideas had been difficult for me to sort out or defend.

Yet, for all the peace these teachers brought, I knew a shadow still lingered. The weight of how I was raised—its rigid doctrines, its fear-based God—hadn't fully dissolved. It was as if I'd cleared the surface of a lake but could still feel currents swirling below, pulling at me. I carried on with my life, inspired but not entirely free. I sensed that deeper healing awaited me, ready to unfold when the time was right.

CHOOSING DAILY—LOVE OVER FEAR

In 2023, the 4th of July rolled around, and I was feeling excited to join friends at a favorite beach nearby. The day promised sandy toes, ice-cold drinks, and the kind of carefree joy only a holiday by the water can deliver. But as I circled the crowded lots, the sun blazing through my windshield, my heart sank—there was absolutely no parking, not a single spot, and I didn't want to keep waiting. Frustration bubbled up, souring my mood as I turned my car toward home, the steering wheel hot under my hands. The thought of spending the holiday alone hurt, and a heavy emotional cloud settled over me. Then, with a whisper of instinct, I remembered I could take myself to another place that always felt like a refuge: a bookstore. The quiet aisles, the scent of fresh pages, and the promise of discovery never failed to lift my spirits. So, I veered off course, pulling into the lot of the trusted Barnes & Noble, its windows glowing with warm light even against the glare of the bright summer day.

Inside, the air was cool, the shelves brimming with stories waiting to be found. I wandered, running my fingers along book spines, hoping for something to pull me out of my funk. That's when I saw it: *The Course in Miracles Experiment* by Pam Grout, its orange cover bold and inviting, practically calling my name. I didn't know it then, but this wasn't a random find—it was a moment of synchronicity, a gift from the Universe. I grabbed the book, then, back at home, settled into a comfy chair on my lanai to crack it open.

From the first page, I was hooked. I was unable to put it down, even though it was structured as a daily guide, meant to be savored one lesson at a time over a full year. Pam's voice leapt off the page—authentic, raw, and funny, like a wise friend spilling her heart over coffee. Her stories of grappling with a fundamentalist upbringing and a fear-based God mirrored my own so closely, it felt like she was speaking directly to me. Her humor sparkled, her vulnerability disarmed me, and her wisdom landed like a soft but seismic shift in my soul. This book was a jewel, glinting with truth and possibility.

Pam's take on *A Course in Miracles* brought its lessons to life with a down-to-earth vibrancy. Each daily lesson was a masterful brushstroke, painting a new way to see the world. Her interpretations were rich, grounded, and artfully told, like stories shared around a campfire, full of wit and heart. I've read it multiple times since that day, turning to its lessons as a daily practice, a ritual as vital as my morning coffee. Each lesson peels back the curtain on the ego's chatter in my mind, revealing its illusions and nudging me back to love. The core truth it shares hit me again like a clear bell:

If it's not love, it's fear. No gray area, no exceptions. This simple choice became a lens for everything—how I speak to myself in quiet moments, how I move through the world, and how I treat others, whether in fleeting encounters or deep connections.

Slowly, the book's teachings began to unravel the deep-rooted belief from my childhood that God was a fearful judge, destined to punish. In its place, a new understanding bloomed, vibrant and alive: God as love, as Source, with an intention for me—and for all of us—to live in joy, no matter what we believe. Coming to this understanding was like watching dawn break over a dark horizon, the light soft but unstoppable, warming every corner of my being. The book became a companion, its pages worn from use, its lessons a daily invitation to choose love, again and again.

A COURSE IN MIRACLES

In June 2024, emboldened by the undeniable clarity I'd found at the Ziva Sacred Secret retreat in Costa Rica—where jungle air sang with possibility and mornings glowed with sunrise meditations—I felt a spark to revisit *A Course in Miracles*. I'd bought the original text months before, its thick, navy-blue cover waiting for me on my book-shelf like an unopened challenge. I'd cracked it open once after I'd first purchased it, only to feel overwhelmed by its dense pages, its patriarchal tone echoing the Bible's stern masculinity. It reminded me too much of the fear-based religion of my childhood, so I'd shoved it aside, untouched. But now, thanks to the retreat's trans-formative energy, I was ready to dive in, setting aside my judgments about its lack of feminine references. I had no idea how profoundly it would reshape my world.

Each morning, I'd settle on a stool in my kitchen, sunlight streaming into the lanai, the water bowl fountains in my pool provid-ing a soothing ambience. With my freshly brewed coffee in hand, I'd open the *Course*, its pages dense but alive with promise. I devoured the text and daily lessons, not as a chore but as a treasure hunt, each paragraph a map to answers I'd sought for years. The words washed over me like a cool stream, bringing peace and clarity about my purpose, the world's purpose, religion, God—everything. I began to see God's will and my will as one, a shimmering thread connecting me to my true self, to who I was meant to be. The *Course* didn't just answer questions; it dissolved them, replacing doubt with a quiet, unshakable knowing.

The text unraveled mysteries from my past, questions that had haunted me about the Bible—sin, sacrifice, and the idea of "unhealed healers" who preached without living their truth. I had no desire to spar with the kinds of theologians whose arguments seemed to tower like fortress walls. But I had long craved a deeper understanding of God that went beyond the fear-soaked sermons of my youth. The *Course* delivered, its messages landing like lightning bolts of truth.

One passage struck me like a bell: "A church that does not inspire love has a hidden altar that is not serving the purpose for which God intended it." I could almost hear the echo of my child-hood church—creaking under the weight of fear, doom, and gloom, with preachers thundering "Resist the devil!" and "Repent!" with unyielding authority. The fear those messages instilled in me had trapped me in a cage, then this single line set me free, affirming what my heart had always known.

Growing up, I'd been taught that if you were a member of our church, you were part of an elite group, the chosen ones destined for God's Kingdom, while everyone else—other Christians, Muslims, Jews, nonbelievers—was "worldly" and wicked. The *Course* also shattered the lingering vestiges of that illusion, painting a vision of unity under a loving Creator. I pictured an expansive, glowing circle, every soul woven together, radiant with equality.

Another line stopped me in my tracks: "You cannot know your own perfection until you have honored all those who were created like you." You mean, every single person? Holy cow, even someone like my grandfather Abram, whose elitist, manipulative ways had cast long shadows over so many members? The *Course* answered: "Those who attack do not know they are blessed. They attack because they believe they are deprived." Suddenly, the world's pain and hate made sense to me in a way it never had before—not as something evil, but as cries from those who'd forgotten their own light. I sat at my kitchen island, journal in hand, staring out at the preserve in my backyard, letting that truth sink in.

In many ways, my family's generational story is one of feeling unworthy, insecure, never enough. The *Course* countered with a breathtaking truth: "To accept your littleness is arrogant, because it means that you believe your evaluation of yourself is truer than God's." I gasped when I first read this, my pen hovering over the page. God, the very Creator who'd spun galaxies into being, cared for my smallest breath and saw me as perfect. "All religion is the recognition that the irreconcilable cannot be reconciled. . . . Sickness and perfection are irreconcilable. If God created you perfect, you are perfect." This shifted everything. I thought of my family's pain, the lack of love they'd endured, and felt a wave of compassion for my upbringing. Even the voices that had told me I wasn't perfect—"fix your wrinkles," "fix this or that"—faded against God's truth. I wasn't broken; I was part of His holy creation, as was everyone else. The *Course* invited me to live big, beautifully, unabashedly—loving myself and every soul I met, despite the human struggle to do so.

One passage became my anthem: "Your Self does not need salvation, but your mind needs to learn what salvation is. You are not saved from anything, but you are saved for glory. Glory is your inheritance, given you by your Creator that you might extend it." I imagined standing in a field, arms wide, bathed in golden light, claiming that glory. Another lesson clarified free will: "You have but two emotions, and one you made and one was given you. Each is a way of seeing, and different worlds arise from their different sights." This is free will. The choice between love and fear shaped everything—my thoughts, others' actions, the world itself.

The *Course*'s vision of peace was a masterpiece to me: "For peace is the acknowledgment of perfect purity, from which no one is excluded. Within its holy circle is everyone who God created as His Son. Joy is its unifying attribute, with no one left outside to suffer guilt alone. The power of God draws everyone to its safe embrace of love and union. Stand quietly within this circle, and attract all tortured minds to join with you in the safety of its peace and holiness." Again, I pictured a circle—vast, radiant, exploding with joy—enfolding every soul, from strangers in my neighborhood to my grandfather, lost in his pain. Each morning, as I read from the text, I stepped into that circle. The *Course*'s words became a daily ritual grounding me in love, guiding me to live boldly as part of God's perfect creation.

GRATEFUL FOR ANSWERS AND PEACE

Now each morning I rise, then settle into my place at my kitchen island, opening my worn copy of *A Course in Miracles*, its navy-blue cover softened from months of use. The text, the teacher's manual, and the daily exercises have become steady companions, their pages alive with a wisdom that shifts and deepens with every read. As I write this, I'm on my second complete journey through, still uncovering hidden gems in a familiar forest. Every line sparks something new—a fresh insight, a clearer truth—lighting up corners of my soul I hadn't seen before.

The process of separating God from the rigid scaffolding of religion has been like stepping out of a shadowed chapel into a sunlit meadow. It all makes sense now that I understand God as love, and not the fearful judge of my childhood sermons. This clarity feels like a cool breeze on a sweltering Florida day, freeing me from the weight of those old doctrines. My daily practice is a sacred ritual, grounding me in this truth. I start with meditation, sitting cross-legged on my comfy lanai chair while the birds singing their choruses, sweet and shrill. My breath slows, syncing with the rhythm of my heartbeat, as I sink into stillness, letting love wash over me like a gentle tide. Then comes my gratitude prayer, whispered softly. I give thanks for the light in my life—for all of Creation, for the blessings and guidance I have received, grateful to live this beautiful earthly life.

Journaling follows as I wait for my coffee to brew, my pen dancing across the pages of a leather-bound notebook, capturing thoughts as they spill out. I set intentions for the day, writing them like promises to myself: *Today, I choose love over fear.* I seek guidance from the Holy Spirit—*Show me what to do, how it will unfold, who I should connect with.* The words feel like seeds planted in fertile soil, each one moving me toward living fully in love.

I'm painfully aware that fear still creeps in, sneaky and familiar, almost daily, whenever the human ego climbs into the driver's seat. It's like a storm cloud rolling over a clear sky, casting shadows of doubt or judgment. In those moments, after I've taken some deep breaths, or come back from my daily walk, I picture God waiting patiently, a gentle presence just beyond the haze, arms open with love and forgiveness. All I need to do is turn back, to choose love again. And when I do, it's as if the clouds part, and peace rushes in like a river of light, warm and golden, flooding my heart. The world sharpens—colors seem brighter, sounds seem clearer, my steps seem lighter—as I move through the day carried by that divine current, anchored in the certainty that love is always there, waiting for me to return.

⋮

39

Surrender's Sacred Dance: Healing Through Forgiveness and Love

After closing the chapter on my thirty-five-year career in financial services and consulting, I stepped into a new groove, leaving behind the relentless churn of corporate life. The world suddenly felt wide open. I sketched loose plans for the next few months, and then each month, a gentle guide for the weeks ahead.

After the first month of joy and the second of profound healing, I decided the third month would be dedicated to pure, unbridled fun. The freedom to shape each day in the way my heart desired felt like a burst of color in my soul. I'd wake to sunlight spilling through my curtains, free to decide whether I would meet friends at the beach, go for a bike ride, or simply chill at home with a great book by the pool. It was a glorious, untethered time, a gift that rekindled a childlike joy.

I thought the next month would shift to action, my old corporate reflexes kicking in. I could almost hear the sharp clack of keyboards, the demands of the deadlines that once defined me. I scribbled a list of milestones—tasks, goals, achievements—my pen moving with the familiar itch to conquer. But as I stared at the page, something else stirred in me. I realized that the urge to charge ahead, to measure my worth in checklists, was beginning to feel more like an ill-fitting suit. So I turned inward, seeking guidance from Spirit. I determined that each morning, I'd settle into my favorite chair and journal my intentions: *Guide me today, Holy Spirit. Let my path unfold.* I let life flow like a river finding its course, trusting it would lead me to my truth. The ability to live this way—without fixed plans, open to divine whispers—was a blessing, a grace I held close with gratitude.

For thirty-five years, my journey had been one of action. I'd poured my heart into my career, driven by a need to climb, to succeed, to prove I was enough in a world that seemed to demand proof. That hustle shaped my identity, as I came up with game-changing ideas for my industry, managed client programs, drafted proposals, met every goal, sealed every deal with a sharp nod.

So it was revealed to me that my mission for the next month was to be bold in a new way—to become the truest and most joyful version of myself. Of course this wouldn't be a quick transformation; it demanded deeper healing. The grind of corporate life had left its mark on me—stress was woven into my bones, and I knew I had to break the habit of valuing completed tasks over joy savored. And my past, with its rigid, fear-soaked upbringing, still cast its faint shadows on my life. Healing became my quiet work, unfolding in moments of reflection, pen in hand, as I faced old wounds.

FORGIVING, FIRST MYSELF

I'd begun writing this book during my month of joy in May 2024. But several months in, as my writing stirred old memories and unearthed shame that sometimes surged like a sudden storm, I had to pause, trembling as old feelings roared. Forgiveness became the cornerstone of the healing I needed most, a soft flame I lit first for myself. While sitting at my kitchen island or walking in my neighborhood, I'd whisper forgiveness for mistakes I'd made, choices I regretted, moments I stumbled. Some days, the weight was too much; I'd have to set the document aside, tuck it onto a mental shelf, and find my way back to love. I'd light a candle in the afternoon, its warm glow dancing on the walls with incense burning on my altar, and meditate, letting love flood through me. In those moments, often with tears streaming down my face, I forgave myself again, knowing each step—however shaky—was part of becoming the radiant, whole version of myself I was always meant to be.

The words from *A Course in Miracles* resonated so deeply in my spirit: "Ask not to be forgiven, for this has already been accomplished. Ask, rather, to learn how to forgive." I sat with that truth in the quiet of my living room. The enormity of it felt like a wave crashing over me, powerful and clear, washing away years of tangled guilt. It was as if the Universe had whispered a secret I'd always known but never heard: Forgiveness wasn't something to beg for—it was already mine. My task was to learn how to extend it, to let it flow like a river from my heart. This realization sent me down a path of surrender and forgiveness, a journey both daunting and luminous, like stepping into a forest where every shadow hid a lesson and every clearing promised peace.

Surrender puzzled me—what did it mean to let go of a lifetime's burdens? I imagined standing at the sea's edge, where the horizon stretched boundless and blue, my arms weighed down by the regrets, fears, and insecurities I was carrying, clutching them all like weathered stones. Surrender, then, was trusting that the soft, powdery sand would cradle my bare feet as I cast each stone into the churning waves, watching them sink into the depths. Forgiving myself became the first step of a process that felt like peeling back layers of an onion, each one stinging with raw truth.

I'd sit at my desk with my journal open to write. The force

urging me to dig deep was undeniable, like a gentle but insistent hand on my shoulder, guiding me to open my heart. I faced what I'd buried—unforgiving thoughts about myself that had rooted like weeds. Memories surfaced: past decisions that left me wincing or choices made from fear rather than love. These moments were like shadows, blocking the light of my own worth. I saw everything I'd clung to—mistakes I made, insecurities that had whispered lies— drowning out more rational thoughts. I remembered moments when self-doubt had steered my decisions, leading me astray.

Sometimes, the truth was ugly and raw—a mirror reflecting parts of myself I'd rather have ignored. But as I wrote, I felt the weight begin to lift. The act of forgiving myself wasn't a single moment but a practice, a daily ritual of choosing love over fear. I'd close my eyes, breathing deeply, imagining my heart as a blooming flower, its petals unfurling to release the past. With each breath, I surrendered a little more, letting go of the need to punish myself, trusting that the Divine had already deemed me whole. The peace that followed was extraordinary. My soul became lighter, and I felt ready to walk forward unburdened.

MY PHYSICAL EARTHLY SHELL

During this healing month, I looked deep into how I viewed my physical body, and a wave of shame washed over me—not because of what I saw, but because of how I'd judged it. For years, I'd scrutinized God's creation with a critic's eye, picking apart what I deemed flawed. I'd chastise myself for savoring something unhealthy. I'd compare myself to others—sometimes smugly, sometimes despairingly—measuring my worth against their polished exteri- ors. Facing this truth was like staring into a raw, unfiltered spotlight, more daunting than a dentist's drill. Embarrassment burned in my chest. How had I let myself spiral here? What had I been thinking, tearing down what my Creator had crafted with love?

I continued to surrender, a daily act as vital as breathing. Who was I to judge what God had declared perfect? I didn't sculpt these bones, weave this skin, spark this soul—He did. Yet, the world's noise is relentless, a constant barrage of society's standards. Billboards glow with airbrushed faces, social media scrolls by with its filters and fixes, commercials hawk pills, injections, even surgeries—these billion-dollar empires promise to "perfect" what is already whole. I see it now clearly: a culture hooked on remedies, chasing the illusion of flawlessness.

I marvel at the brilliance of creative and scientific minds crafting solutions to ease life's burdens—pills for pain, treatments for healing. But I wonder about our dependence on it all, the fact that we have to lean on them to fill gaps left by nutrient-poor food, tainted water, and the unseen toll of modern life. Our smartphones, our screens, our breakneck pace—they jolt our nervous systems in ways our ancestors never knew. We're evolving, yes, but at what cost? I seek not to pass judgment here, only to probe my own motives. Why do I reach for a "fix" when I ignore the perfection of my creation? Why do I fixate on the physical—sagging skin, deepening wrinkles—when the Spirit within me dances with joy and love?

A line from *A Course in Miracles* echoed in my mind: "When you equate yourself with a body, you will always experience depression." It landed like a truth I'd always felt but could never name. It's not the kind of depression that chains you to your bed, but a quiet ache, a nagging sense that something needs fixing. So, I taught myself to choose differently. I stood before the mirror, with soft eyes, tracing the lines etched by laughter, the curves shaped by life. Could I love my aging skin and wrinkles and see in them the same beauty I saw in others without judgment? I could so easily imagine others' spirits glowing beneath their own imperfect shells, radiant and eternal, so why not mine?

Forgiveness has become my daily ritual, a shield against the ego's sly tricks. When the voice of the human ego sneaks in, whispering comparisons or critiques, I try to catch it now. I pause, breathe, and return to love, picturing a golden light washing over me, dissolving the ego's lies. I am grateful for the inner urging that shifted my perspective, this gentle nudge from Spirit, reminding me of my worth. No past mistake—none of the choices I'd once flogged myself for—could dim the truth: I am perfect in God's eyes. Each day, I affirm my commitment to see myself, and everyone else, through the lens of love, forever worthy, forever whole.

NEXT, FORGIVING ALL OTHERS (SERIOUSLY, THOUGH)

Forgiveness for others came easily in some moments. On those occasions, it was like a gentle breeze sweeping away minor slights. When I felt wronged—after experiencing a sharp word or a careless act from a friend—I could release it, picturing my heart as a glowing lantern, its light dissolving resentment and guiding me back to love. But *A Course in Miracles* pushed me further: It insisted that true peace required forgiving *all*. Every single soul. Really? My mind reeled. What about the colleague who betrayed my trust, their words stinging like a slap? Or the client whose unkindness left me seething, their dismissal echoing in my chest? Were all the jerks, bad actors, and even the seemingly cruel people I'd known worthy of forgiveness? I sat with this in stillness, wrestling with the idea. Could it be possible that no one could hurt me unless I gave them that power? The thought was a seed, planted deep, demanding I ponder it.

The *Course's* wisdom struck me again: "All attack is Self-attack.... Blame must be undone, including self-blame." I saw it now—every judgment I'd hurled at others was a boomerang, wounding me most. So, I embarked on a quiet experiment, a journey inward. I dug deep, unearthing where I clung to being right, where I made others wrong. The floodgates opened. Memories surged. Each was a story I'd polished like a trophy, a narrative of victimhood I'd held tight. Who was I without these tales of "what happened to me"? The question hung in the air, heavy as the scent of wax and wick.

Letting go wasn't pretty at first. It felt like dismantling a shrine, tearing down idols I'd built from old wounds—anger at a past relationship's betrayal, frustration with a colleague's arrogance, resentment toward situations that left me raw. Yet the *Course*'s truth cut through every time: "Nothing can hurt you unless you give it the power to do so." No one had that power—not the people I'd feared, not the ones I'd deemed "better" or "smarter" in the competitive haze of my career. My career, which I'd once equated with my identity, wasn't who I was. I saw all those I'd placed on pedestals— colleagues, mentors, even adversaries—not as giants but as fellow souls, flawed and human, just like me. I began to forgive them, one by one, letting go.

The relief was visceral, a physical unburdening deep in my core. It was as if I'd shed a heavy coat. My body felt lighter, my breath deeper. I felt it most one evening, sitting in the stillness. Tears welled, not from pain but from joy, a bubbling spring of peace that filled me until I thought I'd burst. It was the same gleaming freedom I'd tasted during the medicine ceremony in Costa Rica, where the sacred rituals had cracked me open. Now, here in my own space, that same peace flooded back in. I wept, my heart singing with a joy so profound it echoed the Bible's promise: *a peace that "passeth all understanding."* It was as if the Universe had wrapped me in its arms, whispering, *You are free.*

MY OWN SURRENDER EXPERIMENT

When I first set out to write this book, I stood at the edge of an uncharted sea, my heart brimming with the stories and messages I felt called to share. The horizon was huge, the path unclear, but the urge to create was a steady drumbeat within me. To anchor myself, I enrolled in Gabby Bernstein's Bestseller Masterclass online. With her guidance, I crafted an outline and began to write. But as words spilled onto the page, a sinking realization hit: My prose was flat, a monochrome sketch where I'd hoped for a brilliant painting. My stories felt lifeless, lacking the color and imagery I craved. I went back, laboring to infuse them with life. Still, I knew I'd need help to make them sing, to draw readers into the world I saw so vividly in my mind.

Writing was like navigating a complex web, and I often found myself at dead ends. Some days, the task was too daunting. Other times, the act of writing cracked open old wounds, unearthing memories that burned with shame and agony. I'd sit, pen trembling over my journal, as scenes from my past played like a grainy film: choices I regretted, words I couldn't unsay, moments when I'd lost myself to fear. The ugly times were easy to recall, crowding out the light, whispering that my life was a pitiful string of failures. Questions swirled like a storm: *Who was I then? Who am I now? Why did I make those choices?* Each one was a mirror, reflecting not just my past but also the healing I still needed to embrace.

One evening, stuck in this quagmire, I decided to follow the advice I'd read from seasoned authors to take a break from writing and simply read for inspiration. I reached for Eckhart Tolle's *Stillness Speaks*, its slim volume promising solace. Almost immediately, a message slipped in like cool water: Everything I'd done in the past had simply matched the level of awareness I had in that moment. Nothing more, nothing less. Clarity always arrives later, he said, so

I realized that beating myself up over what I couldn't see then was pointless. Reading those few sentences, the tightness loosened. I could finally offer myself the same gentle understanding I was able to give anyone else and then gently step forward. I closed the book, tears prickling my eyes as I pictured my younger self stumbling along yet doing her best with what light she had. This truth softened me, letting me reflect on my past with more kindness. I returned to my own book, rewriting passages that had once dripped with old grievances, their weight no longer mine to carry. I could be honest now—sharing the pain without clinging to it, free of blame, while weaving in the joy that had always been there, too.

This journey has taught me about time and about how God sees us—not as a collection of mistakes but as eternal beings bathed in love. I couldn't erase the words or deeds I wished could somehow be undone, but I could reframe them. I'd sit in meditation each morning, picturing my past as a river flowing into an ocean of grace, every misstep dissolving in its depths. Returning to love became my mantra, a steady thrum guiding me home.

MY QUEST TO OVERCOME LONELINESS

When I read the statement "The lonely ones are those who see no function in the world for them to fill; no place where they are needed" in *A Course in Miracles*, I sat pondering this deeply. I could see how it applied to others—those adrift, searching for purpose—but what about me? I *had* a purpose, a calling that lit me up. So why did I still, at times, feel the ache of loneliness, a sadness that settled like dust in a forgotten corner? I sought answers during my daily walks, letting my mind wander. Another truth nudged me: It was the Law of Attraction. When I let myself sink into loneliness, it was like sending an invitation for more loneliness to arrive, a spiral I'd unwittingly started spinning.

I've always felt part of that rare breed—someone who can venture anywhere and do almost anything alone. It's not always what I *wanted*, but I've embraced it. I've traveled the world solo, my suitcase rolling behind me through countless airports. I've spent several Christmases on the beach alone, the sand warm beneath my toes, waves whispering secrets as gulls wheeled overhead. I've criss-crossed the United States and have explored India's vibrant chaos, Australia's sunbaked horizons, Rio's crowded streets, London's misty charm, Rome's ancient whispers, Florence's Renaissance glow, Costa Rica's lush jungles. I've dined alone countless times, savoring flavors while watching the world unfold around me. I've swayed at concerts, cheered at sporting events, and strolled beaches, my own company enough. I've attended weddings and funerals solo. I'd strike up conversations with strangers or sink into comfortable silence, blessed to have seen so much, done so much.

Yet, I'd be lying if I said I never wasted energy longing for a partner with whom to share it all. My first time in London, I came in early for a work trip, but I nearly stayed holed up in my hotel room before my work commitments began, so intense was my wish for a loved one to navigate the city with me. But I shook it off, stepping into the crisp air, boarding a hop-on, hop-off bus that wound through the streets, revealing ancient spires and sleek skyscrapers. I sipped champagne atop The Shard, London sprawling below like a living map, its blend of history and modernity sparkling in the dusk. I marveled at the grandeur of St. Paul's Cathedral, where Diana was wed; at Harrods, I savored tea, scones crumbling sweetly. When I let go of loneliness, the present bloomed, alive and joyous.

Here in my community in the present moment, I'm surrounded by couples whose warmth I cherish, one of the few single souls. Some of my neighbors have become dear friends, their laughter filling my home during gatherings. Yet, I've sometimes wallowed in sorrow over being the odd one out, choosing regret over connection, letting the human ego whisper that I'd always be alone. I'd catch myself teetering on the brink of spiraling, fighting to shift my gaze to the goodness in my life—friends, purpose, freedom. Most days, I'm buoyant, trusting I'll share life with my person, but some days, the ache pulls harder, a tide dragging me into negativity.

In October 2024, a medical procedure requiring anesthesia brought this into sharp focus. I'd planned to take an Uber to the hospital then arranged for my friend Rene to pick me up post-procedure, as required. But Rene insisted on driving me there too, despite the early hour. Her kindness stirred something deep in me—I burst into tears, gratitude flooding me. In the hospital, the staff's efficiency and care cocooned me, but each transition—from reception to labs, pre-op to post-op—came with the same question: *Is someone waiting for you?* I fought tears, the words piercing like a needle. Alone in a sterile room, I sobbed, the ego insisting that I was unworthy, destined to never be with a partner again. But I kept choosing love, picturing a golden light wrapping around me, whispering, *You are enough.* I got through it, not just surviving but thriving, surrendering to the truth that I was still okay alone. Seeing Rene's familiar smile after the procedure was a balm, a reminder of the friendship and love already in my life.

Then for Christmas, I was determined to rewrite the loneliness of the year before, when I'd fled to Rome, burnt out from work and feeling isolated in my new hometown. That trip, though beautiful, was shadowed by my focus on what I lacked—a partner. This time, I vowed to choose joy. I transformed my home into a festive haven, stringing twinkling lights and hanging ornaments that glinted like tiny stars. I hosted friends, neighbors, and family, their chatter and laughter filling the air alongside the holiday scents. We shared stories, clinked glasses, and danced to holiday tunes. The miracle was my shift in perception—I chose connection over isolation, joy over lack. Loneliness had no foothold.

I've come to see that the *A Course in Miracles* passage I quoted at the beginning of this section rings true for me, too. Even with purpose, I've sometimes chosen loneliness, whether single or in a relationship. When I start to feel this way, I picture myself connected to every soul, every star, rooted in Source. Life is unfolding as it should, and I have everything I need, my heart open to the path ahead, guided by love's unerring light.

RELEASING THE NEED FOR OUTSIDE VALIDATION

Years ago, I eagerly read *The Five Love Languages*, its pages promising to decode the ways we give and receive love. As I read, I saw clearly that my primary love language is Words of Affirmation. I craved praise like a parched garden thirsts for rain. Private whispers of encouragement, public nods of recognition—they were my oxygen. Without them, I wilted, the sting of being overlooked cutting deep. Not getting a "well done" at work or being met by a friend's silence after a shared triumph left me aching; I felt as if my worth hung on their words.

Then, in the summer of 2024, as I dove into Michael Singer's book *The Untethered Soul* again, I read his sentiment around the absurdity of needing others' validation. Thinking that our worth depends on fleeting, uncontrollable opinions is much like chasing shadows. We have accumulated hurts and fears that make us crave approval to avoid feeling vulnerable. Sitting on my couch, a soft throw draped over my knees, this truth stung like a slap. Why did I care so much about what others thought? Why did their approval sometimes feel like my only lifeline? Why wasn't my own internal validation enough for me? I set the book down, staring at the flickering candle on my coffee table, its flame dancing as if mocking my lifelong chase for external praise. Had I been that foolish, building my self-worth on the shifting sands of others' opinions?

The questions lingered, heavy as the scent of wax in the air. The ego still crept in, whispering for applause, but a shift was stirring. I began to see that my own validation—and God's—was all that mattered. I was worthy, enough, whole. I was the only constant companion in my life's journey, awake with myself 24/7 through every triumph and stumble. People—friends, family, colleagues—came and went like seasons, their presence a gift but not my foundation. If I tried my best, if I stood proud of my efforts, that was enough. I pictured myself—my heart a glowing ember, no longer tethered to others' words. The release was electric. My shoulders lifted, and my breath deepened. Suddenly the world brightened.

I saw how I'd set others up to fail, casting them as actors in a play they didn't know they were in. I'd expected friends to cheer my every step, family to affirm my choices, bosses to laud my work, even strangers to offer a nod of approval. When they didn't—because they were busy with their own lives or simply unaware of my silent script—my expectations were shattered, leaving me wounded. I'd placed them on pedestals they never asked for, from the colleague who missed my presentation's brilliance to the stranger who didn't smile back. How absurd, I thought, laughing softly in the quiet of my home, the realization sparkling like the candle's glow.

When I stop letting others define me, when I surrender the hunger for their validation, when I reclaim the power I have given away, when I give up being a people-pleaser, life becomes magical. Everything becomes so much more peaceful, just as it was meant to be.

YEARNING FOR BELONGING

In the spring of 2025, lounging on the beach under a warm Sunday sun, I watched the waves crash and felt memories come flooding back. Nearby, a group of Mennonite families caught my eye—

women in long dresses and hair coverings, their young faces already marked by motherhood. I wondered: Do they feel free? Trapped? Like outcasts? Their men wore typical swim shorts, blending in, while the women alone bore the weight of modesty. It stirred old questions about my past and how, so often, I felt out of place, just wanting to fit in.

My whole life, I've wrestled with this desire to belong. It's crept up in unexpected ways, sometimes twisting into desperate pleas for acceptance that I'm not proud of. Those moments shaped me, but they don't define me. Now, I can look back and smile—maybe even laugh—at the absurdity of it all. Those were just things I experienced and lived through. I don't need to carry them anymore.

LOVE AND RELATIONSHIPS

My life's journey has been a sacred pilgrimage into the heart of love, relationships, and the divine essence within me. Guided by a gentle, unseen hand, I've uncovered profound truths about my soul's longing for connection, peeling back the layers of my being with reverence and grace. I've explored my attachment style, tracing its delicate threads through the tapestry of my past relationships, seeing how it shaped my heart's dance with others. In quiet reflection, I've discerned where my expectations wandered from divine alignment, clarifying what truly matters—a partnership rooted in love, cocreation, and spiritual growth.

This sacred quest drew me to the tender memories of my childhood, where I faced long-buried emotions, listening to the whispers of my inner child. Through this holy work, I've cradled old wounds, offering forgiveness to myself for choices born of fear, and embracing my inherent worthiness. I know I am worthy of a radiant, soul-deep partnership, one through which we will cocreate a life of harmony and evolution together. Yes, during my awakening, I've discovered another luminous truth: I am a vessel of love, brilliant and whole. Love flows from the eternal spark within me, not from another soul. Whether I walk alone or hand in hand with a beloved, I choose to keep my heart open, a sacred chalice overflowing with divine love, unshackled by the need for external completion.

I've faced the shadows of fear—fear of vulnerability, of being fully seen, of standing alone in the vastness of existence—and found them to be mere illusions before the light of Spirit. Vulnerability is a sacred offering, a gateway to deep connection, allowing my soul to shine unguarded. I've let go of the fear of solitude, finding solace in the eternal presence of the Divine, knowing I am never truly alone. Over the years, I've learned the sacred art of communication and conflict, weaving words and understanding with grace, creating bridges to authentic connection.

My soul yearns to share this earthly journey with a partner, yet I trust the divine orchestration of my healing. This season of inner work, guided by the hand of God, is preparing my heart for a sacred union, one that will shimmer with perfect beauty when the appointed time arrives. Reflecting on past suffering, I see now that it was part of my holy journey, refining my spirit into one more capable of a love that transcends my wildest dreams—a love that mirrors the infinite, boundless heart of the Divine. With every step, I am becoming a symbol of this sacred love, ready to embrace a partnership that reflects the eternal light within us both.

⋮

Releasing Old Wounds: A Poetic Path to Joyful Freedom

BLAME

It feels so simple, so righteous, to cast blame,
To tilt the spotlight outward, shielding my shame.
Hiding the shadows, the flaws I disown,
I crown myself right, declaring you wrong.

Yet blame is a thief, draining life's joyful glow,
A heavy yoke, unforgiving, where burdens grow.
Sinking, I wallow, chained to despair's embrace,
Cloaked in a darkness that veils my true face.

But oh, to surrender—a bold, sacred art,
Forgiveness unfurls like a bloom in the heart.
Releasing the weight, I rise, light and free,
Love's gleaming tide flows boundless through me.

I wonder how much of our lives are shaped by clinging to old wounds, as if they were badges that explained every misstep or dark thought. For years, I was shackled to the past—every moment that felt like it happened to me became a piece of my identity. Some days, those stories felt like a warm cup of tea on a crisp morning, comforting and familiar, wrapping me in their bittersweet glow.

Other times, they were a crushing weight, chaining me to shame, guilt, and fear, leaving my chest tight and my breath shallow. I wasn't free; I was trapped, my shoulders sagging under burdens I didn't know how to shed.

Resentment would flare like a sudden fever, or self-pity would creep in, heavy and aching. Why was I raised this way? Why didn't I feel the love and safety every child craves? Why did life feel like a constant battle? Not every moment was heavy—there were stretches of joy, laughter spilling freely, my heart light. But beneath it all, a gnawing longing for freedom pulsed, a quiet ache to break loose from the ego's cruel whispers. That voice in my head was relentless, taunting me with doubts, making me feel like an impostor, never quite enough. My mind raced, my body tensed, locked in a silent war against myself.

A therapist once asked me to share an early childhood memory. The one that surfaced was sharp and vivid: I was four and had been left behind at a campground in Kansas. My family, plus a few others from our Fairwood church, had driven there in a van to visit relatives. I'd been playing near the clotheslines behind the tents, and when I returned, the tables were empty. Panic hit like a wave. I ran to the next campsite, sobbing, inconsolable, certain I'd been abandoned. In reality, my parents noticed my absence within minutes and came back for me. But that moment seared itself into my soul. For years, I blamed every feeling of loneliness or abandonment on it, building a narrative that defined me. Why did that memory linger? It was real, and it was terrifying—but I gave it too much power, attempting to analyze it instead of letting it go as something I simply experienced.

Painful memories of punishment also clung to me like heavy chains, their cold grip stoking feelings of anger that smoldered deep within. The sting of a brush, the snap of a ruler, or the impact of bare hands on my bottom—these specters haunted my heart, especially when the reasons for my "wrongs" remained shrouded in mystery. As a child, my tender spirit flinched more deeply than most, which meant I was left with confusion that lingered long afterward as well. Yet, when I finally surrendered these moments, naming them as mere experiences that shaped but did not define me, a massive release washed over me. It was as if a crushing boulder lifted from my chest, dissolving into a cascade of light, freeing my breath and softening my heart. I was able to see that my parents, too, were ensnared in their own web of culture and custom, their actions woven from beliefs they held as truth, doing their best in a world that taught them such discipline was right. With this understanding, compassion burst forth, and I stepped forward, unburdened, into a brighter, gentler peace.

In my early twenties, another therapist, asked, "Marcia, did you feel loved by your parents?" I bristled. "Of course they loved me," I said. He pressed, "That's not what I asked. Did you feel loved?" The question landed like a punch. I had to admit: No, I didn't. When I eventually shared that with my parents, I was aware that it might feel like a betrayal to them. But their genuine apologies showed harm wasn't their intent. Still, I couldn't understand why I was affected so deeply.

Reflecting now, I see that every child craves something unique, a need that those of my parents' generation often struggled to recognize. Raised in an era when their own parents had given them little individual attention, they simply may not have known how to nurture each of us in our own way. Over the years, I've explored how birth order shapes a child's experience. I was sandwiched between my older siblings, Wendy and Roger, and my younger brother, Steve, whose big blue eyes and happy spirit marked him as the baby until my sister Rose arrived years later. So as the middle child, I often felt like a shadow slipping through the family's bustle, my presence fading in the lively chaos of our crowded Fairwood home.

Over time, I saw the immense pressure my parents faced. Leading the church, they were shaped by a harsh environment rooted in the founder's draconian beliefs that had influenced their own parents. According to many witnesses, the founder had wielded fear like a weapon, demanding members sever family ties if any of them questioned obedience to God. He is said to have fostered a constant state of anxiety and fear through tyrannical intimidation, manipulation, and coercion. Prior to being known as The Kingdom, the movement had been called Shiloh. It has been said that there was a painful absence of self-confidence known as the Shiloh complex. Both sets of my grandparents grew up in this environment, and the damage it wrought was carried out in myriad ways that then impacted my parents and other family members as well. I know that my parents tried their best with what they knew at the time; we've had conversations about it all over the years. They were taught to put God first, then the church, *then* family.

Of course this had an impact on my life and the choices I made. For too long though, I wallowed in that. I didn't know how to release it and lacked the tools to see the situation as just an experience I'd lived through. Eventually, I learned how to spot that lack when it showed up for me—as people-pleasing, which was driven by the fear of being judged by my actions. I had to learn to love myself, to understand what receiving love from others and from God truly meant. Looking back, I see more clearly now how those patterns wove through my relationships—romantic and platonic alike—and how I needed boundaries to protect my heart.

When I first read *The Vortex* by Esther and Jerry Hicks, their contention that we, as souls, choose our families before birth felt absurd. Why would I pick this childhood, this struggle? I was grateful that my parents gave me life, but I was stuck in a narrative of resentment. Casting blame felt good—until it didn't. The resistance, all the negative energy, started to drain me. My PTSD would flare before visits with my parents, my stomach churning with anxiety. I knew there had to be a better way.

A quiet spark flickered in my soul: What if I did choose this path? Every jagged turn and shadowed valley of it? For years, I carried my childhood like a heavy pack, its weight woven from memories of struggle, uncertainty, and other moments I'd labeled as "bad." But what if I reframed it all? What if I looked through a softer lens, seeing not just the pain but the strength it forged as well? In this context, Michael Singer's teachings invited me to stop rejecting my past and instead meet it with gratitude, to recognize it as the quiet teacher that carved my strength. He reminded me that true spiritual growth isn't about rearranging the circumstances of life or erasing what happened; it's about learning to observe everything (even the painful parts) with an open heart, without letting them pull me under. The real freedom, he said, comes not from battling what is, but from changing how I respond to it.

When those ideas settled in, something inside me unclenched. The childhood I'd spent years trying to outrun no longer felt like a burden to fix or a stain to scrub away; it became simply a chapter I could witness with kindness. In that moment, an old, heavy door I didn't even realize I'd been pushing against eased open on its own, and soft light poured in from the other side.

Reframing my story wasn't about rewriting history or pretending the hard moments didn't sting. It was about standing in the present, heart open, and choosing to see my younger self not as a victim but as a brave apprentice to life's lessons. My childhood, with its messy edges, taught me grit—how to stand up after a fall, how to find cracks of light in the darkness. By thanking my path, I began to see every struggle as a teacher whispering, "You are stronger than you know."

Singer's idea of accepting without attachment felt revelatory. I'd spent years tangled in memories, replaying so many moments I wished I could change. But what if I let them be, just witnessing them like clouds passing across the sky? I started practicing this in small ways. When an old memory surfaced—say, the sting of feeling overlooked—I'd pause, breathe, and let it float by without diving into the hurt. It was like watching a wave roll to shore without letting it pull me under. This shift freed me to focus on the present, to pour my energy into creating rather than regretting.

Changing my reaction, as Singer urged, was the hardest but most liberating step in my healing process. Instead of fighting the pain of past moments or bracing against the way they echoed through current challenges, I started choosing my response. Each time I chose a new reaction, I felt lighter, as if I were rewriting my inner script, not attempting to control the world around me.

How could I use my story to help others? Could I let go of my attachment to the past without losing who I am? I realized there's only one path forward: to release, forgive, and choose love. First, I forgave myself. I stopped dissecting the darkness and instead leaned into light, letting it bathe me in its warmth. I know now that my past doesn't define me—it's just something I lived through. Now, I'm learning to shine.

Here are a few lessons I've learned about the art of reframing. See if these might help you turn your own past into power:

1. Reframe your past as your greatest teacher.

Stop battling your history. It's possible to view every hardship as a lesson that built your strength. Thank your past for its teachings, and use those gifts to shape a bolder, brighter present. Your scars reveal your superpowers.

2. Choose your response to reclaim your freedom.

You can't change the past or every current problematic situation, but you can master your response to them. Pause, reflect, and choose actions aligned with your strength and values. Each time you choose a more deliberate reaction, you're building a life of freedom and purpose.

⋮

From Bounds to Bliss: Igniting Infinite Abundance

Our minds, chained by ancient lineage, bind us to scarcity's cell,
Taught to see a world where all is finite, a meager well.
Beyond mere wealth, this creed confines our soul's expanse,
We deem the rich as thieves who steal the poor's last chance.

Clutching tight to coin or millions, we hoard in fear,
Trapped within a cage where loss looms ever near.
We tally every cost, convinced we're always cheated,
Certain that another's gain leaves us defeated.

We compare, we covet, then rage ignites within,
Suffering blooms, a thorned vine born of imagined sin.
So wed to woe, we seek proof our misery's just,
Lost in endless want, craving what turns to dust.

This binds not just wealth, but time, kindness, and love's embrace,
A cycle of lack, a heart's unyielding, barren chase.
But what if we saw life's bounty as boundless, ever flowing?
Shed the victim's cloak, let our spirits start growing?

Rejoice in another's triumph, their light a shared spark,
Born of the same Creator, who wove stars through the dark.
The One who carved our cosmos with intricate, tender care,
And graced the rose with beauty, its scent a fragrant prayer.

Growing up, wealth was a foreign concept, like a language I'd never learned. My parents, living without a salary in our Kingdom community, had nothing to invest, and the stock market was deemed a forbidden realm. I never felt poor, though. I knew our town and school brimmed with affluent families, their lives sparkling with new computers at Christmas while I unwrapped a hand-sewn bathrobe from my mother. Yet, I didn't feel deprived. We had enough—food on the table, a roof overhead. When I started babysitting and earning my own pocket money, I felt a thrill, suddenly able to buy clothes that were new and not hand sewn.

Unfortunately, our culture and society have been perpetuating poverty consciousness over abundance for centuries. If we apply the Law of Attraction, this focus on lack, both individually and collectively, has no choice but to persist. We need a cultural shift that begins with each of us. First, we must understand and acknowledge that the Universe's resources are limitless. Next, we must recognize that we have the power to both ask and receive. This is a fundamental teaching from Jesus. Most of us have not been taught that we have this opportunity in front of us, so we stay steeped in our limiting beliefs.

A number of years ago, after a period of seeking, I began to picture my life as a river, with money, time, energy, and relationships all streaming freely. I let go of the urge to clutch tightly, to hoard, to tether myself to things. Not that I gave everything away—I just shifted my mind-set. And the moment I did, abundance rushed in like a tide. A surprise bonus here, a raise there, but more than that— new friendships, unexpected kindness, bursts of joy.

MANIFESTING

This shift sparked my manifestation practice in earnest. Seeing it as a dance with the Universe, I stopped obsessing over how or when my desires would arrive, and then I watched as miracles began to unfold, vivid and real. I thought of it like playing the lottery: You can't win if you don't play, but why fixate on the odds? Why demand the Universe deliver in one specific way? I started focusing on the why behind my desires. I found that it's so often not about the thing itself but about the emotion that thing carries, the way it makes your heart sing. By trusting the flow, I found abundance wasn't just a dream—it was a living, breathing reality, washing over me in waves.

I had another profound aha moment when I realized that the seemingly negative experiences in my life were actually manifestations of my desire for spiritual transformation. Initially, it had felt like the Universe was testing me—"Seriously, I have to navigate this situation or deal with this person?" It was easy to feel exasperated, slipping into a victim mind-set, thinking life is just hard or that I was cursed with bad luck. But by shifting my perspective and recognizing these challenges as spiritual assignments guiding me toward a more enlightened path, I could reframe my thoughts. I began to observe my reactions, seeing these experiences as mere moments in time—nothing more, nothing less.

Stepping into an abundance mind-set has reshaped my life, teaching me that the Universe's gifts—money, time, love—are limitless when we release the chains of scarcity. Challenges, once interpreted as burdens, became spiritual assignments, guiding me toward growth and deeper understanding. By focusing on the "why" behind my desires, on the joy, security, or connection they would bring, I've learned to trust the flow, inviting miracles that make my heart sing. Embracing this mind-set, I've found not just abundance but a life brimming with infinite possibility as well.

This journey has taught me the following and I hope these nuggets of wisdom may also resonate with you:

1. Embrace the flow of abundance.

Shift your mind-set from scarcity to possibility, trusting that the Universe's resources—love, time, money, connections, joy—are boundless. Let go of fear and focus on the feelings behind your desires, inviting miracles that light up your life.

2. See challenges as spiritual invitations.

Reframe life's obstacles as opportunities for growth, not burdens. By observing your reactions and trusting the journey, you can transform even the toughest moments into stepping-stones toward a more enlightened, abundant path.

⋮

$$42$$

From Fearful Faith to Divine Love: Awakening to a God Beyond Religion

I separate God from religion's grasp,
Casting off fear's man-wrought mask.
I attune to the Creator's boundless heart,
Whose love, unjudging, sets us apart.

Each soul crafted for lives bold and grand,
Called to love fiercely, by divine command—
To cherish God, self, and all humankind,
In this, suffering fades, and peace we find.

From childhood, religion cloaked me like a heavy shroud, its threads woven with control, fear, and suffering. Churches never felt like sanctuaries; their repressive doctrines left me restless, yearning for a divine spark beyond their walls. Long ago, I realized God wasn't confined to pews or pulpits. In my darkest moments, when hope flickered like a dying ember, I felt a steady, warm presence—God's quiet comfort, undeniable and alive. That same divine love meets me in still moments of guidance, in the awe of Creation's beauty, in synchronicities that wink like stars, or when I choose to live heaven on earth.

Recently, a passage from *A Course in Miracles* and its chapter "The Unhealed Healer" struck me like a lightning bolt:

All unhealed healers follow the ego's plan for forgiveness in one form or another. If they are theologians, they are likely to condemn themselves, teach condemnation, and advocate a fearful solution. Projecting condemnation onto God, they make Him appear retaliative, and fear His retribution. What they have done is merely to identify with the ego, and by perceiving what it does, condemn themselves because of this confusion. It is understandable that there have been revolts against this concept, but to revolt against it is still to believe in it.

It was as if a dusty curtain parted, revealing a sunlit truth: Centuries of man-made religion had been built on fear, not love. The passage clarified that "unhealed healers" try to give what they haven't received, the ego clouding divine truth. The call to avoid "revolting" against these distortions led me back to the Art of Allowing, a practice that brought peace and set me up to forgive the confusion, sorrow, and angst of my religious upbringing.

Reflecting on my grandfather Abram, I wondered if he was a wounded soul, seeking control to mask his pain. His actions, including his manipulative affairs within The Kingdom, clearly left scars, yet his four daughters felt his love deeply and were able to separate the man from the leader. However, I struggled to do the same. His dismissive nickname, "Marcia Pest Wakeman," lingered like a bruise, but I realized I finally needed to forgive him. Before his death from stomach cancer in his sixties, he reportedly repented. I now believe that God, his Creator, loved and forgave him—and I needed to do the same, offering compassion to a flawed soul.

I've come to see that, for some, religion is a saving grace, rooted as it is in spiritual principles. Even The Kingdom, for all its flaws, lifted many lives. I've read the Bible cover to cover, but much of it feels distant to me—all the ancient words, contradictory passages, or human translations twisted by the ego. Yet, certain verses offer comfort, like soft light through a window. I've wrestled with claims that the Bible is the unequivocal Word of God, puzzled by how different people draw vastly different meanings from the same text, often bending it to their own views.

A few years ago, my father proudly shared that he and my mother live in a town with a mass amount of churches and that they are attending the most conservative one. I don't fully understand their choice, but if it brings them peace, that's enough for me. I've learned to release the need to judge their path or defend my own.

I found unexpected clarity on a trip to Italy in 2016. Friends of mine had recommended that I take a guided tour in Florence, insisting it was worth the time despite my aversion to long, dull tours. They were right. The guide was mesmerizing, transporting us through history as we wandered the ancient city. He pointed out symbols on weathered buildings, wove tales of the Renaissance, and captured my imagination. One moment particularly stood out to me: He explained how baptism in the Catholic Church had evolved over the years. In prior centuries, contaminated water in cisterns had led to countless deaths, especially among children. So the Catholic Church adapted, shifting from full-immersion baptisms to sprinkling water on the head in order to save lives. This revelation shattered my childhood judgments about the "wrong" practices of Catholics and vividly showed me how specific context shapes tradition. It freed me from snap judgments and deepened my belief that we often condemn what we don't understand.

The confusion of The Kingdom stemmed not just from its Old Testament focus but from misinterpretations of the New Testament and Jesus's teachings, a pattern I see in many Christian faiths. *A Course in Miracles* offered me clarity through passages like this: "Remembering the name of Jesus Christ is to give thanks for all the gifts that God has given you. Jesus has led the way. Why would you not be grateful to him? His words have reached you in a language you can love and understand. Other teachers exist in different tongues and symbols." This resonated deeply. God uses many teachers—Jesus, yes, along with others as well—to share a universal message of love, tailored to different hearts. It reconciled my confusion about non-Christian faiths, affirming that divine love speaks in many languages.

The *Course* also affirmed that "I have made every effort to use words that are almost impossible to distort, but it is always possible to twist symbols around if you wish." I knew that the Bible, translated across centuries, carries human imprints—the ego, cultures, and contexts—that can obscure its spirit. Focusing on the message of love, not literal words, brought me peace.

Additional passages unveiled the truth that Jesus's message was about love, not condemnation, despite the Apostles' human missteps:

> These are some of the examples of upside-down thinking in the New Testament, although its gospel is really only the message of love. If the Apostles had not felt guilty, they never could have quoted me as saying, "I come not to bring peace but a sword." This is clearly the opposite of everything I taught. Nor could they have described my reactions to Judas as they did, if they had really understood me. I could not have said, "Betrayest thou the Son of man with a kiss?" unless I believed in betrayal. The whole message of the crucifixion was simply that I did not. The "punishment" I was said to have called forth upon Judas was a similar mistake. Judas was my brother and a Son of God, as much a part of the Sonship as myself. Was it likely that I would condemn him when I was ready to demonstrate that condemnation is impossible?

This clarity freed me from the Bible's contradictions, letting me embrace its heart: "As you read the teachings of the Apostles, remember that I told them myself that there was much they would understand later, because they were not wholly ready to follow me at the time."

I've released the need to judge religions or defend my beliefs. For years, I wondered how I'd find deep peace without feeling wrong or judged. My faith in God steadied me through confusion, but only recently have I found the clarity I craved. I've arrived at the kind of peace Jesus described, a peace that "passeth all understanding." I no longer need to reconcile my past or have all the answers in the now. I also don't need to make others wrong for their own beliefs. We were made to live bold, beautiful lives, loving God, ourselves, and all beings equally. Jesus's miracles weren't exclusive; we can access that same divine power. I've witnessed countless miracles in my life—moments of grace, guidance, and love. Our Creator uses many teachers beyond Jesus to heal, and just as miracles aren't measured by their magnitude of difficulty, neither are our mistakes. The human ego shows up daily, but I return to love—for God, for myself, for all humanity.

Here is some wisdom around organized religion that has helped me along the way. I now offer it to you:

1. Embrace divine love beyond dogma.

Let go of fear-based beliefs that confine your spirit. Seek a connection with the Divine—whether you call it God, Source, or Creator—in ways that resonate with your heart, trusting that love, not judgment, is the universal truth.

2. Find peace in the release of judgment.

Forgive the flaws of others and yourself, recognizing that everyone is a work in progress. By focusing on love and understanding, you can find a profound peace that transcends past wounds and opens your life to boundless possibility.

⋮

43

Beyond Flesh, Glowing Spirit: Unveiling Our Divine Essence

've been reflecting deeply on our physical bodies—how we fixate on their form yet often overlook their deeper essence. Our culture pours immense weight into the particularities of our tangible selves: the flesh we sculpt, the style we adorn it with, the care we lavish on it. Our culture equates the body with both our identity and our worth. Yet, beneath this surface lies a radiant truth: We are far more than our physical shells. Imagine a world where our bodies shimmer with the vibrant energy of our spirits, and each unique constellation of soul, personality, and divine light is revealed to be far more than the mere flesh we inhabit.

Growing up at Fairwood, my view of the body was steeped in shame and control, an oppressive doctrine that cloaked me like a heavy veil. As a young girl, I was taught to hide myself in long dresses and loose-fitting clothes, with no jewelry, no makeup, and definitely no short hair. Wearing my first bra, a quiet milestone, felt like a forbidden act; even hidden beneath layers, I trembled at the thought of being seen. Shame clung to me like a second skin, whispering that my body was something to conceal, not celebrate. So sheltered was I that I didn't even understand how pregnancy occurred. When an older girl at school became pregnant, I silently prayed, "Please, don't let that happen to me," my innocence wrapped in both fear and mystery. It took years of unlearning my deeply ingrained discomfort with my body to simply allow myself to wear a sleeveless top or to shed the slip beneath my dress.

This fixation on the body ripples far beyond my personal experience in the way it fuels conflicts that tear at our world, whether it's debates over gay rights, transgender rights, abortion, or sexuality itself. These aren't abstract issues; they're woven into the fabric of our lives. I've seen it in my own circle: Friends divided over abortion, their beliefs clashing like storm clouds. My gay brother Steve and his husband Pete, whose love shines as pure as any despite facing a long road to family acceptance. My trans relatives, radiant souls deserving of unconditional love, who are met with judgment at every turn. Why do we focus so much on the body? Digging into this question—what do I believe, and why—has been a sacred unraveling, a shedding of centuries-old beliefs that elevate flesh over spirit. I've caught myself tempted to judge those who judge, but gazing into the mirror of my soul, I've learned to release that impulse. Culture, religion, and family shape us like clay, molding our views until they feel like truth. Breaking free is like stepping into a luminous world where spirit outshines skin.

Our bodies are also vessels of sacred sexuality, yet many of us were taught to see this gift as shameful, not divine. In churches where sexuality is suppressed—and even beyond their walls—the result is often the opposite of intended purity: There is abuse, unwanted pregnancies, abortions, and affairs that flourish in the silence. By stifling open expression and dialogue, we fail to teach the sanctity of our desires, leaving generations to wrestle with guilt instead of embracing the holy fire within.

In my own journey, unexpressed emotions—grief, anger, fear—have settled into my bones, dimming the vitality of both my mind and body. No statistic can capture it, but the truth is undeniable: Our bodies do indeed carry the weight of what remains unspoken in our hearts. I've grown keenly aware of the interplay between the spiritual, mental, and physical planes. Unhealed spiritual wounds seep into the mind and body, manifesting as dis-ease. When I finally began tuning into the energy of my body, everything shifted. I started breathing deeply, letting emotions flow like a river rather than damming them up. Before entering a room or answering a call, I take time to pause, choosing to lift my spirit—like flipping a switch to release negativity and invite connection. We've all felt it: Someone burdened by unhealed pain can dim a room like a gathering storm, while another, radiant with joy and presence, lights it up like sunlight piercing through clouds. It's the person's spirit, their aura—not their appearance—that draws us in, magnetic and uplifting, a beacon of divine energy.

A Course in Miracles offers a transcendent vision: "Let the body have healing as its purpose." More profoundly, it urges us to "see the flesh or recognize the Spirit. But choose the Spirit, and all Heaven bends to touch your eyes and blesses your holy sight, that you may see the world of flesh no more except to heal and comfort and to bless." Imagine a world where we look beyond the body to the spirit, where every glance is a prayer, every touch a blessing. Then peace, joy, and love would ripple outward like a tidal wave of light, transforming our world in its radiant wake. If we embraced this collectively, our planet wouldn't just change—it would glow with the eternal brilliance of the Divine.

My journey has taught me that there is great benefit in the following two lessons:

1. Look beyond the flesh to see the spirit.

Shift your focus from the body's appearance to the radiant essence within. By recognizing the divine spark in yourself and others, you foster love and connection that transcend physical differences and cultural divides.

2. Heal through presence and release.

Let your body be a vessel for healing by releasing the weight of unexpressed emotions. Embrace your sacred energy—whether through breath, a sacred pause, or a moment of intention—and allow your spirit to shine, transforming pain into a beacon of joy and peace.

⋮

Dancing in Kairos: Unshackling Time to Live in the Divine Now

In silence, I sit, attuned to the void,
The boundless expanse where my soul is deployed.
Embracing the vastness of earth's gentle hum,
I learn to just *be*, letting presence become.

The gift of the now, a treasure divine,
The past but a whisper, no longer a sign.
No dread of tomorrow, no fear's heavy chain,
I rest in the calm where uncertainty reigns.

My heart fixed on love, I let life unfold,
Like nature's soft rhythm, unforced and untold.
The grass softly sways, reaching up to the sky,
The flowers unfurl, no question of why.

The sun spills its glow, the birds carve their flight,
The fish glide through currents, untroubled by night.
In silence, pure gold, I surrender, set free,
Returning to Source, where my power's in me.

Connected in love, my spirit takes flight,
Whole in this moment, I shine with my light.

As I recently turned the pages of *The Power of Now* by Eckhart Tolle again, coming back to it felt like rediscovering a hidden treasure chest, each chapter unlocking an energetic, pulsating truth. The words danced before my eyes, alive with a clarity that refreshed my spirit. This wasn't just a reread—it was a revelation. My journey of practicing presence, both in the past and more recently, took on a new hue, enabling me to see the world anew. I couldn't tear myself away from the book; it held me captive, each sentence sparking a cascade of aha moments that lit up my mind like a display of fireworks on the 4th of July.

Tolle's insight about the Past, Present, and Future wove a golden thread through my thoughts. He doesn't just explain—he unveils. "Time is precious," we often hear, or even say to ourselves, but Tolle flips this notion upside down. Time, he argues, isn't precious at all. It's the Now that's the true gem, shimmering with infinite possibility. The more we chase the shadows of the past or strain toward the mirage of the future, the more we let the Now slip through our fingers like sand. I saw my own behavior in this truth, caught in the act. I saw how much energy I'd poured into regretting yesterday's missteps or daydreaming about tomorrow's promises. It was like I'd been carrying heavy sacks labeled "what was" and "what might be," leaving my hands too full to embrace the vivid moment in front of me.

This mind-set isn't just personal; it's cultural, fused into how we're raised. From childhood, we're fed stories of delayed rewards: Follow the rules, check the boxes, and only then you'll earn your ticket to a shining future—maybe even to heaven itself. Religions often lean into this promise, painting life as a waiting game that must be played in the hopes of winning some distant prize. But are we living, or just biding our time? Even the longevity gurus, with their eyes fixed on stretching out their earthly years, might be missing the dazzling pulse of the present. Are they savoring the Now, or are they too busy building a bridge to a far-off tomorrow?

For the past year and a half, I've been gifted a rare pause—a life unmoored from the daily grind of a job. I chose to let the river of life flow so I could drift a while without a set map, to savor the freedom of minimal planning. Yet, even in this spacious time, I caught myself drifting toward the future: Where will I travel next? Should I stay in this neighborhood? When will love find me again? What's the next chapter of my story, and how will I fund it? These questions weren't wrong, but they were like pebbles in my shoe, pulling me out of the moment. When I paused to reflect, I saw the subtle resistance I'd been carrying—old habits of worry and control so familiar they felt like second skin.

Eckhart Tolle's gentle reminder landed softly but firmly: Every shade of fear comes from living too far ahead of this moment, borrowing trouble from a future that hasn't arrived, while missing the steady ground of right now. When I bring my attention back to pure presence, the fear simply has nowhere left to stand. The Present, he insists, is the only key that unlocks the chains of the Past. This insight wasn't just intellectual—it reverberated deep in my bones, a truth my body recognized before my mind could catch up. In the book, he dives into the dance between Mind Energy and Spiritual Energy, and I found myself leaning in, captivated, eager to make that shift as well. It's as if my soul were whispering, *This is it. This is the way.* Surrendered Action began to take shape in my imagination—a vivid vision of moving through life with intention but without grip, like a kite soaring on the wind, guided yet free.

And then, a quiet miracle: I saw how Source had been answering my prayers all along. Not in the neat, predictable packages I might have expected, but in breathtaking, serendipitous ways. Events aligning, connections sparking, circumstances shifting like pieces of a cosmic puzzle falling into place. The guidance I seek flows endlessly from the Holy Spirit when I'm open, when I let go of resistance and trust life's unfolding. Even when I stumble, even when resistance creeps in, I'm held—gently guided back to forgiveness, to surrender, to love.

Then came another email from Emily Fletcher, a spark that set my heart ablaze. She introduced me to the Ancient Greek concepts of time, painting them in vivid strokes. Chronos is linear, clock-bound time that passes relentlessly. It's the busy calendar, the endless to-do list, the ticking clock that makes you feel like time is running out. Kairos is the moment outside of time, rich with significance and meaning. It's the flow state, the serendipitous moment of clarity, the season of change where life unfolds with ease and purpose. My whole life, I've been chained to Chronos—action-oriented, punctual to a fault, annoyed by others who dawdled. I was taught that being late was disrespectful, a waste of someone else's precious time. But now I see the flip side: Cutting short a conversation, rushing to the next meeting, failing to be fully present are all a disservice too. Balance, I realize, is the key.

When I read about Kairos, it was like a bell ringing in my soul. This is the luxury I've tasted over the past year, the gift of stepping out of Chronos's grip. But it's bigger than these twelve months. It's a lens that reframes my entire fifty-five years on this earth. I see the curious, happy-go-lucky five-year-old I once was, skipping through life with wide-eyed wonder. I see the lost, angry teenager, wrestling with pain. I see the party girl. I see the driven career woman, often lonely but relentless. I see the friend, the spiritual seeker, the passionate, generous soul. All these versions of me, spanning decades, now weave together into the woman I am today—and the woman I'm becoming. It's not just freeing; it's a divine, joyful bliss that feels like a homecoming.

This is my vision: To live as a messenger, a light worker spreading love, unshackled from victimhood or warriorhood. To love boldly, expansively, without fear. To dance in the Now, where every moment sparkles with Kairos magic. I want to live and love big—not just for myself, but as a shining light for others, a testament to the beauty of being fully, gloriously present.

I urge you to explore the following opportunities and may you find peace in doing so:

1. Embrace the Now as your treasure.

Let go of the past's shadows and the future's mirage to fully inhabit the present moment. By anchoring yourself in the Now, you unlock a boundless well of peace, joy, and possibility that transforms how you live and love.

2. Dance in divine flow.

Release the need to control life's rhythm and trust the unfolding of Kairos moments. Like a kite soaring on the wind, move with intention but surrender to the divine current, allowing serendipity and grace to guide your path.

⋮

(**45**)

From Chaos to Compassion: Cultivating Peace in a Divided World

As *A Course in Miracles* says, "Every thought I have either brings peace or war, either love or fear." This is a reminder of the power that resides within each fleeting thought. It's as if my mind is a garden and every thought is a seed that blooms into either brilliant flowers of peace or thorny vines of conflict. Right now, as I write this in the swirling storm of 2025, the world feels like a canvas splashed with chaos. The United States is caught in a political maelstrom, the resultant tidal wave of division crashing across the globe. For some, this moment is a fireworks display of triumph, their hearts soaring with hope; for others, it's a dark blanket of despair, heavy with uncertainty. Beyond politics, the world churns with wars that scar the earth, violence that shatters lives, and fraud schemes that slither through society like shadows. I stand at the edge of this tempest, both captivated and chilled, my heart flickering between fascination and horror.

In this moment, I'm drawn back to the Art of Allowing, this gentle whisper that urges me to soften my gaze. It's like stepping out of a stormy sea onto a quiet shore, where I can simply *watch*—not judge, not grasp, but witness. I'm called to see every human, no matter their stance or story, through a lens of compassion. The truth is, I don't hold all the facts; none of us do. Judging what's right or wrong feels like trying to piece together a puzzle with half the pieces missing. Instead, I choose to let compassion flow, a warm light that softens the edges of the world's sharp divides.

Blaming or resisting our age-old political systems for their limitations feels futile, like shouting at the wind. Instead, I believe transformation begins within each of us. When we strive to embody our highest selves—choosing compassion, integrity, and understanding—we create ripples that spread outward, touching hearts and communities. This collective awakening can gently guide the world back to its sacred foundation of love, restoring the harmony envisioned long ago.

It's startling but understandable to me how many people confine themselves to black-and-white opinions and beliefs, refusing to open themselves to another person's point of view. Most of us humans don't do well with change. It's scary and risky. It shakes the very core of our belief systems and ideologies that many of us have defended since adolescence. We naturally declare a belief, then gather evidence to support it. Most of the topics that are central to politics cause divisiveness for this very reason. Can we leave judgment aside and turn toward love, even if we don't agree? Can we spend time attempting to really understand the other's position, where they are coming from, and relinquish our convictions as needed?

I've never been one to raise a megaphone or a protest sign; activism has never sparked my soul. I confess, I've even silently judged those who do—those who march, who shout, who fight for change. Yet in my quiet condemnation, I missed the divine spark within them, the Spirit that God breathed into each of us. By judging, even in the privacy of my own mind, I was building walls of resistance, mirroring the very conflicts I criticized. Whether we resist or cling desperately to the past, we're choosing fear over love, like turning away from a sunrise to dwell in shadows.

So I pause. I seek forgiveness—for myself, for my judgments, for the world. I let compassion wash over me like a gentle tide, cleansing the resistance that clouds my peace. *A Course in Miracles* reminds me, "To know peace, you have to offer it." I've felt this truth in my bones—when I move past fear and choose love, it's as if the world exhales with me. Imagine if each of us did this, consistently, like stars lighting up the night one by one. Could we weave a tapestry of peace so radiant it blankets the earth?

Eckhart Tolle's distinction between "Life Situation" and "Life"—our very Being—feels like a key unlocking a hidden door. The political drama, the endless news cycles, the clamor of opinions—they're just the surface ripples of my Life Situation. But my true Life, my Being, is a still, deep ocean beneath, untouched by the storms above. When I anchor myself in that stillness, the chaos loses its grip. I can witness the world's upheavals without being swept away, like a tree standing firm in a gusting wind, rooted in the eternal Now.

This isn't just about politics—it's about every corner of existence. I've seen friends, family, strangers all weighed down by the world's "bad" situations: senseless violence that cuts like a blade, accidents that steal breath, illnesses that dim spirits, deaths that leave hearts hollow. I've heard activists shame those who don't join their fight, as if visible resistance is the only path to change. But I've learned that resisting anything—whether it's a petty irritation at someone's harmless quirk or a gut-wrenching reaction to global tragedy—only feeds its power. It's like pouring fuel on a fire I want to extinguish. We never know the full story behind any event. We see the outer wounds, the physical toll, but not the invisible healing of the Inner Spirit, the quiet grace that brings peace beyond our understanding. We don't see the unconscious choices, both personal and collective, that ripple out from unhealed pain to create what we label as "negative."

I also learned from Eckhart Tolle's *Stillness Speaks* that the moment we stop resisting, even the things that feel impossible to accept, an unexpected grace flows in. The quiet surrender to *what is* (not because it's okay, but because it already is) becomes the widest doorway to peace. This truth glows like a lantern in the dark. When I dwell on the past or fret about the future, I'm stealing from the Now, dimming its brilliance. Compassion doesn't mean standing idly by—it can mean acting, helping, healing, but only from a place of joy and love. Action born of resistance is like planting seeds in barren soil; it only breeds more struggle. But when I move from a place of presence, my actions become offerings, like flowers laid at the altar of the moment.

Picture this: a world where each of us chooses love over fear, presence over resistance. It's a vision that shimmers like a sunrise, where every thought, every act, radiates peace. I don't need to fight the world's chaos; I need only to anchor myself in the Now, to let compassion and grace flow through me like a river. In that stillness, I find peace, a joyful living connection to the Divine—a spark that can light up the world.

A couple of thoughts for your consideration:

1. Choose compassion over judgment.

In a divided world, let love guide your thoughts, even when you disagree. By seeking to understand others without judgment, you plant seeds of peace that ripple outward, fostering healing and connection.

2. Anchor in the Eternal Now.

Release the pull of past regrets and future fears to embrace the present moment. By grounding yourself in stillness, you tap into a wellspring of grace that transforms chaos into compassion, lighting your path and the world around you.

⋮

46

Fear Versus Love: A Symphony of Healing and Awakening

In shame's sharp sting, I've craved to fade,
Words or deeds astray, my heart dismayed.
Eyes locked on missteps, shadows of the past,
Aching for a key to rewind, recast.

Yet healing sings a gentler lore,
Let go, forgive—unclench the core.
Step bold into dawn's forgiving glow,
I turn to love, where wholeness flows.

On a recent quiet Sunday evening, I closed the final pages of *Power vs. Force* by David R. Hawkins, a book gifted to me by the Universe through my new friend Paula. The book's words lit a spark, reminding me of life's synchronicities—ask and the Universe answers, often in ways that shimmer beyond imagination.

My dear friend Rene had spoken of Paula for months, insisting our souls would align. Skeptical, I hesitated; my comfort zone is a cozy haven, and small talk often feels like a tightrope. Yet, trusting Rene's warmth and the promise of connection, I joined her, her husband Kim, Paula and her husband, and another couple for an afternoon that unfolded like a gift.

Initial pleasantries gave way to something deeper. As we shared our stories, they inquired about the book I was writing and my quest for meaning. Paula's eyes sparkled as she recommended authors who had shaped her own path. Rene had accurately captured the magnitude of Paula's glow, and I felt the pull of connection. Eager for wisdom, I downloaded *Power vs. Force* the next morning, devouring it by evening, my journal brimming with insights. The book wove science—behavioral kinesiology and physics—into a tapestry of consciousness and energy, echoing *A Course in Miracles'* dance of love versus fear. Though the science sometimes soared beyond my grasp, its truths landed intuitively, igniting two revelations that have propelled my healing.

First, there's the notion of consciousness. My recent healing journey has unveiled depths of love, joy, and peace I'd never touched before—these were not fleeting emotions but states of being. David Hawkins's consciousness scale in *Power vs. Force* maps negative states like fear and shame to "force" and positive states like love and peace to "power." I've tasted these higher states, yet I slip back when the ego shows up or my nervous system frays. Hawkins's list of power-based adjectives versus force-based adjectives became a mirror, helping me reflect on where I linger and where I aspire to dwell. The list remains a clarion call to shift my perspective, to choose love's higher vibration over fear's heavy pull. It's a tool that awakens my desire to live with intention.

Second, I gained a new perspective on spiritual healing from the religious oppression of my past. Hawkins offered a sharp warning about the dangers in this area. He pointed out that Americans often approach spiritual teachers with excessive innocence. This happens partly because spiritual pursuit does not have a long tradition here as it does in older cultures. In places like India, people are well aware that false gurus are common. That healthy skepticism does not come naturally to many in the West. Charismatic figures from abroad frequently arrive with polished presentations, dazzling displays of seeming insight, and an uncanny ability to imitate genuine sincerity.

They captivate even experienced seekers. They convince them to abandon their lives, sell everything, and follow blindly. Later those followers face deep disillusionment.

Hawkins described this as spiritual seduction. It is a clever blend of partial truths wrapped in misleading contexts that make the teachings appear authentic at first glance. When the deception eventually comes to light, the resulting pain can be devastating. It is far worse than ordinary losses. Some people never fully recover from the betrayal and despair. He emphasized that the greatest weapon of these false prophets is their sheer persuasiveness.

In my youth, as I've shared, I was deeply shaped by The Kingdom—a movement founded by Frank Sandford, whose charisma held a powerful, though quieter, sway over its followers. It was a spiritual seduction that left lasting scars. Reading this brought me back, once more, to the letter my father wrote in my early twenties. He shared a therapist's insight: what we had endured closely mirrored PTSD. That simple validation became a lifeline—it told me I wasn't broken, just wounded. Revisiting this truth now, not as a tether to suffering but as a key to forgiveness, has set me free. By honoring those unhealed choices—mine and others'—I forgive myself fully and offer that same grace to the world. My path forward is clear: to bless and uplift those still seeking their way, rooted in the unshakable truth that love always overcomes fear.

⋮

From Fearful Myths to Daily Grace: Choosing Heaven on Earth

Once I saw them as realms apart,
Heaven, a mystic dream, a starlit art.
Hell, a chasm of flame, destruction's pyre.
Chase Heaven's checklist, climb ever higher—
Sacrifice, repent, strain through the strife,
Or face Hell's abyss, an eternal life.
What Creator would craft such a grueling race,
Binding our days to a far-off place?
Waiting, not living, tethered to dread,
Missing the moment where presence is fed.

Then truth unveiled a gentler call:
Heaven or Hell—I choose them all.
In suffering's grip, I dwell in Hell's shade,
But in love's embrace, for self, for Creator, for kin,
I find Heaven on Earth, where peace blooms within.
A blissful now, where joy's light is spun,
Each day I choose, and the choice is one.

've come to know that I crafted my own suffering when life veered from my hopes, when moments clashed with my heart's desires, plunging me into a self-made hell on earth. Looking back, the agony lingers—why did I dwell in that shadow, blind to the choice of a brighter lens? Yet, a radiant truth now breaks through: Those struggles were not in vain. Each trial forged a bridge to others, letting me shine a healing light for those lost in similar darkness. Regret fades like mist at dawn; every hardship bloomed with purpose, a quiet sunrise of meaning, and that is more than enough.

This clarity struck like a bell: I choose heaven or hell in every moment, every day. The old myth of a distant afterlife—heaven's gates or hell's fiery chasm—dissolved as I questioned why a loving Creator would bind us to endless repentance, judging our humanness for eternity. Instead, I see now that free will grants us the power to shape our own reality. By choosing love—for myself, my Creator, and for all souls—I weave heaven into the here and now, a vibrant peace that blossoms within. God's love, unwavering for His creations, holds steady, inviting me to choose joy, moment by sacred moment. And I know that when my earthly shell is no longer, my Spirit will soar to a permanent Heaven.

These truths have reshaped my path, offering lessons for anyone seeking peace. First, we can choose joy over suffering by shifting our perspective, embracing each moment as an opportunity to find light even in hardship. Second, letting go of fear-based beliefs about judgment frees us to live fully in the present, trusting in our Creator's boundless love. Finally, small acts of love—for ourselves and others—craft a heaven on earth, weaving a tapestry of grace that transforms our daily lives.

⋮

48

Unity Over Separateness: A Journey Toward Connection

Through my time spent studying and healing, I've come to see how deeply we're conditioned to embrace separateness—disconnected not only from Source but from each other and the natural world. From childhood, we're steeped in messages that foster division: "Don't talk to strangers." "People can't be trusted." "Stay cautious." Growing up in New England, this felt especially true; forging connections was like breaking through stone. When I moved to the South years ago, I was startled by strangers greeting me with a warm "hello." I'd glance over my shoulder, assuming they meant someone else—how could they address someone they didn't know like that? At first, their boldness unsettled me. Now, I can't imagine not offering a greeting in return.

Walking through my neighborhood, I notice a mix of responses to my nods or hellos. Some meet my gaze with warmth; others pass by, eyes averted, perhaps still bound by conditioning or simply lost in their thoughts. I used to feel a flicker of irritation at their silence, but now I choose to send them a silent blessing instead. It shifts something in me—replacing judgment with love feels lighter, freer. I'm not yet the person who greets every passerby in a store or on the street, but why not aspire to it? A smile costs nothing and might just brighten someone's day. When I step out of my inner world to share light, I feel it returned to me, a quiet confirmation that connection matters.

I've also become more aware of the energy I carry. I've brought my own negativity or frustrations with me into new environments and then felt the heaviness ripple outward into the room. Balance is my pursuit now—harmonizing the yin and yang, the masculine and feminine energies within me. The book *The Light Shall Set You Free* presents a core principle: Everything in existence is deeply interconnected through Divine Oneness, so our thoughts, words, and actions don't just affect our own lives, they actively shape and influence the entire world around us. Choosing love over fear raises our vibration, aligning us with the Divine's design. We are not separate, not alone. By tapping into this unity, we can transform negativity into positivity, cocreating a world that reflects the oneness of Source. This is our power, our freedom—to live not in fear but in love, contributing to a Universe that thrives on connection.

⋮

$$49$$

The Power of Thought: Flowing with the Rhythms of Life

After immersing myself in the book *The Light Shall Set You Free*, I've been captivated by the Law of Rhythm, a universal principle that thrums through existence like a heartbeat. It teaches that all things move in cycles, like a pendulum swinging from right to left, or tides ebbing and flowing along a moonlit shore. The sun climbs the sky in a blaze of gold, only to sink into the velvet embrace of night. These rhythms weave an order of renewal into the Universe, a dance that can feel disruptive or serene, depending on the lens through which we choose to see it.

Life's rhythms pulse through every moment, from a sunset's fiery splendor—crimson and amber streaking the horizon—to the quiet mystery of night that cradles or unsettles us. Dawn's soft light breaks, a reprieve or a spark of apprehension for the day ahead. Without rain's gentle patter, we'd take the sun's warmth for granted; without winter's sharp bite, spring's tender blooms wouldn't stir our hearts. Living in Florida's endless summer, I cherish the sun's embrace, free from the dreary bone-chilling winters of my New

England childhood. Yet weather shapes our inner tides more than we admit—a dreary, rain-soaked day cloaks our mood in gray, while a bright morning lifts our spirits like a kite soaring on the wind. When I pause to marvel at the Universe's intricate design—the shifting seasons, the ebb and flow of life's changes, both in nature and within my own heart—I find balance, a quiet awe at the delicate threads that connect it all.

Attuning myself to this rhythm has also taught me the transformative power of thought. I have a choice in reshaping how I navigate these cycles. Change, like a daunting tide, often crashes against the comfort of the familiar, tempting me to cling to what I know or to dwell in fear of what's missing. But that mind-set only deepens the void, like a shadow stretching in fading light. The miracle lies in choosing love over fear, repeatedly, like a river carving a new path through stone. Each loving thought is a spark, guiding me toward freedom and lighting the way through life's inevitable swings.

Though they may outwardly seem opposed, faith and attitude actually dance together, each shaping the other in a subtle, profound rhythm. Perception, often narrow like a fogged window, can trap us in a limited view. But when I open my mind with curiosity, seeking the broader perspective, miracles unfold. I begin to see not just what is, but what could be as well. Am I swept away by life's currents, the clamor of media, the opinions of strangers, the weight of others' expectations, or the echoes of past beliefs? Or do I trust the quiet pulse of my intuition, my inner compass pointing to truth? By aligning my thoughts with love and possibility, I move in harmony with life's rhythms, transforming challenges into opportunities.

When I embrace the rhythm of life's highs and lows without clinging to them, letting them flow like a river between its banks, clarity dawns like mist dissolving at sunrise. Some things won't change, but I can choose how to see and respond, shaping my reality with every thought. This is the actual power of thought: not to force my will on the world, but to nudge myself into the flow of life's cycles, with my heart open to love and my mind alive with possibility, dancing in step with the Universe's eternal rhythm.

This journey has revealed a simple yet profound truth: By aligning our thoughts with love and openness, we can dance with life's rhythms, transforming each moment into an opportunity for peace and possibility, no matter the cycle we face. And the secret lies not in fighting the pendulum's swing but in staying centered—so our reactions to the swings grow gentler, and we remain steady.

⋮

50

Gratitude's Sacred Shift: A Path to Love

A Course in Miracles offers a piercing insight:

> Gratitude is a lesson hard to learn for those who look upon the world amiss. They see themselves as better off than others, finding contentment in another's greater suffering. How pitiful and deprecating are such thoughts. For who has cause for thanks while others have less? Your gratitude is due to Him alone Who made all cause of sorrow disappear from the world. Gratitude goes hand in hand with love.

This teaching sliced through my understanding of gratitude, untangling it from the trap of comparison. True gratitude isn't a fleeting relief born of witnessing another's deeper suffering; it's a radiant recognition of our shared humanity, all of us threaded together by the Divine's boundless love. Compassion, not superiority, weaves us into the fabric of love, dissolving the divisions that culture so often sows.

When self-pity threatens to pull me under, I know now that shifting my perspective is a necessity. So I reach for small, intentional acts of gratitude—pausing to savor a fleeting moment of beauty, like sunlight dancing on leaves, or stepping into nature's warm embrace. A coach once gifted me a simple tool: When a negative thought or memory creeps into my mind, I whisper, "Not relevant right now," gently clearing space for light. Another mentor, taught me a simple, playful way to nudge intrusive thoughts or old fears out of the way. Whenever one appears, I gently acknowledge it with a lighthearted inner nod and then let it pass without grabbing hold. It feels like greeting an uninvited guest with a smile, then quietly showing them the door. That small gesture has turned so much inner noise into something I can almost laugh at and wave good-bye to.

Most transformative is my morning ritual, a sacred start to each day. Before rising, I take Pam Grout's advice and declare that it will be an "Amazingly Awesome" day (her "AA 2.0" approach). Spoken aloud, this intention melts away any morning grumpiness, aligning my heart with possibility. Then, after meditation, I offer a gratitude prayer, its words setting a glowing tone. In my journal, I capture the previous day's miracles—tiny glimmers of joy, unexpected answers, or synchronicities that hum with the Universe's quiet connection. These rituals weave gratitude and love into the tapestry of my life, reminding me that we are all held in the Divine's embrace, free from sorrow, united in grace.

This journey has illuminated a profound truth: Gratitude is a sacred choice that transforms the lens through which we view our lives, magnifying the love that surrounds us. By choosing to see beauty in small moments, we shift from lack to abundance, opening our hearts to joy. Releasing comparison fosters compassion, connecting us to others through shared humanity. And daily rituals of gratitude ground us in the Divine's boundless embrace, making every day a step toward love's radiant path.

⋮

51

Butterfly Kisses and Serpent Whispers: Grateful for Divine Signs of Peace

One morning recently, I woke heavy with sorrow, my heart a tangled knot of unanswered questions and raw ache. Tears carved hot trails down my cheeks as I lay in bed, my chest tight, as if it might burst from the weight of it all. In quiet desperation, I whispered pleas to God, to the Angels, to anyone listening—begging for guidance, for clarity, for a shift in perspective to ease the storm within. Silence answered, deep and unyielding.

Seeking answers, I laced up my sneakers and set out for my daily walk through the streets of my neighborhood. The air was warm, the sun shining brightly, but my soul still churned, searching for peace. Almost every day, delicate white butterflies—their wings kissed with faint traces of color—flutter alongside me, their joyful dance gently lifting my spirits. Occasionally, a bright orange butterfly will appear, its striking wings like a burst of sunlight, though I hadn't seen one in weeks. In my despair, I sent a fervent prayer skyward, my voice cracking: "Please, show me a sign. Let it be an orange butterfly— clear as a thunderbolt, undeniable as a snake."

I walked on, steps heavy but hopeful, scanning the world around me. Palms swayed lazily, their fronds casting lacy shadows on the pavement, and birds chattered in the canopy above. I reached my usual turnaround point but something urged me to keep going, just a little farther. Then, there it was—a brilliant orange butterfly, its wings glowing against the green. It fluttered in the grass before me, weaving through the air as if sent just for my eyes. Tears spilled again, but these were tears of gratitude, my heart unfurling like a flower in the sun. I whispered thanks to God, to my guardian angels. My body softened, peace washing over me like a cool tide. I turned back, my steps lighter, when—astonishingly—just a few paces later, a sleek snake glided across the path, startling me a little. My breath caught. Two signs, unmistakable and electric, as if the Universe had shouted back, *I hear you.* Bliss flooded me, carrying me through the rest of the day on a current of wonder.

And then the next morning, as if to seal the miracle, another orange butterfly joined me on my walk. This one didn't just dance nearby—it swooped close, brushing my cheek with the softest kiss of its wings, a fleeting caress that felt like a love letter from the cosmos. This was no mere coincidence; it was God answering my cries, wrapping me in an embrace of hope and connection that shimmered long after its wings had vanished.

This orange butterfly and its serpent companion represent just one miraculous chapter in a book of countless signs from the angels, each a whisper from the Divine reassuring me that I'm never alone. Sometimes the signs are bold, like that morning's messengers, blazing into my life with the clarity of a lightning strike. Other times, they're softer—a delicate feather on my path, a song lyric that hits like a knowing glance from the Universe—arriving with gentle timing that appears only when I'm ready to see. Each one, quiet or loud, is a reminder that I'm guided, cradled by a presence that sings with love. When I call to the angels, their subtle embrace wraps around me, a shimmering veil of peace, warm and eternal, soothing my soul with the certainty that I'm held in the arms of the Divine.

In life's darkest moments, divine signs—be they gentle or bold—remind us to stay open to love and presence, guiding us toward peace that soothes the soul. In that spirit, I would remind you of the following:

1. Open your heart to divine signs.

Trust that the Universe is speaking to you through moments that may range from subtle to bold—you may be touched by a butterfly's dance or a song's timely lyric. By staying open and attentive, you can find guidance and peace in the signs that surround you.

2. Embrace the peace of presence.

When sorrow weighs heavy, seek solace in the present moment and call out for divine support. The answers may come in unexpected ways, offering a comforting reminder that you are never alone on your journey.

⋮

52

From Questions to Clarity: Discovering My Divine Core

The question *Who am I?* has trailed me like a shadow across the winding paths of this earthly journey, flickering in and out of focus. At times, it's been a soft hum, the glimpse of an answer just enough to keep me moving forward, content with a fleeting glance at a larger truth. Other times, it's a restless ache, a yearning that pulls me deeper into the search, like a diver plunging into the ocean's depths, chasing glimmers of light below the surface. For years, it was easy to wrap myself in the titles of my career—*Consultant, Manager, Partner*—labels that hung like polished medals on my chest. But those were costumes I dressed up in, roles I played, not the essence of who I am. As I continue to peel them away, digging deeper, I seek the core beneath the surface. *Who do I want to be?* The question thumps like a heartbeat, hinting at transformation, a chrysalis waiting to crack open.

Then come the moments that sting, when shame creeps in. I may think or even say something unkind, my words slicing where instead I meant to soothe, and I long for an undo button to erase the hurt. I judge others silently, annoyed by their quirks, their choices, my mind spinning a web of criticism I can't seem to stop. In those moments, I vow to be better, to never let the ego steer me astray again. But the promises feel heavy, like chains forged from fear and self-rebuke. I stand before the mirror of my soul, afraid to look too closely, haunted by the question *Who am I?*

Yet, in moments of quiet, a gentle whisper from Source calls me back. It's as if loving arms of grace wrap around me, warm and unshakable, cradling me through the storm of my own imperfections. I'm reminded that these missteps—these flashes of frustration, judgment, or unkindness—aren't who I am. They're the unhealed parts of me, rising like waves to the surface, asking to be seen, not shamed. I turn to the well of love within, listening, opening, honoring those parts instead of pushing them away. I thank them for showing me where I've strayed, for guiding me back to the truth: I am not my mistakes. I am not the ego's fleeting tantrums.

Surrendering to Spirit, I let go, and in that release, I find freedom. It's like stepping out of a cramped, shadowy room into a wide, sunlit field. I don't need to strive harder or punish myself to be "better." I was created by the Divine. My purpose isn't to wrestle with the world's chaos or add to its suffering—it's to offer peace, to extend love, starting with myself. This is the human dance, a daily, hourly practice of returning to love. *Did I love today?* I ask myself. As if in response, another answer blooms softly: *I am enough. I am.*

Guidance arrives in small, peaceful victories. A warm smile shared with a stranger, a nod to someone weighed down by struggle, patience held steady on a frustrating call, calm when others lash out in pain—these are my offerings. *I see you, and God sees you,* I silently affirm. I'm here to serve, to bless, to sprinkle hope like seeds in a world that often feels parched. My gifts—unique, practical, divinely given—are tools to uplift, to inspire, to remind others that life doesn't have to be a ceaseless battle. Each act of love, no matter how small, ripples outward, a quiet rebellion against the chaos.

This seeking, this returning to love, will be my lifelong pilgrimage. I'll keep turning to my Creator, asking the Holy Spirit for guidance, trusting that the answers will come—not as I might expect, but as they're meant to. I don't need to chase perfection, that elusive mirage of a man-made culture that measures worth by works, sacrifices, and comparisons. *Am I good enough?* The question fades as I breathe deeply, my soul exulting in newfound freedom. I'm unlearning centuries of inherited beliefs—dogmas that demanded struggle, judgment, and striving. Instead, I let the gift of life flow, unimpeded, sparkling with grace.

This is me, being and becoming, a lustrous dance of presence and possibility. I stand in gratitude, my heart alight with peace, knowing I am enough—exactly as I am, exactly where I am. The question *Who am I?* no longer feels like a problem to solve. It's an invitation to live, to love, to shine, and to let the Divine unfold through me, moment by glorious moment.

This journey of uncovering my divine core has revealed timeless truths that extend beyond myself, to anyone seeking their own true essence. Embracing imperfections as teachers fosters self-compassion, guiding us back to our personal center. Small acts of love—a smile, a moment of patience—ripple outward, sowing hope in a weary world. And for those tethered to corporate titles or facing retirement, releasing these labels unveils a deeper identity, rooted in divine purpose, ready to shine in new chapters of life.

⋮

Conclusion

Each decade of my life has woven a richer, more vibrant thread into the tapestry of who I am, each one brighter than the last.

My teenage years were a whirlwind of confusion and yearning. I was caught between wanting to fit in and aching to break free. Those years felt heavy, like I was searching for something I couldn't quite name. My twenties were all about the hustle—charging forward without a clear map, animated merely by a deep drive to keep going. Early career wins fueled me, and the laughter and late nights with friends lit up my world, even when I wasn't sure where I was headed.

In my thirties, I began to unfurl, like a bud catching the first warmth of spring. The good days started to outshine the shadows, and hope took root. My career became a canvas where I painted through self-doubt, guided by mentors, friends, and family who believed in me. Growing up, my voice was often stifled—debate or difference wasn't welcome—so learning to speak up in the business world and personal relationships was liberating. Each step, each conversation, was a lesson in owning my voice and carving my path with clarity and purpose.

Turning forty felt like stepping into a sunlit clearing. No one warned me how freeing it would be—not because it was all about me, but because, suddenly, it wasn't. I stood taller, armed with enough wisdom to shape my response to life's highs and lows rather than just reacting to it all. Challenges, I learned, weren't about surrendering to fear or victimhood; they were invitations to rise with courage and grace. Yes, at forty, I truly began to live. The years before certainly weren't empty; they were my chrysalis, a time of proving, defining, and discovering what matters. Only after those years could the shift come upon my life, like a sail catching the wind. Confidence bloomed, wisdom deepened, and I sought my purpose with fresh urgency.

A colleague, inspired by Simon Sinek's *Start with Why*, once challenged my coworkers and me to uncover our personal "why." I wrestled with it, expecting a grand revelation. Instead, it was beautifully simple: I'm here to make things better—more efficient, less chaotic, less fearful. As a consultant, I glowed when clients thrived. As a leader, my heart swelled watching teammates excel or find their strengths. As a friend, lifting others through hardship became my joy. Making a difference, however small, is my why—it's why work often felt like purpose in motion.

Now, in my fifties, another transformation unfolds, unexpected and profound. Turning fifty during COVID's isolation—no big trips, just quiet moments alone—was a challenge, yet I didn't just survive; I thrived. Leaving Atlanta after twenty-five years for Florida's open skies was a gift I didn't see coming. Closing my financial services career, a chapter rich with gratitude, shifted my focus from "work hard, play hard" to a deeper craving: for connection, peace, and alignment with the Divine. I'm learning to let go of what no longer matters—things I once thought were everything. My spiritual path now lights the way; each step I take is a prayer, each moment a chance to weave my life into a greater story of love and unity.

As for the next chapter of my life, the pages are blank, and I'm learning to embrace their mystery. I no longer need to map every step, to grip the wheel with white knuckles. Instead, I rise each day and take a step back, letting life unfold. I ask Spirit to guide me: *Who am I to serve? How will I show up?* The answers come softly, in whispers of intuition, in synchronicities that show up as chance encounters, in moments of quiet knowing. I trust they'll arrive, as sure as the dawn, and I'm grateful for the freedom to let them find me, guided by a love that never fails.

What I've come to know is that life is a series of seasons, each one shaping us in ways we might not see until later. The struggles, doubts, and triumphs of our early years aren't just obstacles—they're the raw materials of our growth. We must embrace them, learn from them, and trust that every step, even if it's shaky, is leading us toward a purpose that's uniquely our own.

Keep seeking, keep growing, and let your journey unfold with courage, curiosity, and love.

⋮

Appendix

Cherished Authors Who Have Transformed My Perspective and Guided My Healing Journey

I am deeply grateful for the authors and spiritual teachers who have crossed my path, their wisdom lighting the way through my healing journey like stars in a vast night sky. Their words have been lanterns, guiding me from fear to freedom, from pain to profound peace. Each book, and each teaching they contain, has woven a thread into the tapestry of my transformation, offering clarity, courage, and connection to the Divine within. Below, I honor the voices that have inspired and uplifted me, their insights a sacred gift that continues to resonate.

Gabrielle Bernstein

Happy Days: The Guided Path from Trauma to Profound Freedom and Inner Peace

A compassionate companion for healing deep wounds that lead me to inner serenity.

May Cause Miracles: A 40-Day Guidebook of Subtle Shifts for Radical Change and Unlimited Happiness

A gentle nudge toward being on the lookout for daily miracles. This book transformed my perspective with small, powerful steps.

Super Attractor: Methods for Manifesting a Life Beyond Your Wildest Dreams

A vibrant guide to aligning with the Universe's flow, sparking joy and abundance.

The Universe Has Your Back: Transform Fear to Faith

A road map for releasing fear and trusting divine guidance, a beacon in my darkest moments.

Emily Fletcher

Stress Less, Accomplish More: Meditation for Extraordinary Performance

A practical guide to meditation, blending mindfulness with productivity that helped calm my mind and amplify my purpose.

Pam Grout

The Course in Miracles Experiment: A Starter Kit for Rewiring Your Mind (and Therefore the World)

A playful, accessible take on profound spiritual truths, making *A Course in Miracles* a joyful practice.

Living Big: Embrace Your Passion and Leap into an Extraordinary Life

An invitation to embrace bold, expansive living, that ignited my courage to dream bigger.

Esther and Jerry Hicks

The Law of Attraction: The Basics of the Teachings of Abraham

A vibrant introduction to manifesting desires, empowering me to cocreate with the Universe.

The Vortex: Where the Law of Attraction Assembles All Cooperative Relationships

A guide to aligning with love and purpose that pulled me into the flow of divine connection.

Michael A. Singer

Living Untethered: Beyond the Human Predicament

A guide to transcending limitations that anchored me in spiritual clarity.

The Surrender Experiment: My Journey into Life's Perfection

A testament to the power of surrender that inspired me to trust life's unfolding.

The Untethered Soul: The Journey Beyond Yourself

A transformative exploration of inner freedom that helped me release the chains of ego.

Eckhart Tolle

The Power of Now: A Guide to Spiritual Enlightenment

A luminous call to embrace the present that illuminated my path to presence and peace.

Stillness Speaks

A quiet, potent guide to inner stillness that helped anchor me in the eternal Now.

Gary Zukav

The Heart of the Soul: Emotional Awareness

A compassionate guide to navigating emotions, fostering emotional clarity and healing.

The Seat of the Soul: An Inspiring Vision of Humanity's Spiritual Destiny

A soul-stirring exploration of spiritual growth that helped deepen my connection to my authentic self.

Acknowledgments

To my mother and father, Ellie and Joe, the weavers of my first breath, I bow in reverence. You gifted me life. No shadows of grievance darken my heart; the past, with its thorns and blooms, has carved me into who I stand as today. I am a mosaic of those yesterdays, blessed beyond the measure of stars in a midnight sky, forever grateful for the roots and wings you bestowed.

To my brothers, Rog and Steve, you are my unwavering champions, your support a steady light that lifts my spirit and fuels my journey.

To my dear friends—Ang, Kaylin, Kim, and Rene—who have cheered me on through this book's unfolding, your encouragement is a gift I hold close, etched in my heart with boundless gratitude.

To my brilliant editors, Anastasia Voll and Allison Felus: I never could have done this without you.

And to every soul who touched this journey, named or unspoken: thank you. You are written between every line.

About the Author

Marcia Elizabeth Wakeman is the founder of SoulFullJoy, where she guides individuals and teams toward a brighter, more fulfilling path. With a remarkable thirty-plus-year career in financial services technology and consulting, Marcia has transitioned from a visionary intrapreneur to a passionate entrepreneur.

For those feeling weighed down by the frustrations of corporate life, Marcia offers tools and perspectives to reignite joy in their journey. For those haunted by fear, doubt, or guilt from oppressive religious upbringings, she provides a compassionate promise of healing. And for anyone yearning for more love and inspiration in their life, Marcia's guidance lights the way. She embraces the truth that if it isn't love, it is fear—yes, even in the corporate world.

Marcia offers personalized workshops tailored to your unique needs and provides coaching to support your growth. As an inspiring speaker, she is also available to share her wisdom and energy with audiences far and wide.

For over three decades, Marcia has empowered hundreds of clients, colleagues, and friends to unlock their potential, achieve success in their careers or businesses, release deep-seated fears, and embrace a life filled with meaning and joy.

To those feeling crushed by the corporate grind, shadowed by the weight of oppressive religious upbringings, or simply yearning for a brighter spark of joy in their lives, she's eager to walk alongside you, sharing light to guide your journey toward freedom and fulfillment.

Visit her website at SoulFullJoy.com or follow her on Instagram @SoulFullJoy01 to connect and view her offerings and tools.